# THE BEATLES, POPULAR MUSIC AND SOCIETY

# The Beatles, Popular Music and Society

## A Thousand Voices

Edited by

Ian Inglis
*Senior Lecturer in Sociology*
*University of Northumbria*
*Newcastle upon Tyne*

First published 2000 by
**MACMILLAN PRESS LTD**
Houndmills, Basingstoke, Hampshire RG21 6XS
and London
Companies and representatives
throughout the world

ISBN 0–333–73205–7 hardcover
ISBN 0–333–76156–1 paperback

A catalogue record for this book is available
from the British Library.

This book is printed on paper suitable for recycling and
made from fully managed and sustained forest sources.

10   9   8   7   6   5   4   3   2   1
08   07   06   05   04   03   02   01   00   99

Printed and bound in Great Britain by
Antony Rowe Ltd, Chippenham, Wiltshire

Published in the United States of America by
ST. MARTIN'S PRESS, INC.,
Scholarly and Reference Division
175 Fifth Avenue, New York, N.Y. 10010

ISBN 0–312–22235–1 clothbound
ISBN 0–312–22236–X paperback

For my own Fab Four

**Annette, Eleanor, Christopher and Susannah**

# Contents

# List of Tables and Figures

# Acknowledgements

The editor and publishers are grateful to the following for permission to reproduce copyright material:

*A Day In The Life*
Words & Music by John Lennon &
Paul McCartney
©Copyright 1967 Northern Songs

*Good Night*
Words & Music by John Lennon &
Paul McCartney
©Copyright 1968 Northern Songs.

*Back In The USSR*
Words & Music by John Lennon &
Paul McCartney
©Copyright 1968 Northern Songs.

*I'm So Tired*
Words & Music by John Lennon &
Paul McCartney
©Copyright 1968 Northern Songs.

*Helter Skelter*
Words & Music by John Lennon &
Paul McCartney
©Copyright 1968 Northern Songs.

*She's A Woman*
Words & Music by John Lennon &
Paul McCartney
©Copyright 1964 Northern Songs.

*Eleanor Rigby*
Words & Music by John Lennon &
Paul McCartney
©Copyright 1966 Northern Songs.

*Rain*
Words & Music by John Lennon &
Paul McCartney
©Copyright 1966 Northern Songs.

*Day Tripper*
Words & Music by John Lennon &
Paul McCartney
©Copyright 1965 Northern Songs.

*A Hard Day's Night*
Words & Music by John Lennon &
Paul McCartney
©Copyright 1964 Northern Songs.

*And I Love Her*
Words & Music by John Lennon &
Paul McCartney
©Copyright 1964 Northern Songs.

*From A Window*
Words & Music by John Lennon &
Paul McCartney
©Copyright 1964 Northern Songs.

*Yellow Submarine*
Words & Music by John Lennon &
Paul McCartney
©Copyright 1966 Northern Songs.

*Please Please Me*
Words & Music by John Lennon &
Paul McCartney
©Copyright 1962 Universal/Dick
James Music Limited, 47 British
Grove, London W4.

*We Can Work It Out*
Words & Music by John Lennon &
Paul McCartney
©Copyright 1965 Northern Songs.

*Eight Days A Week*
Words & Music by John Lennon &
Paul McCartney
©Copyright 1964 Northern Songs.

# Notes on the Contributors

**Andy Bennett** is Lecturer in Sociology at the University of Surrey. Prior to studying for his doctorate at Durham University from 1993 to 1996, he spent two years in Germany as a *Musikpadagoge* (music instructor) with the Frankfurt Rockmobil project. He is currently writing a book on youth, music, identity and locality.

**Mike Brocken** is a Lecturer and Archivist in the Institute of Popular Music at the University of Liverpool. He is the author of *Some Other Guys!* (1996). He has recently completed his doctorate on the British folk revival, and is currently co-writing Joe Flannery's biography.

**Gary Burns** is Associate Professor and Assistant Chair in the Department of Communication at Northern Illinois University. He is President of the American Culture Association and editor of *Popular Music and Society*. He co-edited *Television Studies: Textual Analysis* (1989) and *Making Television: Authorship and the Production Process* (1990). His articles have appeared in *Popular Music, South Atlantic Quarterly, Goldmine, Wide Angle*, the *Journal Of Popular Film and Television*, and other periodicals.

**Martin Cloonan** is Research Fellow in Lifelong Learning at the University of Stirling. His main research interests lie in the politics of popular music. His first book was *Banned! Censorship of Popular Music in Britain 1967–1992* (1996), and he is the co-editor of a forthcoming volume on censorship and music.

**Guy Cook** is Professor of Applied Linguistics at the University of Reading. His books include *The Discourse of Advertising* (1992), *Discourse and Literature* (1994) and *Principle and Practice in Applied Linguistics* (with Barbara Seidlhofer, 1995) and he is currently preparing *Language Play, Language Learning*.

**Jon Fitzgerald** is Senior Lecturer within the Contemporary Music Program at Southern Cross University, Lismore, Australia. His doctoral thesis examined the development of popular songwriting during the early 1960s, and his articles have been published in numerous journals. He is a member of the editorial board for *Perfect*

*Beat: the Pacific Journal of Research into Contemporary Music and Popular Culture.*

**Ian Inglis** is Senior Lecturer in Sociology at the University of Northumbria, Newcastle upon Tyne. His articles about the Beatles have been published in numerous journals, including *Popular Music*, *Popular Music and Society* and the *International Review of the Aesthetics and Sociology of Music*. His other research interests include the activities of fans, and popular music and history.

**P. David Marshall** is Director of the Media and Cultural Studies Centre in the Department of English at the University of Queensland, Brisbane. He is the author of *Celebrity and Power: Fame in Contemporary Culture* (1997) and is currently preparing *Modes for Cultural Analysis: an Introduction to Media and Cultural Studies*. His current research includes the emergence of the Australian celebrity, self-promotion in television, and the mediatization of the Internet.

**Neil Mercer** is Professor of Language and Communications at The Open University. He is a psychologist with a special interest in the ways in which language is used to share knowledge and develop understanding. His books include *Common Knowledge* (with Derek Edwards, 1987) and *The Guided Construction of Knowledge* (1995).

**John Muncie** is Senior Lecturer in Criminology and Social Policy at The Open University. He completed a doctorate on bohemianism in 1978, and contributed a series of pieces on popular music to The Open University's *Popular Culture* course in the early 1980s. Since then, he has remained an active researcher of representations of youth, moral panics, and 'youth as a social problem'. His books include *The Trouble With Kids Today* (1984), *The Problem of Crime* (1996) and *Youth and Crime: A Critical Introduction* (1998).

**Bob Neaverson** is Lecturer in Film and Media Studies at the University of East Anglia and City College, Norwich. He is the author of *The Beatles Movies* (1997).

**Ed Whitley** graduated from and subsequently completed his MA at Brigham Young University, Provo, Utah. He is currently working towards a doctorate in American literature at the University of Maryland, College Park.

# Introduction:
# A Thousand Voices
Ian Inglis

Speaking in November 1997, at a luncheon in the Banqueting Hall in Whitehall, to mark her golden wedding anniversary, Queen Elizabeth II reflected: 'What a remarkable fifty years they have been for the world ... Think what we would have missed if we had never heard the Beatles'. It was a particularly apposite remark for, while it may appear trite to repeat it, the Beatles have indeed changed the world, and our perceptions of it, in a way that only a handful of popular entertainers – Chaplin, Monroe, Presley, Dylan – have been able to do. Indeed, as we enter the new millennium and indulge in the pastime of enumerating and evaluating the twentieth century's more significant achievements, the Beatles are predictably prominent across a variety of categories – historical, sociological, cultural and musical.

It thus seems surprising – even remarkable – that while there exists an abundance of commentaries in the form of biographies and interviews, compilations and chronologies, anecdotal memoirs and professional recollections, there is an absence of any sustained sociological interrogation of the group, its music, and the debates they provoked. What may be more surprising is that this absence has persisted throughout and despite a period of academic life in which increasing intellectual attention has been directed at the broad area of 'cultural studies'. While 'the changing terrain of popular culture has been explored and mapped by different cultural theorists and different theoretical approaches' (Storey 1993: 18), the group described as 'the most important single element in British popular culture of the postwar years' (Evans 1984: 7) has been largely excluded from those analyses. The collection of articles presented in this book seeks to begin to correct that imbalance, and to demonstrate that the Beatles' career, while certainly unique in terms of its achievements and influence, is simultaneously illustrative in its ability to inform many of the perspectives through which popular music is studied and to illuminate many of the issues with which those studies are concerned.

On one level the story of the Beatles is deceptively easy to relate, not least because it has been retold, reproduced and reinvented on so many occasions. John Lennon met Paul McCartney in Woolton, Liverpool, on 6 July 1957, and shortly afterwards invited him to join his group (then known as the Quarrymen). In 1958 McCartney introduced Lennon to George Harrison; these three remained the nucleus of the group amid numerous variations in personnel (of which the most important was Stuart Sutcliffe's membership from January 1960 to June 1961), changes of name (Johnny And The Moondogs, the Silver Beetles, the Beatles), and a performing history largely confined to Merseyside (with occasional spells in Hamburg) for the next five years. At the beginning of 1962 they agreed to place their management in the hands of Brian Epstein, a local businessman. In August of that year, several weeks after the group had accepted a provisional recording contract with EMI's Parlophone label, drummer Pete Best was replaced by Ringo Starr. In October 1962, 'Love Me Do', their first official single, was released and was a minor chart entry; and in February 1963, 'Please Please Me' became their first British Number One. In January 1964, 'I Want To Hold Your Hand' was their first US Number One, and for the rest of the decade the Beatles dominated popular music around the world. They toured extensively until August 1966, when they elected to abandon live performances in favour of studio work. Epstein died in August 1967, and in 1968 the Beatles established their own management and recording company, named Apple. In April 1970, after increasing involvement in individual projects, the group effectively disbanded. John Lennon was shot dead on 8 December 1980, in New York City. A reunion of sorts took place in 1995, when contemporary studio technology was used to permit McCartney, Harrison and Starr to add their vocal and instrumental contributions to some of Lennon's demo tapes from the 1970s. The remaining three Beatles still, intermittently, pursue their separate careers.

There are two drawbacks to a historical account like this. The first is that as with *any* history, the pursuit of an autonomous, absolute truth is an untenable goal. In assembling and assessing historical documents (even contemporary ones) the researcher inevitably confronts obstacles introduced by incomplete source material, deliberate or unwitting distortion, and confusion stemming from previous judgements about the inclusion or exclusion of documentary evidence.The individual decisions that each researcher takes to overcome these obstacles would therefore suggest that 'the belief in a hard core of historical facts existing objectively and independently of the interpretation of the historian is a preposterous fallacy' (Carr

12). In the history of the Beatles, one of the group's principal biographers has himself warned of the proliferation of 'myths and rumours, multiplying stronger than ever around this scarcely-imaginable, true story' (Norman 1981: xvi). Furthermore, the consequences of these inclinations have been noted by Paul McCartney: 'People are printing *facts* about me and John. They're *not* facts. But it will go down in the records. It will become part of history. It will be there for always. People will believe it all' (Davies 1985: 473).

The second weakness is that while it might be accurate as a *chronological* record, such an account is incapable of conveying fully the scale and force of the impact that the Beatles carried with them, initially within the popular music industry, and later – and crucially – across a range of related areas and activities. Mellers has asserted:

> The Beatles' significance, as a part of social history, is inseparable from the ambiguity of their function ... If this multiplicity of function is a source of much semantic confusion, both on the part of the Beatles themselves and of those who comment on them, it is also a source of their strength. (1973: 183)

A quarter of a century on, it is practicable, in reviewing the Beatles' career, to confirm and extend the above insight, and to argue that the ambiguity or multiplicity of function and role that characterized the Beatles is not separate from or coincidental to their musical success; instead, it *defined* and substantiated that success. Hence this book's subtitle 'A Thousand Voices' is indicative of the nature and extent of the activities into which the group was drawn. But unlike the fool on the hill, whose thousand voices were heard by nobody, the Beatles *were* heard and listened to and acted upon. In so much of their personal, musical and professional behaviour, they were perceived – rightly or wrongly – as innovators, who were consequently elevated into spokespersons for a generation. Whether the subject was the legalization of drugs, the war in Vietnam, traditional and alternative religions, the relationship between the performer and the recording company, the politics of musical integrity, the connections between popular music and other media forms, the Beatles and their opinions were sought out and heard: they were *given* a multiplicity of voices by the community within which they were active and successful.

It is this breadth which provides the thematic perspective uniting the contributions that follow. The book does not – cannot – attempt to replace previous and partial investigations of the group with a 'definitive version' or 'new reading'. That is not its task. But spanning the diversity of themes on which the authors choose to concentrate is an undertaking to locate those issues in their appropriate political, cultural and sociological contexts, and to recognize and emphasize the reciprocal influences between the Beatles, popular music, and the broader social environment. They are, therefore, contributions to those discussions which surround contemporary attempts to understand better the dynamics of the group's career, rather than *post hoc* accounts of a particular segment of the history of popular music. To this end, it is important to consider not only what the Beatles *were*, but also what they *were not*.

Four broadly inclusive perspectives can be discerned within the following chapters; their ordering reflects a general association of interests, rather than a strict hierarchy of topics. The first three contributors are all, in different ways, concerned with *context*. While it is a truism to state that cultural phenomena need to be contextualized before they can be comprehended, it is a necessity that is often unheeded. Indeed, much writing on the history of popular music in general is characterized by an impulse to present it as a series of separate and revolutionary events: 'One moment [Elvis Presley] was singing in a school talent show, the next he was appearing on nationwide television' (Friedlander 1996: 43). 'Epstein ... finally got [the Beatles] a contract with EMI and everything began. From there on in, it was fast and straight-ahead' (Cohn 1969: 131). The first of these examples fails to disclose that the background to the arrival of Elvis Presley (or someone very like him) was less than spontaneous, by overlooking the strategy for commercial success that had been established and outlined by the founder and head of the Sun Record Company, Sam Phillips, long before he met Presley: 'If I had a white man who had the Negro sound and the Negro feel, I could make a billion dollars!' (Hopkins 1972: 47). The second neglects to record that 'everything began' for the Beatles when John Lennon and Paul McCartney first met and started to make music together, several years before the contract with EMI. What they both betray, like many similar examples, is a desire to concentrate on immediate and apparently disruptive incidents and dates, which may well add to the historical drama of popular music, but which detracts from our understanding of it as cycle or process. It is a tendency which serves to clarify Palmer's separation of 'the two primary approaches to rock and roll history – the history of creative flashpoints and the history of an ongoing tradition' (1995: 12), whose balance has long been distorted and now needs to be adjusted in favour of the latter approach. Thus, in Chapter 1, Ian Inglis considers the emergent and fashionable success of the Beatles within the context of the changing intellectual conditions in postwar Britain. In Chapter 2, Mike Brocken assesses the specific, and hitherto unrecognized, attractions of rock and roll for the Liverpool gay community in the late 1950s and early 1960s, and the significance this was to have for the development of Merseybeat and the Beatles. John Muncie, in Chapter 3, examines the reciprocal nature of the contributions that may have existed between the Beatles and the formation and operation of those subcultures of youth which were dominant during the group's existence. All three seek to provide contexts, within which the career of the Beatles can be objectively appraised and appreciated.

The following three chapters address the *music* of the Beatles for, notwithstanding the earlier remarks about the multiplicity of roles that accompanied their professional lives, its continuing impact on audiences, other musicians and scholars has remained unequivocal over four decades. Indeed, many of the most thoughtful analyses of the Beatles are to be found within accounts which focus – at least, initially – on their musical characteristics (Mellers 1973; O'Grady 1983; MacDonald 1995; Hertsgaard 1995) but which go on to reveal much about the dynamics between group members, their pursuit of commercial success, their transition from performance to production, and their facility for personal and professional (re)invention. In Chapter 4, Jon Fitzgerald investigates the early years of the Beatles-led British Invasion of the USA, through a comparison of the songwriting techniques and strategies of Lennon–McCartney and those of the other successful British composers of the period. Guy Cook and Neil Mercer, in Chapter 5, present an innovative and computer-based text analysis of song lyrics which reveals startling (and fascinating) variations in the language of the Beatles' early and later songs. And in Chapter 6, Ed Whitley provides a re-evaluation of one of the group's more controversially-received albums – *The Beatles* – by employing a postmodernist discourse to analyse its textual properties.

The next three chapters return to the *career* of the Beatles through a consideration of some of its many facets. Both in its general sociological application, and certainly in its specific relevance to popular music, the concept of career has been successfully distanced from its traditional definition as a series of frequent and predictable advances within a stratified professional or occupational setting. While 'a career in showbusiness' might imply nothing more contentious or enlightening than 'a job as an entertainer', such a usage is clearly insufficient to allow for a critical discussion of the numerous institutional and organizational practices encountered by the Beatles. It is far more appropriate to ground such discussions in terms of the usage favoured by Goffman: 'any social strand of any person's course through life' (1961: 119). He stresses that 'one value of the concept of career is its two-sidedness ... [which] allows one to move back and forth between the personal and the public, between the self and its significant society' (ibid.: 119). The application of this approach to the Beatles quickly suggests that their negotiation of movement between these two environments (the personal life of a Beatle and the public spectacle of the Beatles) is, arguably, one of the more striking aspects of the group's career, as is illustrated by the three case-studies included here. In Chapter 7, Martin Cloonan examines the occasions on which the Beatles were subjected to, and responded to, threats or real instances of censorship, and speculates on the motivations behind such (attempted) restrictions. In Chapter 8, Bob Neaverson investigates the relatively neglected area of the Beatles' participation in movies, and assesses their contemporary and historical significance – for the group itself, for the subsequent development of popular music practice, and for the form and fortunes of British cinema. In Chapter 9, P. David Marshall considers the manner in which the unprecedented international fame of the Beatles – and its particular formulations – provided a template for many subsequent careers in popular music, and shaped our expectations and definitions of celebrity in contemporary culture.What all reveal is the essential and persistent interplay – enacted in various locations – between the group's 'image of self and felt identity' and its position as 'part of a publicly accessible institutional complex' (Goffman 1961: 119) that quickly came to typify the world the Beatles inhabited.

Fittingly, the final two chapters concentrate on the Beatles' relevance for *contemporary issues* within popular music. Although they had done much to confront and dismantle some of the more restrictive structures and cultures of a resistant record industry, it remains true that at the time the group disbanded, many of the technologies, accessories, practices and developments now commonplace were in their infancy, if imagined at all. This, combined with a reluctance by some critics to identify them as musical innovators – 'Because the Beatles very rarely made important innovations in expressive styles, they had very little lasting stylistic impact on popular music. Their influence tended to be transitory' (Gillett 1971: 315) – has led to rigorous questioning of the extent of their reputation and relevance today. In Chapter 10, Gary Burns assesses the contents and omissions in the group's first meaningful explorations of music video – a genre almost unknown during the 1960s – which were produced as part of the 'reunion' around 'Free As A Bird' and 'Real Love' in 1995. And in Chapter 11, Andy Bennett evaluates some of the contrasting stylistic and lyrical concerns which link the Beatles with the Britpop bands of the 1990s, many of whom repeatedly and publicly turn to the group for inspiration, and for whom it would appear the Beatles have assumed an iconic or talismanic significance.

One of the principal satisfactions to be derived from participation in a collaborative project such as this is undoubtedly the exchange of information and ideas with other authors. My own experience with the contributors here has more than confirmed this, and I wish to record my thanks to them for their enthusiasm, encouragement and advice, which have made the preparation of this book such a rewarding and enjoyable activity. In addition, many people gave freely of their time, energy and assistance throughout its evolution. They include Pete Best, John Bird, Karen Brazier, Annabelle Buckley, Gary Burns, Michelle Hills, Greg Hoare, Mary Mellor, Deborah Scott, Kevin Sheridan, Caroline Smith, Pete Smith, Victor Spinetti, Pauline Sutcliffe, Sarah Wilson and Sandy Wolfson. In some ways, the responsibility for the book lies with my parents, Nancy and Norman Inglis, who, among other things, bought me my first record-player and took me to see the Beatles; and I would dearly love to have been able to discuss its contents with Philip Burns, who would, I know, have relished the opportunity to point out my numerous errors and oversights. Over and above all these debts and acknowledgements, however, my deepest gratitude, as for so much in my life, is to Annette Hames, who so generously understands the little child inside the man, and every day teaches me that love really is all you need.

## REFERENCES

Carr, E. H. (1961) *What is History?* London: Macmillan.
Cohn, Nik (1969) *Awopbopaloobop Alopbamboom.* London: Weidenfeld & Nicolson.
Davies, Hunter (1985) *The Beatles (Revised Edition).* London: Jonathan Cape.
Evans, Mike (1984) *The Art of the Beatles.* New York: Beech Tree.

Friedlander, Paul (1996) *Rock and Roll: a Social History*. Boulder, Colorado: Westview.
Gillett, Charlie (1971) *The Sound of the City*. London: Sphere.
Goffman, Erving (1961) *Asylums*. New York: Anchor Books, Doubleday.
Hertsgaard, Mark (1995) *A Day In The Life*. New York: Delacorte.
Hopkins, Jerry (1972) *Elvis*. London: Macmillan.
MacDonald, Ian (1995) *Revolution in the Head*. London: Pimlico.
Mellers, Wilfrid (1973) *Twilight of the Gods: the Beatles in Retrospect*. London: Faber.
Norman, Philip (1981) *Shout! The True Story of the Beatles*. London: Hamish Hamilton.
O'Grady, Terence J. (1983) *The Beatles: a Musical Evolution*. Boston: Twayne.
Palmer, Robert (1995) *Rock & Roll: an Unruly History*. New York: Harmony.
Storey, John (1993) *An Introductory Guide to Cultural Theory and Popular Culture*. Hemel Hempstead: Harvester Wheatsheaf.

# 1 Men of Ideas? Popular Music, Anti-Intellectualism and the Beatles

Ian Inglis

> Until quite recently popular culture has lacked a 'serious' discourse. It was invariably disassociated from intellectual life, usually considered its demonic antithesis, and ... completely under-represented in theory, except by negation. (Chambers 1996: 204)

> Each man ... carries on some form of intellectual activity, that is, he is a 'philosopher', an artist, a man of taste, he participates in a particular conception of the world, has a conscious line of moral conduct, and therefore contributes to sustain a conception of the world or to modify it, that is, to bring into being new modes of thought. (Gramsci 1971: 9)

> We learned more from a three minute record than we ever learned in school. (Bruce Springsteen, 'No Surrender')

Although the Bruce Springsteen song 'No Surrender' does not go on to reveal which three-minute record provided so much, in December 1980 on the evening following John Lennon's murder in New York, the singer had prefaced his show at The Spectrum in Philadelphia by declaring: 'The first song I ever learned was a record called 'Twist And Shout' ... if it wasn't for John Lennon, we'd all be in a different place tonight' (Garbarini et al. 1980: 22).

However, attempts to situate the place (or places) to which popular music can direct its listeners are repeatedly confounded by a broad reluctance within popular music to claim publicly for itself anything more than a role as a mere provider-of-entertainment, and by a well-established tendency outside popular music to dismiss those claims (from performers or researchers) which appear to endorse any greater ambition as pretentious and risible. Whether such attitudes reflect a jealously-guarded elitism, manifested in a conscious hostility

1

to newer forms of artistic activity and a reluctance to relinquish cultural advantage, or a real unfamiliarity with the practices surrounding the production and consumption of popular music that encourages the retention of fallacious and stereotypical judgements, the result is the same. Its performers, its products and its participants have been routinely trivialized and consistently referenced through a discourse of anti-intellectualism which admits the physical, the emotional and the behavioural impacts of popular music, but which finds no place for the cognitive. 'Of course, pop is a form crying out not to be written about. It is physical, sensual, of the body rather than the mind, and in some ways it is anti-intellectual; let yourself go, don't think – feel' (Kureishi and Savage 1995: xix).

That this imbalance is now being (or about to be) redressed is by no means certain. While it is undoubtedly true that the sheer scale and diversity of the international popular music industry (an annual global turnover of record, tape and CD sales approaching $40 billion) have stimulated scrutiny from a multiplicity of academic disciplines, it remains equally true that the popular media (and, to some extent, the specialist music media) continue to identify the vicissitudes of a musician's personal life as more significant than the circumstances and consequences of his or her professional output. Although the adoption of such a perspective is by no means entirely absent from critical appraisals of, for example, the poet, the novelist, or the painter, it is rarely as marked as it is when applied to the popular musician, whose position, in this respect, more closely resembles that of the movie star.

And on those occasions when a 'serious' discourse is practised, the research often yields little in the way of agreement. Observations on the political functions of popular music, for example, vary from conclusions which emphasize that 'music and musicians *can* play a very effective role in radically changing the political and cultural environment of which they are a part' (Wicke 1992: 196) to the assertion that 'the most rock can hope to communicate ... is simpleminded slogans' (Rosselson 1979: 46). In fact, if anything, the earlier comparison with movies understates the extent of the uncertainty surrounding popular music and politics, since there has long been an implicit recognition of the role of film as a vehicle for ideas. The Italian government of the 1930s and the United States government of the 1940s were among those who established fiscal programmes that directly rewarded film-makers whose movies presented positive or sympathetic images of their country. And opposition to the possibility of alternative opinions was most starkly exemplified by the

House Un-American Activities Committee investigations into alleged Communist sympathizers in Hollywood in the early 1950s, which united elements of the movie industry, the news media and the political/military establishment in their explicit declaration of the relationship between film and ideology.

By contrast, popular music has largely (though not completely) evaded that kind of official interrogation, and in some ways this is surprising. On the one hand, the lyrics of songs as diverse as the Small Faces' 'Itchycoo Park' (*Marriott–Lane*), Alice Cooper's 'School Is Out' (*Cooper–Bruce–Buxton–Dunaway–Smith*) and Pink Floyd's 'Another Brick In The Wall' (*Waters*) are among many to have contested the authority of traditional sources of knowledge and its delivery. On the other hand, there is abundant argument in support of music's capacity to assemble and communicate ideas, which it would be unwise to ignore. Such testimonies are to be found in numerous sociological and historical commentaries: 'Popular music is one of the ways that we come to know who we are and what we want' (Street 1986: 226). They are also to be found in the personal reflections of many participants and consumers, such as Keith Richards:

> I really wanted to learn when I was a kid. I really did ... and then the assholes manage to turn the whole thing around ... and then you just hate the learning thing. You don't wanna learn anymore. So you get thrown out of school and you get into art college and it's the same thing. [But] there's always some cat who's ... going through his latest Jack Elliott or Woody Guthrie number, and you discover Robert Johnson, *and it all comes together for you*. (Scaduto 1973: 37–8; emphasis added)

Yet while it is undoubtedly the case that a general reluctance to invest popular music with a role in which ideas are seen as significant does continue to exert its influence inside and outside the industry, it is also true that the activities of a small number of performers have attracted attention and investigation for reasons other than those typically associated with the crudely commercial concerns of the industry. In recent years, they have included Madonna's apparent ability to re-invent herself (boy toy–chameleon–diva), and, in doing so, to provide demonstrations of power and control over her own sexuality for others to follow; Paul Simon's collaboration with musicians from Southern Africa and its implications for the status of Third World music; and the poetry of Bob Dylan, who was himself nominated for the 1997 Nobel Prize for Literature.

However, the performers whose musical and professional careers have been most carefully examined in this way remain the Beatles. Their ability to transcend the role of entertainers and to simultaneously assume, or accept, the role of teachers – of men of ideas – has been upheld in a variety of forms. Some, including Timothy Leary's representation of them as incarnations of a deity are embellished and extravagant: 'I declare that the Beatles are mutants. Prototypes of evolutionary agents sent by God with a mysterious power to create a new species – a young race of laughing freemen. They are the wisest, holiest, most effective avatars the human race has ever produced' (Norman 1981: 287). Others are more restrained in their assessment: 'By virtue of their own example, the Beatles gave people faith in their ability to change themselves and the world around them' (Hertsgaard 1995: 191). And some, as in the recollections of Todd Rundgren, point to a more directly personal impact: '[T]he biggest influence of all was the Beatles. At the time, it involved much more than music. It was a whole connection with your peers and an idea of an alternative method of becoming successful besides going to college and becoming a doctor or lawyer' (Somach and Sharp 1995: 230).

Claims of this sort clearly invite a re-evaluation, within the contours of popular culture, of the Beatles in terms that go beyond the purely musical to encompass the intellectual. It is important here to distinguish between two of the most salient criteria by which intellectual contributions are assessed – their longevity and their impact. It may well be (although I would caution against too premature an adoption of the view) that the durability or longevity of ideas deriving from those referred to as 'pop intellectuals' is relatively weak; in an appraisal of the best known (his list of names includes Susan Sontag, Tom Wolfe, Buckminster Fuller, Andy Warhol, Bob Dylan, John Cage and John Lennon) Ross concludes that 'none have retained any lasting theoretical respect of the sort that is still accorded to the older liberal intelligentsia' (1989: 114).

But the force of the impact of the Beatles' activities is much more difficult to dismiss. Inasmuch as the group and its members have been perceived to co-exist at a number of differing levels – as a historical event, as a cultural phenomenon, as musical innovators, and as role models for many millions of young people around the world – their refusal to conform to the conventional wisdoms and routine practices of a particular artistic environment (and the similar refusal of many of the pop intellectuals with whom they have been bracketed) does seem to conform very closely to some of the conditions of intellectual activity outlined by others.

C. Wright Mills, for example, has noted the importance of fresh perceptions: 'The independent artist and intellectual are among the few remaining personalities equipped to resist and to fight the stereotyping and consequent death of genuinely living things' (1963: 299). Gramsci has referred to the intellectual's ability to influence profoundly – even if only for a while – social reality: '[I]ntellectual activity must also be distinguished in terms of its intrinsic characteristics, according to levels ... which represent *a real qualitative difference*' (1971: 13; emphasis added). Eyerman, whose reference to intellectuals generally views them as 'part of an historical process in which human actors reinvent cultural traditions in different contexts' (1994: 4) also proposes a concept of 'movement intellectuals' – individuals whose position within specific social movements permits them to utilize those spaces through which new forms of knowledge and cognitive identities are produced; the analysis may be particularly helpful in its application to popular music, which is specified as 'an important, though relatively neglected, channel for the transference of political and social meanings into the broader culture' (Eyerman and Jamison 1995: 466). Coser is among those who have pointed to the obstinate and provocative independence of intellectuals, often displayed in a refusal to embrace conformity or constancy: 'They are those who "think otherwise" ... not only puzzling but upsetting to the run of ordinary citizens' (1965: x). And Said has offered a broad overview which might usefully serve as a working definition, and which is made all the more useful by its rejection of the tendency to link intellectual work with rigid hierarchies of knowledge – science, politics, religion, literature, and so on: 'The intellectual is an individual endowed with a facility for representing, embodying, articulating a message, a view, an attitude, philosophy or opinion to, as well as for, a public' (1994: 9).

I hope to show that the significance of popular music may be approached in the context of these (interrelated) conditions – resistance, effect, position, independence, articulation – and that it is not inappropriate to consider the Beatles as successful exemplars of such abilities. Not all popular music can lend itself – or would wish to – to such an analysis. But the analysis is not inherently misplaced, and if popular music is to be taken seriously, as a creative form and as a subject for academic inspection, investigations of this nature are not only justified, but desirable.

## THE BEATLES, POPULAR MUSIC, AND THE 1960s

> People tend to listen to the Beatles the way families in the last
> century listened to readings of Dickens, and it might be remem-
> bered by literary snobs that the novel then, like the Beatles and
> even film now, was considered a popular form of entertainment
> generally beneath serious criticism, and most certainly beneath
> academic attention. (Poirier 1969: 162)

> John Lennon: And the thing about rock and roll, good rock and
> roll ... is that it's real ... you recognize something in it which is
> true, like all true art. (Wenner 1971: 101)

There still persists in popular music today a reticence to engage in comparative evaluations of individual songs, performers or genres. Other
than to employ a broad, ill-defined distinction between 'rock' and 'pop'
which promotes the former as possessing qualities of 'creativity',
'authenticity' and 'distinctiveness', and the latter as 'commercial', 'contrived' and 'predictable', there is no consensually agreed set of criteria
which usefully and consistently allows for objective judgements of
quality. A principal explanation for this lies in the historical experience
of rock and roll itself; through the 1950s and into the early 1960s it was
uniformly dismissed as trite, unimportant and inferior by musicologists
who saw in it no lasting value or musical significance. Five decades on,
having refuted the claims of those who forecast its early disappearance,
there is thus an unwillingness within popular music to be seen to be
making similar and categorical value judgements about the advantages
or shortcomings of specific musics. (It must be said that the industry's
own preoccupation with quantity – sales and the charts – is both a consequence and cause of its retreat from the question of quality).

However, by the mid-1960s, it had become impossible to maintain
that such music was merely a temporary aberration. The recasting of
Elvis Presley from demonic rocker to family movie star (and, in the
UK, a similar, though less marked, transition in the career of Cliff
Richard); the emergence of Tamla Motown as the first internationally
successful Black-owned record label; the impact of Bob Dylan and the
development of the 'protest' song; the British Invasion, led by the
Beatles, which repositioned the sites of power in the global record
industry; the central role assigned to popular music within the first
stirrings of a student movement and counter-culture: all led, in
differing ways, to a recognition that popular music could and should
be taken seriously – as industry, as entertainment, and as art.

Above all, this recognition embodied a perception of popular music as a lasting creative form which possessed its own aesthetic, its own structures and cultures, and which had the ability to generate its own and others' ideas; it has been characterized at this period as a form 'pregnant with ideas and innovations' (Eyerman and Jamison 1995: 452). Among its most significant outcomes was the publication in 1967 of *Rolling Stone*, the first music paper to endeavour to exceed the limitations of the fan magazine and the traditional pop weekly; it described itself as 'sort of a magazine and sort of a newspaper ... a new publication reflecting what we see are the changes in rock and roll and the changes related to rock and roll ... *Rolling Stone* is not just about music, but also about the things and attitudes that the music embraces' (Frith 1978: 144).

Related shifts in the cultural re-arrangement of popular music in the 1960s have been noted by, among others, Chambers. Its typical consumers expanded from 'working class teenagers ... feeding garish juke-boxes' to include the 'recently enfranchized grammar school, student and "hip" middle class audience'. Its sites of consumption were no longer just the coffee-bars, but 'fashionable urban residences ... [and] late night on BBC-2'. Its social and cultural context had been transposed from the 'nonconformity previously associated with the twilight world of beats and jazz' into 'the "radical chic" of a "thinking" person's music' (1985: 84).

The ability of agents of popular culture to undermine the monopoly of legitimate sources of knowledge and its transmission, and the communities which sustained them, to which I referred earlier, was aided in the UK by the rapid and irresistible rise of television, which offered an alternative source of information and explanation and promoted new forms of entertainment. In 1950, 6 per cent of households held a television licence; by 1965, this had risen to more than 90 per cent. ITV began transmissions in 1955 to break the monopoly of BBC; an additional channel, BBC 2, was introduced in 1964. Pulled in opposing directions by the legacy of the Reithian ethic of public service broadcasting and the audience demands of commercial broadcasting, British television evolved, *inter alia*, a style of reportage and presentation which came to occupy the terrain lying between the celebrity chat show and the panel of experts. (The archetypal example of such a programme was *What's My Line?*, in which a quartet of guests drawn from show business, public life and the arts would attempt, through astute questioning and reasoning, to discover a person's occupation).

Blurring news and entertainment, and utilizing documentary and
interview styles, television (and the press) provided the perfect public
platform from which those with something important to say, or those
whom television believed would be appealing to viewers, could
communicate with huge and widely dispersed (socially and geograph-
ically) audiences. In the mid-1960s, at the height of what has been
depicted as a extraordinary period of revolution in Britain and the
Western world, this relatively small, established community of
experts, celebrities and commentators was expanded to accommodate
the more articulate and attractive representatives from the new world
of pop. 'Scarcely a day went by without news of the opening of a new
boutique, without a feature on Terence Stamp or Michael Caine or
Carnaby Street, without a picture of Jean Shrimpton or a mention of
Mick Jagger or decorating tips from David Hicks' (Booker 1969: 275).
In sociological terms, this can be seen as a contemporary illustration
of the movement from exclusion to assimilation within the Parsonian
process of social acceptance.

As the undoubted principals in the cast of the 'Swinging Sixties',
the Beatles shared with television a position of reciprocal gain. The
group, like others, relied on the national and global exposure which
television could provide; television welcomed the guaranteed audiences that accompanied each of their appearances. In a development
not witnessed in the entertainment industry before, the nature of
these appearances gradually changed, from singing (or miming) their
hit songs to participating in interviews and discussions in which they
offered opinions, interpretations, guidance, on events and issues
often unrelated to the traditional concerns of the pop star – the war
in Vietnam, the decriminalisation of marijuana, creativity and
control within popular music, the possibilities of religious exploration, and so on. This transition was to become increasingly evident
as the decade progressed. From October 1962 to April 1970, the
group (individually or collectively) made more than 120 television
broadcasts (excluding news coverage and the screening of their
promotional films/videos) in the UK alone, during which time the
proportion of those in which the primary content was musical rather
than discoursive reduced significantly (Lewisohn 1992: 355). In 1962
and 1963, they made 42 appearances, of which 32 (76 per cent) were
mainly musical; in 1964 and 1965, the group appeared 47 times on
television, of which 19 (40 per cent) were mainly musical; between
1966 and 1970, their 35 television appearances included six (17 per
cent) that were mainly musical.

What replaced the musical emphasis was an emphasis on the Beatles as men of ideas. At different times they were allocated and fulfilled each of the varied roles of the secular scholar outlined by Znaniecki in his analysis of the social circulation of knowledge. *The discoverer of truth* is the person who comes across new truths, hitherto unknown, and is hailed as such by a group of followers. *The systematizer* is characterized by the certainty and completeness of the knowledge he or she possesses, when compared to that from other sources. *The contributor* corrects mistakes, rectifies omissions and contributes at least one or two major accomplishments in a singular field. *The fighter for truth* defends his or her own, and others', explanations and theories, often engaging in particular campaigns. *The eclectic* is not confined to one school or philosophy alone, although he or she may eventually develop a distinctive personal domain. *The disseminator of knowledge* develops, expands and institutionalizes his or her knowledge to an unprecedented degree (1940: 117–50).

The similarities between Znaniecki's descriptions of a particular kind of intellectual and the qualities attributed to the Beatles (and other of their peers) are striking. Moreover, it should not be supposed that the role of intellectuals is somehow diluted by their contact with the contemporary mass media. Responding to the criticism that the media undermine the maintenance of intellectual traditions by the temptations of easy fame and fortune which they offer, Shils insists that this is not automatically the case: '[T]here is no reason to conclude that they affect those with strong motivation or outstanding literary or artistic talent' (1972: 85).

This assertion is reinforced by a consideration of one aspect of the group's musical output throughout the 1960s. The archetypal pop song has always been, and continues to be today, the love song – the lament for lost or unrequited love, the celebration of mutual and/or genuine love, and the comment about the nature and significance of love. However, the Beatles' ability and determination to go beyond conventional estimations of commercial viability, while remaining within the mass medium of records, is seen in the way that their lyrical concerns gradually shifted. Of the 76 self-compositions (typically Lennon–McCartney or Harrison) recorded between 1962 and 1965, 74 (97 per cent) were love songs; of the 120 self-compositions recorded between 1966 and 1970, 38 (32 per cent) were love songs (Inglis 1997). In place of love, their new themes explored alienation and estrangement ('A Day In The Life'), rebirth ('Here Comes The Sun'), escape and solitude ('Fool On The Hill'), political involvement

('Revolution'), nostalgia and regret ('You Never Give Me Your Money'), greed ('Piggies'), the effects of drugs ('Tomorrow Never Knows'), interpretations of childhood ('Penny Lane'), divisions within the counter-culture ('Come Together'), the boredom of excess ('Good Morning, Good Morning'). In so doing, the Beatles were in effect realizing their ability 'to make larger artistic statements within the pop format' (Hertsgaard 1995: 301).

Similarly, the conduct of the group's press conferences through the decade posed a disruption to the established conventions of knockabout question-and-answer sessions in favour of longer, more complex interviews in which beliefs and advice were sought. Two extracts will suffice to demonstrate this. The first is from a group press conference in August 1964 in New York.

> Q:   Do you like fish and chips?
> Ringo:   Yes, but I like steak and chips better.
> Q:   How tall are you?
> Ringo:   Two feet, nine inches.
> Q:   Paul, what do you think of columnist Walter Winchell?
> Paul:   He said I'm married and I'm not.
> George:   Maybe he wants to marry you!
> Q:   How did you find America?
> Ringo:   We went to Greenland and made a left turn.
> Q:   Is it true you can't sing?
> John:   (*points to George*) Not me. Him.
> (Giuliano and Giuliano 1995: 27)

The second is from John Lennon's press conference at the Amsterdam Hilton Hotel in March 1969, during his honeymoon with Yoko Ono.

> Q:   Some people are equal, but some are more equal than others, as you know.
> John:   Yes. But they all have equal possibility.
> Q:   Is Holland a honeymoon country?
> John:   It's a beautiful place. Amsterdam's a place where a lot of things are happening with the youth. It's an important place.
> Q:   Are those ideas that appeal to you?
> John:   Yes, the peaceful ideas that the youth have. If we have any influence on youth at all, we'd like to influence them in a peaceful way.
> Q:   What do you see in a conformist institution such as marriage?

John:   Intellectually, we know marriage is nowhere: that a man
should just say 'Here, you're married', when we've been living
together a year before it. Romantically and emotionally, it's something else. (Ibid. 1995: 118–19)

Taken by themselves, the above examples might be explained by
the duration of the Beatles' success; even for the popular media, there
is a point at which enquiries about diet and height cease to be appropriate. But there are numerous additional factors which would
support a contention that during the 1960s the affiliation between
popular music, its leading performers, and 'the arts' began to stray
outside the parameters erected and maintained by what has been
described as 'the dialectical antagonism that surely governs the relationship between the intellectual and the popular' (Ross 1989: 227).

An early example was the reaction of the literary establishment to
the publication of John Lennon's two books of verses, essays and
drawings. *In His Own Write* (1964) was endorsed by *The Times Literary
Supplement* as 'worth the attention of anyone who fears for the impov-
erishment of the English language and the British imagination'
(Coleman 1984: 195), was honoured by a Foyle's Literary Luncheon
at London's Dorchester Hotel, and was later adapted for the stage
and performed at the National Theatre. *A Spaniard In The Works*
(1965) was said in *New Republic* to have 'at one stroke, put the young
non-reader in touch with a central strand in the literary tradition of
the last thirty years in every English-speaking country' (Thomson and
Gutman 1987: 61); interviewed by literary critic Wilfred De'Ath on
the BBC radio programme *World Of Books*, Lennon revealed that his
major influences included Arthur Conan Doyle and Lewis Carroll.

Parallel to Lennon's acceptance by intellectual circles in Britain
was Paul McCartney's unashamed enthusiasm for contact with other
art forms outside rock and roll. 'Paul was very much the bon vivant
and man about town. He was trying to do a crash course in culture ...
It was Paul who was actually hanging out with London's avant-garde
crowd ... Paul met everybody who was anybody in the creative world'
(Flippo 1988: 212–14). Explaining his increasing immersion and
involvement in the worlds of the theatre, literature, art and classical
music, and the new companions with whom he was exchanging ideas
(Bertrand Russell, Harold Pinter, Kenneth Tynan, Arnold Wesker)
McCartney insisted: 'I don't want to sound like Jonathan Miller going
on, but I'm trying to cram everything in, all the things I've missed.
People are saying things and painting things and composing things

that are great, and I must know what people are doing' (Salewicz 1986: 154).

This appetite for knowledge, translated into 'a truly fierce drive to make sense of the world' (Mills 1959: 233) was repeatedly seen in other areas of the group's activities, too. Of their experiences in 1967–8 of the Maharishi Mahesh Yogi's doctrine of transcendental meditation, Ringo Starr explained: 'We have got almost anything money can buy. But when you can do that, the things you buy mean nothing after a time. You look for something else ... we have found something now which fills the gap' (Giuliano and Giuliano 1995: 86). John Lennon expressed the motivation behind his political collaborations with figures such as Michael X, Tariq Ali and Jerry Rubin in 1970 by stating: 'I think we must make the workers aware of the really unhappy position they are in, break the dream they are surrounded by. They're dreaming someone else's dream, it's not even their own' (Coleman 1984: 363). And George Harrison's rejection of the preeminence of the Beatles was emphasized by his comments in 1968: 'All that sort of Beatle thing is trivial and unimportant. I'm fed up with all this me, us, I, stuff and all the meaningless things we do. I'm trying to work out solutions to the more important things in life' (Davies 1968: 339).

The commitment revealed by the Beatles to their role not merely as consumers of ideas, but as facilitators of the circulation of ideas was formalized with the establishment of Zapple, a sub-division of Apple, the management and recording company formed by the group in 1968. Operating as a new, specialist record label, Zapple was intended to grow into a commercial outlet for the spoken word. Recordings of discussions, conversations and readings with Allen Ginsberg, Gregory Corso, Henry Miller, Lawrence Ferlinghetti, William Burroughs, Charles Bukowski and others were planned, and, in some cases, completed and released. Invitations were also extended to Mao Tse-Tung, Indira Gandhi and Fidel Castro. Zapple's initial press release, in February 1969, announced:

Discussions are now in progress with several world figures, as well as leaders in the various arts and sciences to record their works and thoughts for the label ... It is the hope of Apple Corps Ltd that the new label will help pioneer a new area for the recording industry equivalent to what the paperback revolution did to book publishing. (Miles 1997: 475)

While such forays into the worlds of politics, philosophy and religion do not perforce make an intellectual, they do connect with, and illustrate the validity of Znaniecki's reflections on personal intellectual development, wherein he suggests that the essence of true knowledge is the 'conviction that man, the individual man ... can ... discover the ultimate nature of the world and his own nature' (1940: 161).

The group's comments and behaviours, amplified by an attendant mass media, unexpected because of their origin, and contrasted against a contemporary background in which it was widely supposed that 'an intellectual generation ... simply never appeared' (Jacoby 1987: 3), gained a currency which in other times and other circumstances might not have been theirs. Almost by default, the Beatles (and some of their peers) were elected to act as spokespersons for a generation, to define and guide a global counter-culture, to distinguish the valuable from the worthless, to offer new insights and philosophies, to transform the world – to assume the mantle of (surrogate) intellectuals.

Ironically, they may well have been aided in those obligations by the essential fact (identified by all of their biographers) of their irreverence and sense of humour. Mills has noted the importance of 'a playfulness of mind' (1959: 233); and Said has argued that one of the requirements of intellectuals 'involves a sense of the dramatic and of the insurgent ... catching the audience's attention, being better at wit and debate than one's opponents' (1994: xv). Nowhere were these capacities better displayed than in the note which accompanied John Lennon's return of his MBE (awarded in 1965) to Buckingham Palace in November 1969:

> Your Majesty: I am returning this MBE in protest against Britain's involvement in the Nigeria–Biafra thing, against our support of America in Vietnam, and against 'Cold Turkey' slipping down the charts. With love, John Lennon of Bag. (Coleman 1984: 324)

Commenting on public bewilderment at his return of the MBE, his bed-ins in Amsterdam and Montreal in 1969, and his appearance (with Yoko Ono) concealed inside a large white bag during the Underground Arts Movement's 'Alchemical Wedding' Christmas party at London's Royal Albert Hall in 1968, Lennon demonstrated his awareness of the necessity to combine political argument with the manipulation of the media: 'Henry Ford knew how to sell cars by advertising. I'm selling peace at whatever the cost. Yoko and I are just one big advertising campaign' (Connolly 1981: 121).

Unpredictability, irresponsibility, flippancy which, if taken to extremes, may lead to marginality, also serve to illustrate an important historical connection, which in the case of the Beatles, appears particularly apt. 'Among the intellectuals' ancestors we may also reckon the medieval court jester. *The role of the jester ... was to play none of the expected roles*' (Coser 1965: viii–ix; emphasis added). The disjunction between the expected role of the 'pop star' and the increasingly diverse and innovative roles assumed by the Beatles – musical, social, political, professional – became one of the most striking components of their career. The fact that many of their actions were inconsistent, uncertain, unsuccessful and (in retrospect) ill-advised, does not detract from the status of the ideas from which they derived. '[I]t should not surprise us that our age has been characterized as one of conversion. Nor should it be surprising that intellectuals especially have been prone to change their world views radically and with amazing frequency' (Berger 1963: 63).

However one seeks to approach and evaluate the significance of the Beatles, the extent to which the debates provoked by their career can be meaningfully investigated relies on a constant awareness of the principal fact that they are musicians. To state this is not to devalue their other (subsequent) roles, but to recognize that their work, its point of origin, and its impetus were primarily musical. Whatever its nature – literature, painting, poetry, music – 'nothing is as important to the intellectual as the work he creates. Through this work, he affirms his calling, and his creation strengthens his identity' (Coser 1965: 326).

That the Beatles' music was, and continues to be, widely regarded as (among) the best of its kind and time is self-evident, as its critical respect and commercial success suggest. However, these are merely the public manifestations of artistic fortune; the personal certainty of satisfaction is the criterion which guides the intellectual. The craft of composition and the release of the imagination may be the sole activities through which creative performers are able to reassure themselves that their work – and thus, they – possess intrinsic value. This is especially true within the working practices of the entertainment industry, where the over-riding emphasis tends to be on instant gratification, winning formulae and predictable outcomes. Popular music is often seen as exhibiting the most acute embodiment of these concerns, operating as it does within boundaries created by the relatively inflexible demands of airplay requirements, the existence of the charts, assumptions about appropriate subject matter and suitable lyrical content, and, more recently, music video formats.

The ability to confront and overcome these limitations is rare indeed, which is why so many popular musicians have chosen to distance themselves from segments of their work, by invoking a professional cynicism about its merits. While such repositioning is certainly present in some of the Beatles' reflections on their music, there is a much deeper, and more consistent, appraisal of their own work which points to a satisfaction with the way in which it substantiates the identification and justification of themselves as creative musicians. John Lennon's assessment of the group's musical abilities provides one confirmation of this: 'I think Paul and Ringo stand up anywhere with *any* of the rock musicians. Not technically great. None of us were technical musicians. None of us could read music. None of us can write it. But as pure musicians, as inspired humans to make noise, they're as good as anybody!' (Sheff and Golson 1981: 142). Similar sentiments about the group's capacity as composers have been articulated by Paul McCartney: 'People always say to me "Do you think you and John were great?" I say "We were fantastic." It would be kind of stupid to say we're no good' (Coleman 1995: 61).

Equally significant was the ability of the Beatles to engage in musical innovation and departure without seeming to undermine their earlier outputs. So, for example, Lennon defined 'In My Life' (1965) as his first major piece of work, suggesting that from that time 'the *depth* of the Beatles' songwriting ... was more pronounced; it had a more mature, more intellectual – whatever you want to call it – approach' (Sheff and Golson 1981: 121). Yet at the same time, McCartney has found much to be proud of in the group's first single 'Love Me Do' (1962): '[That] was our greatest philosophical song: "Love me do/You know I love you/I'll always be true/So love me do/Please love me do". For it to be simple, and true, means that it's incredibly simple' (Miles 1978: 79).

McCartney's (and the group's) endorsement of a language which is direct and a presentation which is unambiguous have been seen in part to draw on some of the narrative simplicities of the traditional folk song. 'Maybe the most important service of the Beatles and similar groups is the restoration to good standing of the simplicities that have frightened us into irony and the search for irony; they locate the beauty and pathos of commonplace feelings even while they work havoc with fashionable or tiresome expressions of those feelings' (Poirier 1969: 167). In addition, the enunciation of the simplicity of clear statement reveals one of the principles through which intellectual activity and the communication of ideas come to be stimulated.

'The "creative" act, of any artist, is in any case the process of making a meaning active, by communicating an organised experience to others' (Williams 1961: 49).

This last point deserves clarification. Like the creative artist, the intellectual too requires a community within which he or she is to function, and within which the intellectual vocation is possible. These requirements are discussed in Coser's assessment of the place of intellectuals within contemporary mass culture:

> First, intellectuals need an audience, a circle of people to whom they can express themselves and who can bestow recognition [...] Second, intellectuals require regular contact with their fellow intellectuals, for only through such communication can they evolve common standards of method and excellence, common norms to guide their conduct. (1965: 3)

If 'intellectuals' is replaced by 'popular musicians' in the above passage, and applied to the history of the Beatles, the analysis is not diminished, but gains from the inclusion of a singular and pertinent example.

This overall sense of a distinct, dynamic and diversified community in which the Beatles were active and influential has prompted a comparison with the *jongleurs* or 'wandering minstrels' of the Middle Ages, the itinerant poet-musicians who used their musicianship to fulfil a multiplicity of roles – entertainer, critic, chronicler, commentator – and who were simultaneously courted and distrusted by those who aspired to be their patrons. In some ways the comparison may not be valid; technological, geographical and political conditions and opportunities scarcely existed in the way they do today. But in the context of the communication of ideas and the generation of new knowledges that typically contest the privileged existence of older, more established ones, and the public adoption of the adversarial positions they often imply, the cultural and musical history of the 1960s does support such a comparison. 'Who would have thought that the pop music of the 1960s would develop into a force as vital as that of the jongleur of old?' (Peyser 1969: 127).

## CONCLUSION

> Leonard Bernstein:    Three bars of 'A Day In The Life' still sustain me, rejuvenate me, inflame my senses and sensibilities. (Stokes 1980: ii)

Abbie Hoffman:  There was a cultural revolution where the best and the popular were identical. And that is a very rare occurrence in history. The effect of something like *Sgt Pepper's Lonely Hearts Club Band* ... on me and other activists, organisers and counter-culture people around the world was one of incredible impact. (Giuliano and Giuliano 1995: 261)

Wilfrid Mellers:  Through their music they rendered articulate a generation. (Mellers 1973: 188)

The history of mass communications, from the introduction to Britain of William Caxton's printing press in the late fifteenth century to the proliferation around the world of Bill Gates's Microsoft programs in the late twentieth century, has always been dependent on the interplay between two separate but crucially related variables – an audience and a technology. One without the other is redundant. Whatever the size of the population, it only becomes an audience when it has access to a common technology; whatever the specifications of the technology, it only evolves into a system of communication when it has located and contacted an audience.

Not until the 1950s did the technologies of the record player, the transistor radio and the jukebox coincide with the emergence of a new audience, composed of large numbers of young, relatively affluent men and women, who became known as teenagers. The resulting (often inexact) correspondence of supply and demand was able to exploit the convergence of several musical strands – gospel, blues, ballads, folksong (including country) and jazz – which had begun in the 1940s, and which had given rise to a new form of contemporary popular music, called rock and roll. Of course, the simultaneous existence of an audience and a technology does not *per se* guarantee anything other than the possibility of new forms of cultural activity; that the activities surrounding rock and roll were so successful was contingent on a number of other factors, including economic, legal and demographic circumstances. Significantly, it has also been recognized that like cultural activity, intellectual life too depends not only on an audience but on institutions of communication through which its works can be assessed, selected and disseminated. To the extent that there is a common identification between the preconditions for the activation of popular culture (including popular music) and the transactions of intellectual life, it is therefore plausible to continue to think of the two as related, both theoretically and substantively.

These remarks should not be seen to imply that for the Beatles (and others) the pop song became a manifesto carrying a stream of messages, insights and announcements from teacher to pupils. John Lennon's explicit denial of this – 'Forget about the teacher. If the Beatles had a message, it was that. With the Beatles, the music is the point' (Sheff and Golson 1981: 108) – is not, however, so much a rejection of the argument that songs (as texts) possess meanings and can convey messages, but a frank admission that their precise nature is unknown, even to the musician. One is reminded of the observation attributed to Alfred Stieglitz: 'You will discover ... that if the artist could explain in words what he has made, he would not have had to create it' (Norman 1960: 10). Notwithstanding these reservations, there remains much in the music and career of the Beatles that lends itself to a re-evaluation in terms of the social role of the man of knowledge.

One striking, and relevant, example of the association between the popular and the intellectual is provided by considering the condition of Britain in the 1950s, and in particular its intellectual life, which in the early years of the decade was marked by an 'extraordinary state of self-satisfaction' (Shils 1972: 139), and protected and prolonged by the existence of strict social and geographical bounds around what continued to be an exclusive, if pluralistic, community. Yet, by mid-decade, 'out of this comparative placidity, Britain suddenly entered on a period of upheaval ... above all, a new spirit was unleashed – a new wind of essentially youthful hostility to every kind of established convention and traditional authority, a wind of moral freedom and rebellion' (Booker 1969: 32–3). This upheaval centred primarily around a recalibration of the distance between the popular and the intellectual within the world of ideas, as some examples from that world may help to indicate.

In September 1955, *Waiting For Godot*, written by Samuel Beckett and directed by Peter Hall, opened at the Arts Theatre in London, followed in 1956 by John Osborne's *Look Back In Anger* at the Royal Court Theatre, and Brendan Behan's *The Quare Fellow* at Joan Littlewood's Theatre Workshop. Kingsley Amis's *Lucky Jim* (1954), Colin Wilson's *The Outsider* (1956) and John Braine's *Room At The Top* (1957) were among the decade's first novels by new authors. The Institute Of Contemporary Arts' 'This Is Tomorrow' exhibition at the Whitechapel Gallery in 1956 introduced pop art to Britain. The Campaign For Nuclear Disarmament held its first Aldermaston march over Easter in 1958. By 1955, the most popular programme on radio was the comedy series *The Goon Show*, first broadcast in 1952. For many, the definitive exposition of the energies contained in these and other events was achieved in the publication in 1957 of *Declaration*, a collection of essays whose introduction referred to 'indignation against the apathy, the complacency, the idealistic bankruptcy of their environment' felt by 'a number of young and widely opposed writers [who] have burst upon the scene and are striving to change many of the values which have held good in recent years' (Maschler 1957: 3).

While it is important not to romanticize or exaggerate the significance of examples like these, it is equally important not to overlook them. Individually, they may offer instances of the fresh perspectives referred to earlier; *Look Back In Anger* has, for example, been defined as the play which 'announced a new kind of attitude, a new kind of drama, even a new kind of actor' (Levin 1970: 251). Taken together, their proximity is not coincidental, but indicative of a general resurgence of independent artistic and intellectual activity from those formerly excluded from such a community:

one of the most impressive facts about modern life is that in it, unlike preceding cultures, intellectual activity is not carried on exclusively by a socially rigidly defined class ... but rather by a social stratum which is to a large degree unattached to any social class and which is recruited from an increasingly inclusive area of social life. (Mannheim 1960: 139)

Placed in conjunction with simultaneous developments, such as the rapid growth of television, the increasing availability of contraception, the emergence of the affluent society, the abolition of conscription, they contextualize the period in which the promises embedded in American rock and roll had introduced alternatives, in leisure and work, into the lives of many aspiring young British musicians, such as the Beatles. And overall, they illustrate the initiation of a process which in effect dismantled many of the barriers between the intellectual and popular culture. Popular culture itself became a recognized subject for intellectual investigation and comment; and the approved environs of intellectuals expanded from bourgeois literary, artistic and academic precincts to encompass large sections of the mass culture industries. Moreover, these tendencies developed an impetus of their own which quickly led to an exponential rate of growth in the quantity, range and content of the works produced. The novelist Doris Lessing has written that 'when a hitherto inarticulate class is released into speech, it brings a fresh rush of vitality into literature' (1957: 22); in the years that followed, cinema, theatre, broadcasting and music were to reap similar benefits from the democratisation of admission to and membership of such circles.

There is a great temptation to seek to establish an unbreakable connection between the Beatles and the events and developments of the 1960s; understandably so, since the group's musical successes did occur in those years. But, in addition to imposing analytical constraints, this tendency has also, on occasion, been responsible for a reification of the decade, through which it is endowed with spiritual, material, even spatial qualities. Such analyses are not wholly untenable, but certainly incomplete. The Beatles and their peers in the 1960s were not the *inventors* but the *inheritors* of the possibilities first mooted in the 1950s, as they themselves were growing from schoolboys into young adults. John Lennon has been quick to acknowledge this: 'Whatever wind was blowing at the time moved the Beatles too. I'm not saying we weren't flags on the top of the ship. But the whole boat was moving. Maybe the Beatles were in the crow's nest shouting "Land Ho!" ... but we were all in the same damn boat' (Sheff and Golson 1981: 78). His insight is remarkably similar to Mannheim's observation, made some fifty years earlier, that the particular position enjoyed by intellectuals may permit them to accomplish individually things of very much wider significance: 'Thus they might play the part of watchmen in what would otherwise be a pitch-black night' (1960: 143). Inasmuch as the achievements of the Beatles illuminated and enlightened so many paths followed by so many people, his comment might well stand as an apt metaphor with which to finally evaluate the importance of their work.

## REFERENCES

Berger, Peter (1963) *Invitation to Sociology: a Humanistic Perspective*. New York: Doubleday.
Booker, Christopher (1969) *The Neophiliacs*. London: Collins.
Chambers, Iain (1985) *Urban Rhythms*. London: Macmillan.
Chambers, Iain (1996) 'Waiting on the End of the World', in David Morley and Kuan-Hsing Chen (eds), *Stuart Hall: Critical Dialogues in Cultural Studies*. London: Routledge.
Coleman, Ray (1984) *John Lennon*. London: Sidgwick & Jackson.

Coleman, Ray (1995) *McCartney: Yesterday and Today*. London: Boxtree.

Connolly, Ray (1981) *John Lennon*. London: Fontana.

Coser, Lewis A. (1965) *Men of Ideas*. New York: Free Press.

Davies, Hunter (1968) *The Beatles*. London: Heinemann.

Eyerman, Ron (1994) *Between Culture and Politics: Intellectuals in Modern Society*. Cambridge: Polity.

Eyerman, Ron and Andrew Jamison (1995) 'Social Movements and Cultural Transformation: Popular Music in the 1960s', *Media, Culture and Society*, **17**(3): 449–68.

Flippo, Chet (1988) *McCartney*. London: Sidgwick & Jackson.

Frith, Simon (1978) *The Sociology of Rock*. London: Constable.

Garbarini, Vic, Brian Cullman and Barbara Graustark (eds) (1980) *Strawberry Fields Forever: John Lennon Remembered*. New York: Bantam.

Giuliano, Geoffrey and Brenda Giuliano (eds) (1995) *The Lost Beatles Interviews*. London: Virgin.

Gramsci, Antonio (1971) *Selections from the Prison Notebooks*. London: Lawrence & Wishart.

Hertsgaard, Mark (1995) *A Day in the Life*. New York: Delacorte.

Inglis, Ian (1997) 'Variations on a Theme: the Love Songs of the Beatles', *International Review of the Aesthetics and Sociology of Music*, **28**(1): 37–62.

Jacoby, Russell (1987) *The Last Intellectuals*. New York: Basic Books.

Kureishi, Hanif and Jon Savage (eds) (1995) *The Faber Book of Pop*. London: Faber.

Lessing, Doris (1957) 'The Small Personal Voice', in Tom Maschler (ed.), *Declaration*. London: MacGibbon & Kee.

Levin, Bernard (1970) *The Pendulum Years*. London: Jonathan Cape.

Lewisohn, Mark (1992) *The Complete Beatles Chronicle*. London: Pyramid.

Mannheim, Karl (1960) *Ideology and Utopia*. London: Routledge.

Maschler, Tom (ed.) (1957) *Declaration*. London: MacGibbon & Kee.

Mellers, Wilfrid (1973) *Twilight of the Gods: the Beatles in Retrospect*. London: Faber.

Miles, Barry (1978) *Beatles in their Own Words*. London: Omnibus.

Miles, Barry (1997) *Paul McCartney: Many Years from Now*. London: Secker & Warburg.

Mills, C. Wright (1959) *The Sociological Imagination*. New York: Oxford University Press.

Mills, C. Wright (1963) *Power, Politics and People*. New York: Ballantine.

Norman, Dorothy (1960) *Alfred Stieglitz: an American Seer*. New York: Random House.

Norman, Philip (1981) *Shout!* London: Hamish Hamilton.

Peyser, Joan (1969) 'The Music of Sound or the Beatles and the Beatless', in Jonathan Eisen (ed.), *The Age of Rock*. New York: Vintage.

Poirier, Richard (1969) 'Learning from the Beatles', in Jonathan Eisen (ed.), *The Age of Rock*. New York: Vintage.

Ross, Andrew (1989) *No Respect: Intellectuals and Popular Culture*. New York: Routledge.

Rosselson, Leon (1979) 'Pop Music: Mobiliser or Opiate?', in Carl Gardner (ed.), *Media, Politics and Culture*. London: Macmillan.

Said, Edward (1994) *Representations of the Intellectual*. London: Vintage.

Salewicz, Chris (1986) *McCartney*. London: Queen Anne Press.

Scaduto, Anthony (1973) *Mick Jagger*. London: W. H. Allen.

Sheff, David and G. Barry Golson (eds) (1981) *The Playboy Interviews with John Lennon and Yoko Ono*. New York: Playboy Press.

Shils, Edward (1972) *The Intellectuals and the Powers*. University of Chicago Press.

Somach, Denny and Ken Sharp (1995) *Meet the Beatles ... Again!* Havertown, Philadelphia: Musicom.

Stokes, Geoffrey (1980) *The Beatles*. New York: Times Books.

Street, John (1986) *Rebel Rock*. London: Blackwell.

Thomson, Elizabeth and David Gutman (eds) (1987) *The Lennon Companion*. London: Macmillan.

Wenner, Jann (1971) *Lennon Remembers*. London: Penguin.

Wicke, Peter (1992) 'The Role of Rock Music in the Political Disintegration of East Germany', in James Lull (ed.), *Popular Music and Communication*. Newbury Park, California: Sage.

Williams, Raymond (1961) *The Long Revolution*. London: Chatto & Windus.

Znaniecki, Florian (1940) *The Social Role of the Man of Knowledge*. New York: Columbia University Press.

# 2 Coming Out of the Rhetoric of 'Merseybeat': Conversations with Joe Flannery

## Mike Brocken

Brian Epstein was 'not gay'. He was a 'queer', a 'puff', a 'pansy' ... but he was not 'gay'. The expression simply did not exist in the Liverpool of the 1950s and early 1960s. To be 'gay' was to be happy, exhilarated, confident ... qualities that had no connection with what were then considered to be acts of perversion and gross indecency. To be 'queer' was to be one of the dregs of conventional society, on the hinterlands of a netherworld.

Sadly, it appears that for many writing today about Liverpool during the 'Merseybeat'[1] era, these oppositions still apply. There remains a formulaic belief by some 'Merseybeat' specialists that a 'rock narrative' *per se* continues to be the 'alternative' way of knowing about popular music activity in the city during the 1950s and early 1960s, grounded in references to 'Cunard Yanks'[2], 'prellies'[3] and sex. Yet these histories, full of gender stereotypes and based, still, on a concept of rock and roll as a distinctly macho orientation, are ineffective and incomplete while they continue to ignore their own inherent institutionalization and gender reinforcement. Any critical capacity has disappeared from narratives concerning the Beatles and 'Merseybeat', leaving us with a universalizing didacticism that rejects accounts which do not fit easily into canonical descriptions. Brian Epstein, therefore, remains a 'queer'. The problem that faces those who persist in writing about 'Merseybeat' in this customary manner is that, ultimately, any historical narrative requires remapping and further theoretical reconstruction. For the Beatles, that time is long overdue.

Joe Flannery was also 'not gay'. Joe was a pivotal influence upon Brian Epstein in the important second phase of the Beatles' career (the transition from regional to national celebrity). Joe managed a number of groups and performers via his Carlton Brooke Agency (including Lee Curtis – Joe's brother – and the All Stars, Beryl Marsden, Steve Aldo, the Nocturns) and later went on to manage the Star Club in Hamburg, together with its associated franchises, during that club's heyday between 1963 and 1967. It was Flannery who suggested to Epstein that the Beatles should wear suits, ask for more money, and adopt a more professional stance (for example, it was his idea that the Beatles stay in their dressing room, rather than mingle with fans, after their gigs). Joe Flannery handled the entire Pete Best 'affair' for Brian Epstein – 'Brian didn't really want his hands to be dirtied by the affair'[4] – and is one of the very few people who really understands *why* Best was removed from the Beatles in 1962. Most Beatles 'experts' would be shocked to discover just how much Joe Flannery was involved in turning the Beatles into a thoroughly professional performing group, since he has remained relatively silent about his close personal and business relationship with Brian Epstein as a covenant with the Epstein family; but he *was there*, and is one of the few 'Beatle people' in Liverpool who still has the ear, friendship and respect of the surviving Beatles.

I have spent more than two years researching into Flannery's personal history and involvement in 'Merseybeat' and, via many discussions and interviews with Joe and those around him (then and now), have come to appreciate that while the impetus of the Beatles grew out of important social and economic circumstances in the years following the end of the Second World War, it was also part of a historical interpretation of *hidden* performance and social histories of that era in the UK, as well as a rereading of the social uses of performance. In fact, the influence of Liverpool's homosexual community on 'Merseybeat' in general and the Beatles in particular was a highly significant part of this re-evaluation. As an intricate and important aspect of the Beatles' career, it has hitherto been either ignored, or else stereotyped into a quasi-farcical 'homosexual manager signs boys' narrative (see Rogan 1988).[5]

Popular music traditions are now correctly recognized as representing our historical heritage. However, this 'understanding' often fails to recognize the complex social processes within which pop historicity came to be constructed initially. To the extent that popular music histories are often written as 'rock' histories, they carry a considerable number of male motifs of 'authenticity'. Indeed, many rock histories are so strewn with macho/ideological leanings and prejudices of one sort or another that they simply reproduce an 'internal' narrative. There is, however, room for a history of the Beatles without the limitations of internal narratives. There are, in fact, many inter-weaving histories existing simultaneously, and, although we cannot record them all, the popular music historian must always be sensitive to the critical question of balance.

As stated above, like Brian Epstein, Joe Flannery was/is also 'not gay'. Unlike the unfortunate Epstein, however, Joe is still available to discuss his experiences and influences, and, in so doing, to provide an alternative reading of a singularly important period in the evolution of popular music. Flannery's history presents an opportunity to furnish ourselves with a challenge to the (often) tedious metanarrative ramblings of the 'Merseybeat Mafia', those apparent specialists who continue to roll out their 'Merseybeat' can(n)on, blasting out the same old sequential anecdotes time and time again. Indeed, Flannery is seldom consulted by these 'experts' (Dave McAleer, Mark Lewisohn, Alan Clayson) because, like many Beatles fans, they are rather non-quantitative historians who are reluctant to incorporate findings from diverse sources on trust, fearing that such evidence may challenge their predetermined notions of rock's essential authenticity and barbarism – the rock writer's *violence symbolique*'.

Thus, while the impact of rock and roll on the city of Liverpool has been repeatedly documented, the impact of what we would now call the gay community (the 'queers' and 'puffs' of 40 years ago) on the furthering of rock and roll as a meaningful social practice has never been regarded as a significant part of that historical–musical jigsaw puzzle. Instead, in accordance with the rock historical/mythological use of words such as 'organic', 'alternative' and 'authentic', we have been presented with a picture of Liverpool as a 'macho', 'hard' city, full of wide-boys, con-men and thieves. Ironically, while rock writers have continued to explore these sets of stylistic devices, they have not expanded the scope or reputation of their genre at all, but have merely presented it within a shallow, hierarchical discipline in which only their own enquiries and assertions are illuminated (the current crop of writers on *New Musical Express* is an acute example of this form of cultural capital). This is neither 'organic' nor 'alternative'. The characteristics of the *Rolling Stone* school of rock writing – a striving towards objectivity, the down-to-earth styles, a casual and/or cool attitude, the sense of 'Merseybeat' being 'what it was' – has ulti-mately explained very little, and only constituted itself at the centre of that meaning. Rather than select and idealize one chosen group or period, a need exists to contextualize the period more fully and to re-evaluate one's predispositions and assumptions from a variety of different standpoints. This can only assist our understanding of the Beatles, their music, and their locality.


THE FLANNERY FILE

After a tortuous time following his National Service in the early 1950s, when his engagement to a local girl broke down (not because of his sexuality, but because of his fiancée's infidelity), Joe Flannery was to find a level of personal salvation in the apparently 'macho' sounds of rock and roll (and skiffle) that projected the stereotypes of US (and British) teenage sexual behaviour. The musics actually assisted Joe's and Brian Epstein's escape from their ceaseless difficulties created by the 'straight' society of the 1950s – not for the reasons suggested by, for example, Rogan (1988), whose discussion of pop managers in the 1950s and 1960s places them in a series of sexual pigeon-holes ranging from motherly affection to sexual infatuation, but because rock and roll music, the 'scene', the activity, at least helped to facilitate a relatively gender-free evaluation of a person's character (perhaps, for both of them, for the first time). Although the dance culture of the 1990s has often been credited with a gender-free communality and *esprit de corps*, and described as almost revolutionary in its encouragement of a sexual behaviour, it is in fact neither revolutionary (haven't people always danced?) nor does it have exclusive rights to gender-free evaluations of 'otherness'. Joe informed me:

> When I began managing my brother's band [the Detours], I found that I was trying to be as discreet as I had to be in my daytime work ... never a word, never an expression, never a glance out of place ... just in case, you know. But it was in the smelly cellars of Liverpool and the suburban dance halls and jive hives that I began to question 'normality'. In these places there were no questions ... or at least very few questions ... about one's place there at all. You were just *there*.

At the same time, there is little doubt that the Liverpool of the 1950s could be a very dangerous place for a homosexual male. The repeal of the Homosexual Act in 1967 which served to legalize private homosexuality between consenting males over 21 was still far off. Even the expression 'homosexual' – a word we familiarly use today almost as much as the term 'gay' – was not common and not easily defined. For example, Joe told me that after the collapse of his heterosexual relationship, he had no idea that he might be gay himself, and had drifted into the few bars frequented by gay men more or less by accident. I verified this with information from other members of the Liverpool gay community of the period, who confirmed that in the cases of Joe and Brian, nothing was ever openly discussed. This was to protect individuals from the possibilities of arrest, blackmail, beatings or, most dramatically, confinement in Rainhill Lunatic Asylum (where, as one man revealed to me, he was given 'aversion therapy', shown heterosexual pornography, and given drugs to either quell or divert his sexual impulses).

## LOCALITY

Further research, together with recollections of my own childhood in Liverpool, helped me to place the locality frequented by many of those involved in the Liverpool gay community of the 1950s. The area is, sadly, no longer a part of the city's rapidly changing landscape, having initially been used as a car park for the St John's Precinct shopping mall, and now (as I write) forming part of the site for the construction of a new hotel within an area to be renamed by its original title: somewhat ironically, Queen's Square. The cobbled square lay riverside of St John's Precinct, in front and to the right of the Liverpool Playhouse; it was here that Liverpool's fruit and vegetable market existed until the late 1960s, when it moved to a site it still occupies on Prescot Road (formerly a speedway and rugby league stadium). On what is now a car park to the right of the present gyratory stood a couple of pubs and a hotel – The Stork Hotel, a cream-painted building with a very elegant entrance. The Stork was residential and, as it was within walking distance of the Playhouse theatre, its cheap and cheerful accommodation was well patronized by travelling actors and the transient salesmen of the day. Together with the occupants of the Stork Hotel's bar and the Magic Clock pub, the square *itself* plays a vitally important part in the origins of 'Merseybeat' for it was only a short walk away from the fruit and vegetable warehouses in Mathew Street and Harrington Street. It was in the cellar of one of these enormous buildings that the Cavern Club opened for trad jazz and skiffle music in 1958. At the time, the cellar that was to become the most famous musical venue in the world was empty, but had previously been used as a wine, as well as a vegetable, warehouse. My own personal memories of the place (which commence in the mid-1960s) are ones of the pungent odours of rotting vegetables from nearby warehouses and stale urine from the inadequate and overflowing drains.

Joe Flannery was initially nicknamed 'the Untouchable' by some of Liverpool's gay community who felt that he should be allowed time to come to terms with his own sexuality, without undue pressure from those who cared. And they did care. There was great cameraderie shown by the gay community, a community steeped in art, theatre and music, and also in the methods of surviving as an 'underground'. Caution and a high level of secrecy were essential, for even the simple act of entering the wrong pubs invited the unwanted attentions of 'queer-bashers' and/or the Liverpool Constabulary. Joe told me that both he and Brian Epstein were sporadically watched by the police, who would occasionally place 'undercover' officers in certain venues in order to catch somebody 'at it'. This was especially ironic since a few closet homosexuals from Liverpool's 'respectable city fathers' also frequented the Stork Hotel and the Magic Clock. Joe and Brian were even followed home by police squad cars:

> The police showed such an interest in Brian that I'm still convinced of two things: firstly, that there was (and probably still is, some-where) a file on Brian's activities in the late fifties and early sixties; secondly, that they handed out a good hiding to him on one occasion. The Epsteins were a special family in Liverpool. They had made a lot of money and were also of the Jewish faith. Now that was OK if you were conventional ... but, step out of line and, well, you can imagine ...

It was amongst the good friends and close confidants in this 'subterraneous' atmosphere that the young Joe Flannery and Brian Epstein began to develop their ideas about show business. Both had attempted (relatively unsuccessfully – Joe as a singer with the Joe Loss Band, Brian as a student at RADA) to enter the entertainment business as performers but, through spending invaluable time with the many local and visiting actors and actresses who used the Stork Hotel (Brian Bedford, Patricia Routledge, Rita Tushingham), other ideas began to germinate.

Although still unaware of his true sexuality, Joe was undoubtedly the first person in whom Brian Epstein confided about his own inclinations. As one might expect between close friends, Joe knew of Brian's homosexuality before the Epstein family. But even while showing sympathy towards his young friend in attempting to understand his predicament, it did not occur to Joe that he too was homosexual. His own Roman Catholic upbringing, together with the social climate of postwar Britain in which sexual matters were seldom if ever divulged, combined to ensure that Joe was unable to confront his own feelings for some considerable time. Despite the affection and honourable distance shown to him by leading members of the gay community, such as Liverpool photographer Albert Marrion, Joe remained unable and/or unwilling to acknowledge the nature of his sexuality:

> I was terrified. People would tell me to let go, but I was terrified. I wasn't really sure exactly what I felt! There were people who would like to watch the men, even though they claimed not to be homosexual, and they were named 'viewers'. I didn't know whether I was a 'viewer' or not ... I didn't know whether I was Arthur or Martha!

Surrounded by repressive conditions, and following Brian's experiences of brutality and blackmail which prompted Joe to begin the search to discover himself, it was rock and roll and the management of his brother's groups (the Teenage Rebels, the Detours, the All Stars) which codified that journey of discovery.

## ROCK AND ROLL DANCE AS METAPHOR

While his companions in The Stork were trying unsuccessfully to help Joe liberate his feelings, the male-dominated rock and roll of the 1950s did become a socially liberating force for him ... and not through the attraction of its boys! Even the very locations of its performance in Liverpool, many of which were suburban, were a source of stimulation. Venues such as the Aintree Institute, Garston Baths, the Queen's Hall in Widnes, the Orrell Park Ballroom, even the Riverpark Ballroom in Chester were the important sites. Managing Lee Curtis took Joe away from the clandestine meeting places around Queen's Square in the city centre, and he was to discover the key to his personal liberty and sexuality through his interest in and understanding of the meaningful social functions of dancing and the beat in these local jive hives. Sounding like an Acid House raver of the late 1980s, Joe explained to me in 1994 how his worries and concerns were diminished once 'inside the beat and among the dancers dancing to the beat'.

At first, I found this difficult to comprehend. How could a person be made more aware of his own sexuality through dancing and, in particular, watching *others* dance (Joe did not always dance himself, except occasionally with his friend, Cilla Black)? How could listening to the heavy beat of Liverpool rock and roll lead to sexual liberation? Following several additional interview sessions, we were able to approach the nexus of what Joe thought he meant, and in so doing, uncover a fresh component of the history of 'Merseybeat'.

He explained that once he began to manage Lee Curtis's various groups, he felt part of something different, something 'other' – but not merely from a 'band' perspective. In his youth, Joe had been an accomplished and enthusiastic ballroom dancer, but felt that by the late 1950s, ballroom dancing had become a meliorating force; it had been institutionalized and developed into:

> a kind of art form for the middle classes, very remote. But the bodily forms that I started seeing in the jive hives were fantastic pieces of timing and great exhibitions of fun. The kids were told that they shouldn't dance like 'niggers', but that just smacked of racialism. In actual fact, they were dancing without *any* preconceptions at all ... black nor white ... I just found it so refreshing – especially when they were doing it to Peter's [Lee's] band and everything was going well ... it was a revelation for me.

He felt a rush of 'collective' association:

> Nothing looked more disorganised when I would look out from behind the scenes at the dancers at, say, the Aintree Institute, but nothing felt more coherent, because I felt (and I think that Brian also felt) that 'normality' was left outside.

He saw the dancers as:

> uncontrolled, brash, physical, exciting ... not pre-planned to any great extent except that the girls might like to dance around their handbags and flirt a little.

The word to which Joe frequently returned was 'uncontrolled' – the very antithesis of the forced and controlled behaviour encountered in the albeit communal atmosphere of the Stork Hotel or the Magic Clock. In contradistinction to the activities in the jive hives, evenings at the Stork were characterized by an almost 'instrumental' precision which was manifested in carefully planned expressions, movements and glances. Joe called this 'knife and fork behaviour'. For Joe Flannery, the bodily awareness of the dancers metaphorically emphasized the taboo and the tolerated in conventional society. On the one

hand, the puritanical forbidding of bodily pleasure beyond certain
norms and modes of 'decent' behaviour in 1959–60 were questioned
by the youthful dancers. On the other hand, his own (and Brian's)
instrumentalism was highlighted – a sense of disciplining oneself,
keeping oneself in check, subduing feelings, constructing a
controlled, permitted repressiveness – which existed outside of the
jive hives (even in the gay community) and was dedicated to 'correct'
behaviour which would not give the game away.

All of this seems a million miles from stereotypical descriptions of
the 'gay' manager 'patrolling' the burgeoning British beat and rock
scene of the 1960s. Joe explained that his experiences in watching the
(usually) younger dancers elicited a 'high', but also a previously
unknown and resistant facet to his character, which enabled him to
become more at ease with himself, and more resistant to the repressiveness and limitations of the traditional body-sense. This ease, he
claimed, was recognized by the young Beatles when they first met in
the Liverpool Jazz Society bandroom in early 1962:

> Brian introduced me to his 'boys' and we immediately hit it off.
> They could see right away that Brian and I were one of a kind in
> many ways (we were different in other ways, mind you). They
> trusted me immediately and this was very flattering. I had heard
> that they were normally very wary of older promoters and agents
> after their previous experiences, but we engaged almost instantly.
> After a few weeks, Bob Wooler had told them that my apartment
> was only around the corner from their beloved bowling alley and so
> they began to spend a great deal of time with me. At times John and
> Paul slept over. Can you imagine what some journalists would
> make of that?! But it was all entirely honourable. They respected
> my route into rock. Even as very young men, they understood that
> it also had an oppositional status for me. Of quite a different
> nature, but, nevertheless, it presented me with another world that I
> could not ignore. Easiness with oneself leads to easiness with
> others, and then confidence builds in others so that they come
> looking for the easiness. That's what Gardner Road [Joe's apart-
> ment] was all about. Don't just ask the Beatles, ask all of the musi-
> cians who frequented the place!

The key point to be learned from this insight into the impact of rock
and roll on Merseyside in the late 1950s is that the music had the
potential to arbitrate meaning in some very irregular and uneven
ways, none of which are included in the 'conventional wisdom' of

most rock historians and/or journalists. For example, while dancing seems to be relegated as a pursuit by many writers, who appear on occasion to believe that bodily functions are secondary to navel contemplations, it offered itself within the 'Merseybeat' days as a significant metaphoric expression. Dance provided Joe with the opportunity to investigate new proposals about relationships between body and society. Location within local institutes and other suburban venues suggested new experiences of space, place and time. The dancers were able to incorporate language, repetition (or anything else) as forms of expression. The whole process of 'Merseybeat' as seen through the eyes of Joe Flannery was one of participation in new possibilities, not the pursuit of good-looking boys in tight-fitting suits. Radio personality and former member of the Merseybeats, Billy Butler, concurs:

> It could be very competitive. A lot of the material was easy to play ... and good to dance to. Don't forget, dancing plays an important part in it all, too. That's often forgotten about ... it was good money if you appealed to the dancers. (Brocken 1996: 118)

Simply to listen to the music and watch its dancers might appear rather mundane today. But rock and roll (or 'beat' music as the Liverpool 'sound' is often retrospectively labelled) and the release that it gave to people as an uninhibited activity was not merely exhibition: it was a resistance *via* exhibition, together with a resistance via a lack of inhibition which gave Joe Flannery ideas about resistance in the sense of his own body, and allowed him space to consider the manner in which conventional society restricts the body by subscribing to values around 'decency'. While all of this may seem routinely plausible at the end of the twentieth century, it was something quite distinctive in the early 1960s – so distinctive, in fact, that it was immediately seen by the Beatles (despite their youth) to give form and meaning to Joe Flannery and Brian Epstein. The cliché of homosexual managers attempting to entrap young musicians is thus given a completely inverse perspective as it becomes evident that not only did Epstein 'sign' the Beatles, but that they also effectively 'signed' him! Given the enormous effect that rock and roll had on stereotypical social contact in the UK of the 1950s, further research into the meanings, uses and effectiveness of music from a semiotic perspective is long overdue, and of paramount importance if we are not to be continually burdened with the 'homosexual svengali' story *ad nauseam*.

In discussing dance further, I questioned Joe about dances such as the Twist, the Pony and the Fly which, from my historical distance, appear quite formal and far from 'uncontrolled'. I told Joe that I remembered my cousin practising steps to the Madison, carefully co ordinating her movements on a piece of card with steps drawn on it; did this not challenge his 'uncontrolled' concepts? He rejected the analysis, for while he appreciated that dance steps were very important for dancers *before* they commenced dancing, it was his belief that most dancers tended to disentangle themselves from ceremony once on the dance floor, because of its inherent excitement. He remembered the Twist as almost uncontrolled, in that it was built around one small movement repeated over and over ... and it was highly strenuous and physical. He recalled: 'Even the Beatles got into the Twist. On stage, Pete Best would perform what they called the Pinwheel Twist to a baying crowd of females ... it went down a storm!'

As a gay male in Liverpool in the late 1950s and early 1960s, Joe Flannery received invaluable *experiences* in the dance halls which enabled him to establish a sort of pattern for the rest of his life. In the months that immediately followed his 'epiphany' in the dance halls, while he continued to establish a thriving retail business, his sense of resistance also grew. By late 1962, the popularity on Merseyside of Lee Curtis and the All Stars briefly rivalled that of the Beatles, and during that period Joe felt more settled within himself than he had in the previous 10 years. His life, however, began to take on two distinct sections: during the day, he felt as if he was 'someone else' working within the limitations of 'normal' society; during the evening, he felt that he was able to be 'himself'.

In early 1963, Joe Flannery was erroneously arrested for receiving stolen goods. Although he was innocent, and was able to prove his innocence quite easily, he decided finally to eliminate his social dichotomy. His brother's popularity in Germany facilitated a move from the UK to Hamburg; Joe burned all of his social and financial bridges in Liverpool and became manager of the Star Club until 1967.

## CONCLUSION

It was an observation of 'otherness' via communality which played a vital role in Joe's move into music management, not an overt interest in 'boys', a fact recognized by the Beatles as they became firm friends and associates. If the emergence of the Beatles and the advent of

'Merseybeat' were, indeed, part of a response to contemporary concerns, and if the potency of rock and roll was linked to a level of optimism about the future and a discontent with the social mores of postwar Britain, then the need for a complex and detailed study of that social location remains of supreme importance. It is now more than 35 years since the Beatles emerged on to the (inter)national stage, and yet the methodologies of many rock writers appear to have remained remarkably uniform. The very pre-eminence of rock's own rhetoric about the Beatles leads to a fundamental historical question: how can we continue to write and rewrite the same linear narratives about the Beatles, when it is quite obvious that they are neither historically valid nor potentially constructive? Perhaps by raising such issues as the associative relationships between the apparently opposi-tional lifestyles of older homosexual males and young heterosexual dancers and rock and roll groups, we might begin to address the vari-able nature of popular music reception. Bringing these historical fragments together may then give us the option to inject 'rock' history with a healthy dose of inconstancy, something that has thus far been distinctly lacking in the work of the 'Merseybeat Mafia'.

## NOTES

1. I use 'Merseybeat' in quotation marks deliberately, for I remain uncon-vinced of its status as a holistic genre.
2. Another over-mythologized piece of 'history', if ever there was one; long overdue for thorough investigation, this truism has lived on the shirt-tails of 'Merseybeat'.
3. Prellies (preludin) were uppers enabling participants to stay awake for hours.
4. This, and all the other direct quotes that follow (unless otherwise indi-cated) are taken from my personal interviews with Joe Flannery, conducted between 1994 and 1997.
5. Rogan's book is a considerable contribution to popular music history, but his propensity to over-simplification knows few boundaries.

## REFERENCES

Brocken, Mike (1996) *Some Other Guys!* Liverpool: Mayfield.
Rogan, Johnny (1988) *Starmakers and Svengalis*. London: MacDonald, Queen Anne Press.

# 3 The Beatles and the Spectacle of Youth[1]

## John Muncie

Paul McCartney:   Don't for heaven's sake say we're the new youth, because that's a load of old rubbish. (Braun 1964: 14)

John Lennon:   Nothing happened, except that we grew up; we did our thing just like they were telling us ... we're a minority, you know, people like us always were, but maybe we are a slightly larger minority because of something or other. (Wenner 1973: 12)

The Beatles have long been viewed as one of the key icons – perhaps *the* key icon – of the 1960s. Between the release of 'Love Me Do' in 1962 and their disbanding in 1970, they produced more than 200 songs and sold more than 200 million records. Their early appearances provoked unprecedented scenes of mass hysteria. The group whose popularity was to be variously gauged as greater than that of Elvis Presley or Jesus Christ are widely acclaimed as one of the most significant forces in the history of popular music, as being a symbol for teenagers worldwide and for revolutionizing British pop culture. Thirty years on, we routinely find their albums appearing in lists of the greatest records of all time (usually *Revolver*, *Abbey Road* and *Sgt Pepper's Lonely Hearts Club Band*), and they are widely regarded as a key reference point for the emergence of Britpop in the mid 1990s.

It is hard to deny their achievements as songwriters or as true innovators in musical style and the 'vocabularies of pop'. But, as McCartney warned in 1964, the Beatles never saw themselves as spokespeople for a generation; in Lennon's view, all that happened was that they grew up. So to what extent should we expect that a social history of the late 1950s and 1960s can be 'read' through the sights and sounds of the Beatles? In particular, what relation did the Beatles have to a succession of 'spectacular' youth subcultures and cultures – teddy boys, mods, rockers, hippies, beatniks, bohemians, skinheads – that surfaced contemporaneously? Which sections of youth did they speak to ... and whose voices were notably absent?

PRECURSORS: ENTER THE TED AND THE TEENAGER ...

Paul McCartney: We started off by imitating Elvis, Buddy Holly, Chuck Berry, Carl Perkins, Gene Vincent, the Coasters, the Drifters – we just copied what they did ... The people we copied were all American, because there was no one good British. (Palmer 1977: 227)

For a decade following the Second World War, British social history was shaped above all by austerity and rationing. But by the mid-1950s, Britain had slowly pulled itself towards economic and social recovery, epitomized by the symbolic commitment to creating a welfare state and education for all. By that time, the country was supposedly riding on a wave of affluence and full employment, and was allegedly witnessing the emergence of a classless society. However, affluence also had its price. Inevitably, it was those lowest in the social hierarchy – working-class, unskilled youths – who found they were excluded from such 'benefits'. The postwar years also brought the 'planning blight' and consequent break-up of many working-class neighbourhoods which had previously existed as close-knit communities. It is against this background that the 'utterly unexpected' rise of the teddy boys has been explained (Fyvel 1961).

The teddy boys' subculture (like a majority of British working-class youth subcultures) was typically male and specifically the creation of working-class districts in London. In a period of relatively full employment it was such sections of the population, traditionally lacking in power and status, that were most likely to find themselves excluded from full-time employment. Despite an educational system which supposedly provided equal opportunity, it was they who had lost out. In the wake of the new affluence and an increasing availability of consumer goods, the teds discovered that there remained a general lack of public leisure provision for the under-twenties. In response, they moved into the only spaces available, and made the local 'caff' and the street their 'home'. Identity of self and group was maintained through territoriality and the defence of working-class places and spaces. Their hair, by military, or perhaps more pertinently by National Service (1947–60) standards, was excessively long and was generally worn with sideburns, a great deal of Brylcreem, some form of quiff at the front, and variations of the DA (duck's arse) at the back. Their preferred drug was alcohol. Their clothes were a bastardization of a pseudo-Edwardian style, created by Savile Row tailors in the early 1950s for young upper-class men about town; it comprised long 'drape' jackets with velvet collars, tight 'drainpipe' trousers, bootlace ties and thick crepe-soled shoes, known as 'brothel creepers'. For Jefferson (1976) such style represented both an arrogant yet half-conscious parody of the upper-classes, and an attempt to defend working-class values and glorify the masculinity and slickness of the Hollywood criminal hero. The term 'teddy boy' first appeared in print in March 1954, when it was clear that they could no longer be simply referred to as the 'hooligans', 'spivs', or 'cosh boys' of the past (Rock and Cohen 1970: 94).

The teds pre-dated rock and roll, but with its arrival the ted was able to give voice to his 'resistance' and 'disenchantment'. Imported from the USA, rock and roll signified an abrupt shift in musical style. Derived from black blues and white country traditions, Melly has seen it as 'a contemporary incitement to mindless fucking and arbitrary vandalism: screw and smash music' (1970: 36). It represented a blatant attack on parental sexual taboos and, for the disaffected young, became one of the few avenues through which self-autonomy could be expressed.

In 1956, at the screening of the film *Blackboard Jungle* in London, Britain witnessed its first 'rock and roll riot'. Later, Bill Haley's UK performances and the first screenings of Elvis Presley's films were to be greeted by a previously unknown hysteria: 'The music was drowned out by screaming, whistling, stamping, roaring, and the gallery shook so much that people below could see the floor buckling above their heads' (Cohn 1969: 21). The ted came to be demonized as the source of all manner of troubles. When the adult world demanded order in the cinemas, coffee bars and streets, the teds, it seemed, responded by jiving in the aisles, razoring cinema seats, and attacking 'intruders' in their 'territories'. They were assured of a hostile political and media reaction. *Reynolds News* (1 May 1954) described them as a 'grave social evil' and they were widely condemned as the end result of the importation of an un-British degenerate culture into the UK (Hebdige 1988: 30).

Although membership of the teds, like the later British youth subcultures of the 1960s, recruited from a relative minority, it has been argued that the 'nihilist ted spirit' did impact on many more, and indeed it was from the 'rock and roll mania' of 1956 that the US term 'teenage culture' was imported into Britain (Melly 1970). The first influential study of the phenomenon was Abrams' *The Teenage Consumer* (1959), an empirical survey of a new consumer group which was purportedly defined in terms of age-specific leisure – milk bars, fashion, clothes, cosmetics, hair styles, rock and roll records, films, magazines, dancing and dance halls – and which implied a classless culture. Abrams' research, however, revealed that the consumer habits of youth were in fact dominated by the interests of working-class males.

In many ways this contradiction between the rhetoric of a classless culture defined by age and the reality of its class specificities was soon collapsed when recording, publishing and film companies gradually realized that there existed a huge market for such interests. Such films as *The Wild One* (1954) starring Marlon Brando and *Rebel Without A Cause* (1955) starring James Dean quickly became cult movies in their celebration of teenage lawlessness. The teddy boys' style too began filtering upwards and outwards from South London and underwent significant changes. Leather jackets replaced drapes, motor cycles allowed greater freedom and mobility. The 'rocker' style emerged. By the end of 1956, Britain's first domestic rock and roll star, nineteen-year-old Tommy Steele, had appeared. His example, coupled with the popularity of skiffle music (pioneered by Lonnie Donegan), meant that semi-amateur music-making by and for youth became a reality. Indeed, it was from these origins that in 1956 a group called the Quarrymen was formed in Liverpool which, over the next five years, was to evolve through the Nurk Twins, the Rainbows, Johnny and the Moondogs, and the Silver Beetles, to become, in 1960, the Beatles. (The name was reputedly derived from one of the gangs in *The Wild One* or from Buddy Holly and the Crickets; either way, the influence was American.)

There is no doubt that the Beatles' musical origins and development drew significantly from pre-existing black exponents of blues, rock and roll and pop. The group's first official recording (with Tony Sheridan) in 1961 was a copy of Ray Charles's version of 'My Bonnie'. During 1963 and 1964 they recorded covers of tracks such as 'Twist And Shout' (the Isley Brothers), 'Roll Over Beethoven' and 'Rock And Roll Music' (Chuck Berry), 'You Really Got A Hold On Me' (the Miracles), 'Kansas City' (Little Richard) and 'Please Mr Postman' (the Marvelettes). In addition 'Honey Don't' (Carl Perkins) and 'Words Of Love' (Buddy Holly) reflected another range of influences from the white US traditions of rockabilly and country.

The relation of the Beatles to rock and roll *per se* was therefore somewhat anomalous – partly derivative and partly a creative synthesis. As numerous commentators have noted, the Beatles' chief impact was to make black American pop music accessible to a white audience in Britain in the 1960s, in much the same way that Elvis Presley had appropriated and represented black blues and gospel musics for a white audience in the USA in the 1950s.

The relation of the Beatles to the teds is, if anything, more obscure. John Lennon has recalled how he went to see the film *Blackboard Jungle*, fully expecting to slash the cinema seats, but was dismayed to find nobody even screaming or dancing (Braun 1964: 35). But the style adopted by the time they were regular performers in Hamburg was more a reflection of a black-leathered Gene Vincent, than of the 'drapes' and 'brothel creepers' of the British teds. An explanation for this may be found in the observation that their musical and cultural reference points were largely American (via Liverpool); and that all of the Beatles (Ringo Starr apart), including original members Stuart Sutcliffe and Pete Best, are best described as middle-class or lower-middle, rather than working class. For them, art school influences were as strong, if not stronger, than those of the street. Lennon's own recollections of his early days at Liverpool Art College in 1957 are revealing: 'They all thought I was a ted ... but I wasn't really, just a rocker. I was only pretending to be one. If I'd met a proper ted, with chains and a real gang, I'd have been shit scared' (Davies 1980: 18).


BEATLEMANIA

Dear Ones:   Yesterday to show my loyalty, I bought a Beatle wig, a Beatle sweatshirt and four Beatle dolls. I spent $24.79. I adore you. Take my heart. It is all I have left.

Fondly, Karen A., Springfield, Mass. (Adler 1964: 81)

'Please Please Me' became the Beatles first Number One single in the UK in February 1963, and was also the title song of their first album, released two months later, which enjoyed an unbroken run at Number One in the British charts for six months. Regular national tours, TV appearances, and two more Number One singles quickly followed. Towards the end of the year they had been invited to appear at the Royal Variety Performance, and were being described in *The Sunday Times* as 'the greatest composers since Beethoven' (29 December 1963). The *Evening Standard* proclaimed 1963 to be the 'Year Of The Beatles' and announced that 'an examination of the heart of the nation at this moment would reveal the word BEATLE engraved upon it'. In December, 'I Want To Hold Your Hand' became the Christmas Number One, the Beatles' fourth Number One single of the year, and (at the time) their most successful single world wide, with sales in excess of 12 million. The following month it gave the group its first Number One record in the USA. At the beginning of April 1964, the Beatles held the top five positions in the *Billboard* US singles chart, plus an additional seven entries lower in the Top 100. In Australia in the same week, they held the top six positions in the singles chart, with a total of 10 entries in the Top 20. Commercially, as well as musically, the Beatles were fast becoming a global phenomenon.

● The widespread cultural and popular acclaim they achieved has been 'read' in a number of competing ways. Harker is clear that given the 'contemporary competition', the Beatles' singles were a 'qualitative improvement', but argues that the group's commercial success also depended on these 'happy little rockers' accepting the trappings of respectability (1980: 84). Out went the leathers, to be replaced by suits; out went the rough edge of rock and roll, to be replaced by more conventional love songs. He is especially dismissive of 'I Want To Hold Your Hand': 'Verbally and emotionally, the crassness of this song knows no bounds. Musically ... it's High School with a dash of beat. Overall, it's thoroughly adolescent, whether by design or by default; and it makes "Twist And Shout" or even "Love Me Do" seem raw and spontaneous by comparison' (Ibid.: 86). Such commercial success however also depended on the ability of a still-growing popular music industry to produce, distribute, market and promote a 'new product'. The Beatles did not receive their MBEs in 1965 for charitable work, or even their music, but for their considerable contribution to British exports. In 1963–4, the 'turnover from Beatles music leapt from nothing to £6 million' (Ibid.: 87); by mid-1964, sales of their records were 'bringing in £500,000 a month' and in the process, 'EMI's pre-tax music profits rose by 80 per cent' (Frith 1983: 135). Whatever else the Beatles were, they were undoubtedly an 'unprecedented business event' (Ibid.: 144).

In his reflections on 20 years of 'youth culture revolution' in Britain – most obviously in the music, fashion, literature and art of the sixties – Melly (1970) has detected an underlying process of 'revolt into style' in which innovative, 'threatening' or oppositional musical styles are routinely diffused by their commercial appropriation. If the Beatles initially reflected a teenage disenchantment with society which was expressed at a cultural level by questioning the elitism of highbrow culture, the boring nature of work, the meaning of freedom, the constraint of puritanical sexuality and so on, then the revolt was remarkably short-lived, as the consumer industries, eager to market any kind of exploitable 'subversion', moved in, offering television appearances, fame and money to the rebellious. Melly suggests that every new youth movement is ultimately packaged, stylized, and committed more to the goals of profit than to social criticism. Deviant styles must become commercially viable or else vanish into obscurity; in fact, the end result is similar in both cases, for commercialism soon ignores 'old' consumer styles and looks for new 'deviant' styles to promote in order to keep market demand alive. The Beatles may have provided fresh meanings to existing styles, or even created new styles themselves, but their diffusion was ultimately dependent on marketing and commercial enterprises over which they had little or no control. This is the 'castration via trivialization syndrome ... what starts as revolt finishes as style – as mannerism' (Ibid.: 107). While this analysis can be directly applied to rock and roll, in the specific case of the Beatles there is uncertainty about the presence of an initial revolt at all; it is certainly not in evidence in any of their early lyrics. The 'stylization' of the group appears to be more of a shift from amateur style to commercially successful style, than one of recording industry emasculation. Either way, looking for moments of 'uncontaminated originality' in any subcultural or musical style may be a fruitless exercise. Latterly, Thornton has argued, for example, that it is impossible to isolate moments of 'authenticity' which are subsequently subverted. As she astutely points out, 'media and businesses are integral to the authentication of cultural practices ... commercial culture and popular culture are not only inextricable in practice but also in theory' (1995: 9).

It is also clear that the Beatles' successs was dependent not just on a teenage market, but was constructed around a popularity that transcended class, gender and age boundaries. Lauded by the press as the epitome of a new vibrancy and optimism of the 1960s – 'you have to be a real sour square not to love the nutty, noisy, happy, handsome Beatles' (*Daily Mirror*, 6 December 1963) – their appeal was considerable. But the adulation was strongest in the ranks of ten to fourteen-year-old white girls. Beatlemania began with a report that fans had mobbed the group after a concert at the London Palladium on 13 October 1963, and lasted until 1966 when they gave their final live performance in San Francisco. On their first tour of the USA in 1964, up to 10 000 teenage girls greeted them at Kennedy Airport. Their TV appearance on the *Ed Sullivan Show* attracted an all-time record audience of 73 million viewers (during which, it is widely reputed, not a single crime was committed across the USA) At their concerts, teams of security guards were required to hold back the crowds, while the music itself was barely audible over the frenzied shrieks of the audience. Everywhere, it seemed, young girls were swooning, weeping, screaming and 'flipping'. Indeed, as Ehrenreich *et al.* (1992) have recalled, it is difficult now to capture the strength and intensity of the hysteria. Star adulation had occurred before, notably with Elvis Presley, but never on the same scale, as Norman Weiss, the group's US agent, has readily acknowledged: 'The Beatles and Elvis Presley are both in show business. After that, any comparison is just a joke. No one, before or since, has had the crowds the Beatles had' (Davies 1968: 221).

Furthermore, the all-pervasive obsession with every detail of the Beatles' lives took on the characteristics of a social movement – and notably one that was led and orchestrated by girls and young women. This has been seen as Beatlemania's most significant feature. It gave young, white women, in particular, a collective identity, a space in which to lose control and to assert their own sexuality: 'To abandon control – to scream, faint, dash about in mobs – was in form, if not in conscious intent, to protest the sexual repressiveness, the rigid double standard of female teen culture. It was the first and most dramatic uprising of *women's* sexual revolution' (Ehrenreich *et al.* 1992: 524). While this latter assertion may be something of an overstatement, it is difficult to escape the conclusion that Beatlemania did provide a rare opportunity through which young, white women could challenge dominant conceptions of femininity. Why it should happen with the Beatles in particular is less clear. Publicity prior to their first US tour certainly played its part, but the group's appeal also lay in their 'mop top' androgyny: 'the Beatles construed sex more generously and playfully, lifting it out of the rigid scenario of mid-century American gender roles ... Theirs was a vision of sexuality freed from the shadow of gender inequality because the group mocked the distinctions that bifurcated the American landscape into "his" and "hers"' (Ibid.: 535).

In hindsight, the greatest contribution the Beatles made to youth culture may have been Beatlemania itself. Of all the social movements and cultural symbols of the 1960s, it was, at least, something that they could genuinely claim to be their own.

ON THE MARGINS: MODS, BEATS AND BRITISH R'N'B

Dear Beatles:   In some magazines they make you appear as if
you're from everyday families. In others you appear sophisticated
and conceited ... Are you one of us?

A Fan (?) Harriet B., Brooklyn, NY (Adler 1964: 38)

From the late 1950s onwards, British society was widely interpreted
by political commentators and sociologists in terms of the earlier
prophesied classlessness and embourgoisement. It was argued that
postwar affluence had by now eroded differences between middle-
class and working-class life chances and styles. Despite contrary
empirical evidence of the perseverance of the class structure and
differential opportunities, working-class youths of the early 1960s
were caught up in the desire to share the fruits of the 'new affluence'.
The use of the term 'mod' reflected such contradictions by referring
both to the image of a consumer-based 'swinging' London and also to
a distinctive youth subculture. It was the province of upwardly mobile
working-class youngsters who had 'made it good' through art school
and the commercialization of style – including Mary Quant, David
Bailey, Jean Shrimpton and Twiggy, as well as the Beatles – but more
precisely of those who found the lower middle-class, non-manual
occupations to which they had aspired just as stultifying as the manual
jobs they had left behind.

As a subculture, the mods originated from East London and working-class estates in the suburbs of the capital. Typically, they were
engaged in semi-skilled manual work or basic white-collar jobs (van
boy, messenger, clerk, office boy). The mods accepted work in so far as
it gave them a greater potential to buy style and status. They lived for
nights, weekends and Bank Holidays The mod style – partly a reflection of their relative affluence and partly an attempt to emulate the
cool and slick style of their Afro-Caribbean 'Rude Boy' neighbours
(the 'shades' and pork pie hats) – was characterized by short hair, smart
well-cut suits, and an almost narcissistic obsession with neat appearance. Mods were the archetypal example of the conspicuous consumer,
whether in clothes, scooters, music or amphetamines ('speed'). But for
Hebdige (1976), they were never passive consumers. The scooter and
clothes were transformed into symbols of movement and solidarity,
while 'speed' enabled a total commitment to all-night dancing in the
clubs and discos. The style they created has thus been 'read' as consti-
tuting a parody of the consumer society in which they were situated.

Their leisure was concentrated in the meeting places of music clubs and ballrooms of London's West End; but here it was the musical styles of Tamla Motown from the USA and bluebeat and ska from Jamaica that provided the backcloth, rather than the music of the Beatles. Previously, many of these clubs had in fact been exclusively for blacks, and the mods' emulation of black style reveals and illustrates the extent to which many British youth subcultures have drawn on a black heritage for their music and their fashion (Hebdige 1979).

If the mods were something of an apolitical or 'imaginary' reaction against the ideology of classlessness, then they equally reacted against the music and style of the previous decade. Rock and roll and the descendants of the teds – the rockers – were dismissed as boorish, out of date and crude. Nor were the mods fans of the Beatles. The Beatles may have been *mod* in the contemporary associations they shared with 'swinging' London and Carnaby Street, but they were never *mods*. When the mods ventured out beyond black dance music, it was to the altogether more uncompromising sounds of British R'n'B as epitomized by The Who, the Yardbirds and the Rolling Stones. While the Beatles' influences stretched back to skiffle, the Rolling Stones' lineage was one of blues and jazz. Their long hair, scruffy clothes and unkempt appearance also reflected something of the political and moral disaffiliation of the beatnik.

Even before the arrival of the teds and rock and roll in the early 1950s, a section of middle-class youth – the beats – were already indicating their disaffection with postwar society. Rather than having deprivation and poverty imposed on them, the beats voluntarily chose a life of poverty by avoiding work. The 'freedom' that was gained has generally been 'read' as a protest against the increasing technological impersonality and bureaucratic ordering of social life. Faced with an extreme pessimism about the future and the possibilities of progress, the beats lived out the present to the fullest in the style of Woody Guthrie and Dean Moriarty, Kerouac's hero of a life *On The Road* (1957). The US beat scene was best captured in Polsky's (1971) empirical study carried out in Greenwich Village, New York in 1960. It was a scene characterized by anti-politicism rather than apoliticism, by work avoidance rather than inability to work, and by the belief that voluntary poverty was an intellectual gain.

Although the movement was predominantly white American, the visual symbols of beat were exported to Britain. Jazz, poetry and marijuana were its hallmarks. The beats' concern for the spontaneous and the creative was mirrored by modern jazz, in which it seemed formal organization was subordinated to improvization. In Britain, the impact of this music was marginal and, ironically, was accompanied by a revival of earlier New Orleans and Dixieland styles which eventually were far more successful. Though less 'wild' and more collectively organized, these styles, especially when their folk and blues roots were pulled out, were however also capable of attachment to a philosophy of romantic estrangement from society.

By the early 1960s, the folk music element of the beats was captured and expressed in the work of Bob Dylan. While the Beatles were singing 'Love Me Do', Dylan was foretelling the coming of a new social awareness in 'Blowing In The Wind', the song that became a classic statement of non-violent protest against US racism and militarism. Quite clearly, at this time the audiences of Dylan and the Beatles were totally polarized – middle-class beatniks versus teenyboppers.

In comparison to other contemporaneous musical movements – R'n'B, folk protest, mods, black soul – the Beatles appear marginal. Their 'symbolic embodiment of the healthy, zany exuberance of British youth by the national press, parents, Prime Minister Harold Wilson and the Establishment could only mean one thing for us' (Chambers 1985: 68). The Beatles were 'safe'. The cutting edge of youth culture was to be found elsewhere.

## HIPPIES, THE COUNTERCULTURAL UNDERGROUND AND BRITISH PSYCHEDELIA

John Lennon:   I am like a chameleon, influenced by whatever is going on. If Elvis can do it, I can do it. If the Everly Brothers can do it, me and Paul can. Same with Dylan. (Sheff and Golson 1981: 165)

The term 'hippie' covers a wide range of bohemian, drug, student and radical subcultures. Out of the beats, there was a hard core of artistic–literary intelligentsia; from the CND movement of the 1950s came a strong contingent of anti-war pacifists and radicals. Indeed, the hippie counterculture in Britain was something of a hybrid of CND's liberal humanitarianism and the beats' retreatism. The hippie, like the beat, was deeply critical of the growing dominance of technology and bureaucracy in both capitalist and socialist societies. However, the hippies' withdrawal was not necessarily one of self-imposed poverty, but involved definite attempts to create a 'new and distinct' way of life that would, they hoped, convert others by example. Nor was the culture manifestly politically orientated. It had no party, no leadership and no manifesto, but lived by its unwritten demands to the rest of society: to seek love rather than violence, to be able to express oneself freely without fear of social sanctions. Above all, the hippies' alternative lifestyle was aimed at revolutionizing society through peaceful means, as was exemplified by Abbie Hoffman's proclamation: 'Revolution is in your head. You are the Revolution. Do your thing' (1968: 14). For Yablonsky (1968) the hippie community was a para-society existing casually beneath the surface – neither subcultural nor countercultural, but an attempt to resonate with a deeper reality of cosmic consciousness. It is largely accepted that this particular brand of bohemianism was born in the early 1960s on the West Coast of the USA, and particularly in the Haight Ashbury district of San Francisco (Wolfe 1969).

The community or 'colony' brought with it some of the trappings of the beat subculture, especially the use of drugs to explore the limits of imagination and self-expression. A lifestyle developed, based on the use of marijuana and, in particular, Lysergic Acid Diethylamide (LSD or 'acid') which, because of its hallucinogenic effects, enabled the user to 'trip' through a multitude of distorted ideas, images and actions in rapid succession. Dedicated users believed that such an experience enabled reality to become clearer in that it could be approached free from all preconceptions. A leading figure was Timothy Leary, who founded the so-called International Federation For Inner Freedom in 1962, and coined the phrase 'Tune in, turn on, drop out'; another was Ken Kesey, whose 'Merry Pranksters' travelled the USA by bus between 1964 and 1965 with the Warlocks – later to become the Grateful Dead. If Leary's interest was partly scientific and partly tied to religious awakening, Kesey's contribution was to make the acid experience spectacular, wild and playful.

At the beginning of 1967, San Francisco was the setting for the first 'Human Be-In', and by the summer 100 000 young people had been attracted into the area. Haight Ashbury was quickly discovered by the media, who introduced the term 'hippie' into circulation. Hippies became figures who attracted sympathy for their philosophy of love and peace, but who were mistrusted for their antipathy to work, their use of drugs and their permissive morality – practices which were to become the main focus for moral panics in the later 1960s. In Britain, LSD was declared illegal in September 1966. Regional drug squads were established in March 1967. Later that year, Keith Richards and Mick Jagger of the Rolling Stones were arrested and convicted for possession of marijuana. From 1967 to 1969, the offices of the under-ground newspaper *IT* (*International Times*) were raided by police, and its editors imprisoned and/or fined on charges of obscenity or conspiracy to corrupt public morals (Stansill and Mairowitz 1971). The underground music clubs, UFO and Middle Earth, were eventu-ally closed after police raids. And in October 1970, the infamous OZ obscenity trial began, following raids on the underground magazine's offices in June; OZ was fined £1000 plus court costs, and prison sentences imposed on its editors – Richard Neville, Felix Dennis and Jim Anderson – which were only dropped after a lengthy appeal (Palmer 1971).

In many ways, 1968 was a watershed year in which bohemian disen-chantment spread to, and was adopted by, student bodies in univer-sities throughout Europe and the USA as a basis on which a radical political movement could be built. Its contemporary origins lay in the Free Speech Movement and subsequent campus protest at Berkeley, California, in September 1964, when the university author-ities attempted to ban all political activity on the campus. In the spring of 1965, the movement was fuelled by President Lyndon Johnson's order for heavy bombing of North Vietnam. And in April 1968, renewed race riots followed the assassination in Memphis, Tennessee, of Martin Luther King. These three issues – US imperi-alism in Vietnam, Civil Rights, and educational control – were to inform a spate of university sit-ins, marches and demonstrations throughout 1968, when a strange agglomeration of black militants, students, drop-outs, draft dodgers, mystical hippies and womens liberationists seemed to be momentarily united. In France, the radical student was particularly motivated by the take-over of the Sorbonne in May by a student/ worker alliance, and the formulation of an ideology of situationism which emphasized the importance of developing the revolution in everyday life. These events were paral-leled in West Germany by the wave of demonstrations which followed an attempt on the life of student leader Rudi Dutschke. Reverberations from Europe were felt most in Britain at the London School of Economics and Hornsey Art College, where students demanded more autonomy in the organization of university educa-tion. And in March and October, the Vietnam Solidarity Campaign organized large – and, as it transpired, violent – demonstrations outside the US Embassy in Grosvenor Square, London.

The 1960s counterculture was thus a loose affiliation of many dis-parate radical and libertarian groups. Nevertheless, elements of this 'new radicalism' remained a dominant force in youth culture style until the early 1970s. Because it encouraged a diverse range of alternatives, from Eastern mysticism to Third World revolution, it was able to draw on a multitude of romantic images and symbols (Hall 1969). Similarly, because of their fusion of the personal and the political, countercultural styles were able to retain a progressive and radical image. In musical terms, it was the acid rock of San Francisco groups such as Quicksilver Messenger Service, Jefferson Airplane and the Grateful Dead, the progressive and electronic rock of Britain's Pink Floyd, and the blues and folk revivals spearheaded by Bob Dylan, which remain the lasting legacies of this countercultural 'revolution'.

The Beatles had first met Bob Dylan in August 1964 when, it is widely assumed, they were introduced to marijuana. Undoubtedly, the Beatles had taken illegal drugs before – notably amphetamines during the night-long gigs in Hamburg in the early 1960s – but marijuana was new to them. By 1966, the group, under Dylan's influence, began to 'abandon their previous nice-boy personae, falling all the while from generalized public favour, and to produce increasingly complex and "meaningful" work' (Davis 1990: 200). The turning point was *Revolver*, released in August 1966, whose songs 'Tomorrow Never Knows', 'She Said, She Said' and 'Love You To' heralded a submergence into a drug-assisted and Eastern religion-inspired journey into the subconscious. In February 1967, 'Strawberry Fields Forever' – hailed as 'psychedelic' because of its backwards music at the fade – was released on the eve of San Francisco's Human Be-In. In the summer of that year, as Melly has recalled, a great deal of critical energy was spent on speculating how much of the newly-released *Sgt Pepper's Lonely Hearts Club Band* was directly concerned with drugs (1970: 113). Did 'Lucy In The Sky With Diamonds' refer to LSD or was it, as John Lennon protested, simply a reference to a picture the Beatle's son had drawn at school? Were the 'friends' of 'A Little Help From My Friends' amphetamines? Was 'Fixing A Hole' a euphemism for injecting heroin? Whatever the truth, or truths, 'A Day In The Life' was banned by the BBC on the grounds that it encouraged drugtaking. But these few songs apart, the Beatles (and British psychedelia in general) was a peculiarly 'childlike' version of its US countercultural cousin. Musically, it often smacked of vaudeville ('When I'm Sixty-Four'); in fashion, it degenerated into dressing up (witness the cover of *Sgt Pepper*); politically, the urgency of the Vietnam War or the Civil Rights Movement was lacking ('Taxman').

In the summer of 1968, at the time of the Grosvenor Square confrontations and the art school revolts, there were no songs for the barricades emanating from the British underground. True, the Beatles recorded 'Revolution', but this carried the largely ambiguous message that political activism 'won't help you to make it with anyone, anyhow'. By this time, the Beatles had become part of the 'pop aristocracy'.

## ABSENT VOICES: SKINHEADS

They were surgically clean, wore their hair cropped, brown boots and jeans with braces. They were looking for 'bother' and seemed to sense that pop music, once a music cutting across class barriers, was now the property of an intelligentsia. (Melly 1970: 122)

Skinheads probably first appeared in East London in 1967, and were generated from sections of the unskilled working-class community. Mungham and Pearson have noted that the specific content of their style represented both a 'caricature and re-assertion of solid, male, working-class toughness' (1976: 7). The exaggerated reflection of their parent culture was demonstrated by their 'uniform' of cropped hair, braces, half-mast trousers and Doc Marten 'bovver boots'. Their association with violence, football hooliganism, and 'Paki' and 'queer' bashing has been, in turn, viewed as an attempt to recover the cohesiveness of working-class communities and to retain some control over their territory – albeit in its most reactionary form (Hebdige 1981).

Frequently, the cause of their anger would be displaced on to the new Asian immigrant communities, and consequently, skinheads were seen as the racist right wing of subcultural style. Despite this, in line with their hard mod ancestors, the skinheads tried to emulate the sharp 'rude boy' of an Afro-Caribbean youth subculture. Accordingly, reggae and ska – for example, the Pioneers' 'Long Shot (Kick De Bucket)' and Desmond Dekker's 'The Israelites' – were adopted for their accessibility and their apparent enhancement of masculine values. But the skinheads steered clear of nightclubs, partly because of the expense and partly because they identified more with the traditional working-class activities located around pubs, alcohol, football and the street. They explored avenues which were tainted by the 'work ethic', puritanism and working-class chau-vinism, and those who had most obviously dismissed such values – middle-class hippies, the Beatles, and their like – became legitimate targets for their aggression. According to radical deviancy theorists,

ad culture remained an affirmation of white working-class
s (Clarke 1976; Hebdige 1981) and a subculture which filled the
gap opened up by the decline of working-class politics and culture –
a gap they attempted to defend with their developed sense of
'community' and 'territoriality'. In particular, such allegiances were
frequently centred on the local football team, where the traditional
values of collectivity, physical toughness and local rivalry could be
acted out. While skinhead style did become a common sight on
British streets in the late 1960s, as it spread outwards from the inner-
city areas it also became more diffuse, evolving into groups known
as crombies (derived from the crombie coat), smooth-heads and
casuals. Once again, the way was open for consumerism to capitalize
on a 'radical' and 'oppositional' style.

But skinhead style has never disappeared. It continually resurfaces
– through Oi music, through soccer hooliganism, through the British
National Party and neo-Nazi groups, particularly in Germany, and at
the harder edge of British working-class culture in general. Is this the
world the Beatles left behind? Is it a world they ever occupied?


## CONCLUSION

In comparison with other groups, before or since, the most remarkable characteristic of the Beatles was probably their ability continually to reinvent themselves. It was perhaps a sign, as John Lennon
recognized, that they were simply into whatever was going on. From
the group's 1950s skiffle origins, through the rockers of the early
1960s, the fab four pop idols of the mid-sixties, to the flower power
icons at the end of the decade, the Beatles always appeared to be at
the forefront of pop culture. As such, they have been widely assumed
to be the key innovators whom others could only copy. Yet what
emerges from this mapping of the Beatles against the youth cultural
and subcultural terrain of Britain in the 1960s is that much of it can
be (and has been) written about without reference to the Beatles at
all (Hall and Jefferson 1976; Mungham and Pearson 1976; Hebdige
1979; Brake 1980). In Osgerby's (1998) postwar social history of
British youth, the Beatles are afforded passing reference on just one
page, and that in the context of teenybop Beatlemania. Indeed, one
attempt to find a unique and original cultural place for the Beatles
might do no more than see them as the forerunners of a stream of boy
bands – the Bay City Rollers, the Osmonds, New Kids On The Block,

Take That, Boyzone – that surfaced from the 1970s onwards. Despite the familiar attributions routinely made about their historical signifi- cance, their innovative musical and visual styles, and indeed their sheer, overwhelming *presence*, as exponents of British mainstream pop *par excellence*, the legacy of the Beatles to the 1990s may simply be that. Whether these contradictions reveal more about the Beatles, the communities within which they allegedly moved, or our willing- ness to re-invent and re-interpret the past by reference to its popular rhetoric rather than its reality, are issues that still deserve to be addressed. But consider the following descriptions: 'possibly the biggest group of all time'; 'everyone, however remote from youth culture, has heard of them'; 'role models for their generation'; 'their energy and personality guaranteed nationwide attention'; ' naughty but nice'; 'something for everyone' (Norman 1997: 38–45). Add a 17 million-selling album, a Number One single in the charts of more than 30 countries, and a movie glorifying a day in the life of the band. All of these could happily apply to the Beatles. In fact, they are all references to the Spice Girls.

NOTE

1.    I wish to thank Andy Simpson, Gordon Hughes and Eugene McLaughlin for their comments on an earlier draft of this chapter.

REFERENCES

Abrams, Mark (1959) *The Teenage Consumer*. London: Press Exchange.
Adler, Bill (ed.) (1964) *Love Letters to the Beatles*. London: Blond.
Brake, Mike (1980) *The Sociology of Youth Culture and Youth Subcultures*. London: Routledge.
Braun, Michael (1964) *Love Me Do: the Beatles' Progress*. London: Penguin.
Chambers, Iain (1985) *Urban Rhythms*. London: Macmillan.
Clarke, John (1976) 'Style', in Stuart Hall and Tony Jefferson (eds), *Resistance Through Rituals: Youth Subcultures in Postwar Britain*. London: Hutchinson.
Cohn, Nik (1969) *Awopbopaloobop Alopbamboom*. London: Weidenfeld & Nicolson.
Davies, Hunter (1968) *The Beatles*. London: Heinemann.
Davies, Hunter (1980) 'Twist and Shout: the Early Days and the Beatle

Years', in George Darby and David Robson (eds), *John Lennon: the Life and Legend*. London: Sunday Times Magazine.

Davis, John (1990) *Youth and the Condition of Britain*. London: Athlone.

Ehrenreich, Barbara, Elizabeth Hess and Gloria Jacobs (1992) 'Beatlemania: a Sexually Defiant Consumer Culture?', in Ken Gelder and Sarah Thornton (eds), *The Subcultures Reader*. London: Routledge.

Frith, Simon (1983) *Sound Effects*. London: Constable.

Fyvel, T. R. (1961) *The Insecure Offenders: Rebellious Youth in the Welfare State*. London: Chatto & Windus.

Hall, Stuart (1969) 'The Hippies: an American Moment', in Julian Nagel (ed.), *Student Power*. London: Merlin.

Hall, Stuart and Tony Jefferson (eds) (1976) *Resistance through Ritual: Youth Subculture in Postwar Britain*. London: Hutchinson.

Harker, Dave (1980) *One for the Money: Politics and Popular Song*. London: Hutchinson.

Hebdige, Dick (1976) 'The Meaning of Mod', in Stuart Hall and Tony Jefferson (eds), *Resistance Through Rituals: Youth Subcultures in Postwar Britain*. London: Hutchinson.

Hebdige, Dick (1979) *Subculture: the Meaning of Style*. London: Methuen.

Hebdige, Dick (1981) 'Skinheads and the Search for White Working Class Identity', *New Socialist*, 1: 38–41.

Hebdige, Dick (1988) *Hiding in the Light*. London: Comedia.

Hoffman, Abbie (1968) *Revolution for the Hell of It*. Chicago: Dial.

Jefferson, Tony (1976) 'Cultural Responses of the Teds', in Stuart Hall and Tony Jefferson (eds), *Resistance Through Rituals: Youth Subcultures in Postwar Britain*. London: Hutchinson.

Melly, George (1970) *Revolt into Style*. London: Allen Lane.

Mungham, Geoff and Geoff Pearson (eds) (1976) *British Working Class Youth Culture*. London: Routledge.

Norman, Philip (1997) 'Spice Lolly'. in *The Sunday Times Magazine*, 21 September 1997.

Osgerby, Bill (1998) *Youth in Britain since 1945*. Oxford: Blackwell.

Palmer, Tony (1971) *The Trials of OZ*. London: Blond & Briggs.

Palmer, Tony (1977) *All You Need is Love: the Story of Popular Music*. London: Futura.

Polsky, Ned (1971) *Hustlers, Beats and Others*. London: Penguin.

Rock, Paul and Stanley Cohen (1970) 'The Teddy Boys', in Vernon Bogdanor and Robert Skidelsky (eds), *The Age of Affluence*. London: Macmillan.

Sheff, David and G. Barry Golson (eds) *The Playboy Interviews with John Lennon and Yoko Ono*. New York: Playboy Press.

Stansill, Peter and David Mairowitz (1971) *BAMN: Outlaw Manifestos and Ephemera 1965–70*. Harmondsworth: Penguin.

Thornton, Sarah (1995) *Club Cultures: Music, Media and Subcultural Capital*. Cambridge: Polity.

Wenner, Jann (1971) *Lennon Remembers*. London: Penguin.

Wolfe, Tom (1969) *The Electric Kool-Aid Acid Test*. New York: Bantam.

Yablonsky, Lewis (1968) *The Hippie Trip*. New York: Pegasus.

# 4 Lennon–McCartney and the Early British Invasion, 1964–6

Jon Fitzgerald

When the Beatles achieved a series of hits on the US pop charts in early 1964, they initiated what is commonly referred to as the 'British Invasion'. During this so-called invasion, numerous male, guitar-orientated, British groups achieved unprecedented levels of success within the USA, thereby challenging the established dominance of US performers. The Beatles also represented a serious threat to the musical status quo by performing and recording a substantial amount of original material (mostly written by Lennon–McCartney) rather than relying on songs written by US professional songwriters. Brill Building[1] songwriter Ellie Greenwich has described the dramatic impact of the British bands and songwriters at this time:

> When the Beatles and the entire British Invasion came in, we were all ready to say, 'Look, it's been nice, there's no more room for us … it's now the self-contained group – males, certain type of material. What do *we* do?' (Betrock 1982: 173)

Lennon–McCartney's US success was soon emulated by other British writer–performers, such as Dave Clark (of the Dave Clark Five) and Mick Jagger–Keith Richards (of the Rolling Stones), and British pop songs established an ongoing presence within the US charts. But although the emergence of original British material within the US charts during the early to mid-1960s represents a significant development in the history of popular music, to date there has been little attempt to document the development of early British Invasion songwriting as a whole. This chapter aims to make a contribution in this area by examining Lennon–McCartney's early work within the context of the British Invasion. Comparisons are made between Lennon–McCartney and three other successful British Invasion writer–performers – Dave Clark, Mick Jagger–Keith Richards and Ray Davies (of the Kinks) – by considering their US chart achievements, songwriting styles and overall contributions to the development of 1960s popular songwriting.

53

As Table 4.1 indicates, Lennon–McCartney were clearly the dominant British Invasion songwriters between 1964 and 1966. Their impact upon the US pop charts in 1964 was dramatic. Table 4.2 reveals that in addition to the 14 songs which they wrote for the Beatles in this year, their compositions provided six US hits for other performers.

*Table* 4.1   US Top 40 hits by the most successful British Invasion writer-performers, 1964–6[2]

|  | 1964 | 1965 | 1966 | Total |
|---|---|---|---|---|
| Lennon–McCartney | 20 | 8 | 6 | 34 |
| Jagger–Richards | 2 | 4 | 7 | 13 |
| Clark (*et al.*) | 6 | 2 | 3 | 11 |
| Davies | 1 | 4 | 4 | 9 |

*Table* 4.2   US Top 40 hits by Lennon–McCartney, 1964–6

| Date | Position | Performer | Song title | Label and no. |
|---|---|---|---|---|
| 25/01/64 | 1 | Beatles | I Want To Hold Your Hand | Capitol 5112 |
| 01/02/64 | 1 | Beatles | She Loves You | Swan 4152 |
| 02/02/64 | 14 | Beatles | I Saw Her Standing There | Capitol 5112 |
| 22/02/64 | 3 | Beatles | Please Please Me | Vee Jay 581 |
| 28/03/64 | 1 | Beatles | Can't Buy Me Love | Capitol 5150 |
| 11/04/64 | 2 | Beatles | Do You Want To Know A Secret | Capital 5150 |
| 25/04/64 | 35 | Beatles | Thank You Girl | Vee Jay 587 |
| 02/05/64 | 1 | Beatles | Love Me Do | Vee Jay 587 |
| 16/05/64 | 10 | Beatles | P.S. I Love You | Tollie 9008 |
| 13/06/64 | 9 | Billy J. Kramer and the Dakotas | Bad To Me | Imperial 66027 |
| 16/05/64 | 1 | Peter and Gordon | A World Without Love | Capitol 5175 |
| 11/07/64 | 12 | Peter and Gordon | Nobody I Know | Capitol 5211 |
| 18/07/64 | 1 | Beatles | A Hard Day's Night | Capitol 5222 |
| 08/08/64 | 12 | Beatles | And I Love Her | Capitol 5235 |
| 15/08/64 | 25 | Beatles | I'll Cry Instead | Capitol 5234 |
| 15/08/64 | 11 | Billy J. Kramer and the Dakotas | I'll Keep You Satisfied | Imperial 66048 |
| 19/09/64 | 8 | Billy J. Kramer and the Dakotas | From A Window | Imperial 66051 |

| 24/10/64 | 16 | Peter and Gordon | I Don't Want To See You Again | Capitol 5272 |
|---|---|---|---|---|
| 05/12/64 | 1 | Beatles | I Feel Fine | Capitol 5255 |
| 12/12/64 | 4 | Beatles | She's A Woman | Capitol 5327 |
| 27/02/65 | 1 | Beatles | Eight Days A Week | Capitol 5327 |
| 20/03/65 | 3 | Beatles | I Don't Want To Spoil The Party | Capitol 5371 |
| 01/05/65 | 1 | Beatles | Ticket To Ride | Capitol 5407 |
| 14/08/65 | 1 | Beatles | Help | Capitol 5476 |
| 02/10/65 | 1 | Beatles | Yesterday | Capitol 5498 |
| 06/11/65 | 10 | Silkie | You've Got To Hide Your Love Away | Fontana 1525 |
| 18/12/65 | 1 | Beatles | We Can Work It Out | Capitol 5498 |
| 25/12/65 | 5 | Beatles | Day Tripper | Capitol 5555 |
| 29/01/66 | 18 | David and Jonathan | Michelle | Capitol 5563 |
| 05/03/66 | 3 | Beatles | Nowhere Man | Capitol 5587 |
| 11/06/66 | 1 | Beatles | Paperback Writer | Capitol 5587 |
| 25/06/66 | 23 | Beatles | Rain | Capitol 5651 |
| 27/08/66 | 2 | Beatles | Yellow Submarine | Capitol 5651 |
| 10/09/66 | 11 | Beatles | Eleanor Rigby | Capital 5715 |

Eight of the Lennon–McCartney songs became Number One hits, and on April 4, *Billboard* listed their songs in the following chart positions: 1, 2, 3, 4, 5, 31, 41, 46, 58, 65, 68 and 79 (Coleman 1990: 29). In 1965 and 1966 Lennon–McCartney maintained a significant presence

*Table* 4.3    US Top 40 hits by Clark, 1964–6, all performed by the Dave Clark Five

| Date | Position | Song title | Label and no. |
|---|---|---|---|
| 07/03/64 | 6 | Glad All Over (S) | Epic 9656 |
| 11/04/64 | 4 | Bits And Pieces (S) | Epic 9671 |
| 20/06/64 | 4 | Can't You See That She's Mine (S) | Epic 9692 |
| 08/08/64 | 3 | Because | Epic 9704 |
| 17/10/64 | 15 | Everybody Knows (I Still Love You) (D) | Epic 9722 |
| 05/12/64 | 14 | Anyway You Want It | Epic 9739 |
| 27/02/65 | 14 | Come Home (S) | Epic 9763 |
| 04/09/65 | 4 | Catch Us If You Can (D) | Epic 9833 |
| 19/02/66 | 18 | At the Scene (D) | Epic 9822 |
| 23/04/66 | 12 | Try Too Hard (S) | Epic 10004 |
| 02/07/66 | 28 | Please Tell Me Why (S) | Epic 10031 |

*Co-writers:* (S) Mike Smith (D) Lenny Davidson

Table 4.4    US Top 40 hits by Jagger–Richards, 1964–6

| Date | Position | Performer | Song title | Label and no. |
|------|----------|-----------|------------|---------------|
| 01/08/64 | 24 | Rolling Stones | Tell Me (You're Coming Back) | London 9682 |
| 19/12/64 | 22 | Marianne Faithfull | As Tears Go By (O) | London 9697 |
| 30/01/65 | 19 | Rolling Stones | Heart Of Stone | London 9725 |
| 10/04/65 | 9 | Rolling Stones | The Last Time | London 9741 |
| 16/06/65 | 1 | Rolling Stones | Satisfaction | London 9766 |
| 19/10/65 | 1 | Rolling Stones | Get Off Of My Cloud | London 9792 |
| 08/01/66 | 6 | Rolling Stones | As Tears Go By (O) | London 9808 |
| 02/04/66 | 31 | Otis Redding | Satisfaction | Volt 132 |
| 05/03/66 | 2 | Rolling Stones | 19th Nervous Breakdown | London 9823 |
| 21/05/66 | 1 | Rolling Stones | Paint It Black | London 901 |
| 16/07/66 | 8 | Rolling Stones | Mother's Little Helper | London 901 |
| 06/08/66 | 24 | Rolling Stones | Lady Jane | London 902 |
| 08/10/66 | 9 | Rolling Stones | Have You Seen Your Mother Baby, Standing In The Shadow | London 902 |

*Co-writer:* (O) Andrew Loog Oldham

in the Top 40, but failed to dominate the charts as they had in 1964. However, all but two of their 14 Top 40 songs from 1965–6 entered the Top Ten, and six became Number One hits.

After Lennon–McCartney, Dave Clark was the most successful British songwriter in the US in 1964, composing six Top 40 hits for his group, the Dave Clark Five – often in conjunction with lead guitarist Lenny Davidson or keyboard player/vocalist Mike Smith. In 1965–6 they were responsible for a further five Top 40 hits (Table 4.3).

Original songs by Mick Jagger and Keith Richards of the Rolling Stones did not make a major impact in the USA until 1965, when 'Satisfaction' and 'Get Off Of My Cloud' both became Number One hits. In 1964, they had written two Top 40 songs – 'Tell Me' recorded by the group, and 'As Tears Go By' recorded by Marianne Faithfull – but their most successful singles of that year were cover versions of 'It's All Over Now' and 'Time Is On My Side'. By 1965, however, all the Rolling Stones' Top 40 hits were compositions by Jagger–Richards, who by 1966 were challenging Lennon–McCartney as the dominant British Invasion songwriters (Table 4.4).

Ray Davies, lead vocalist and songwriter for the Kinks, achieved his first US Top 40 entry in late 1964 with 'You Really Got Me', and

Table 4.5   US Top 40 hits by Davies, 1964–6

| Date | Position | Performer | Song title | Label and no. |
|---|---|---|---|---|
| 24/10/64 | 7 | Kinks | You Really Got Me | Reprise 0306 |
| 16/01/65 | 7 | Kinks | All Day And All Of The Night | Reprise 0334 |
| 27/03/65 | 6 | Kinks | Tired Of Waiting For You | Reprise 0347 |
| 10/07/65 | 23 | Kinks | Set Me Free | Reprise 0379 |
| 04/09/65 | 34 | Kinks | Who'll Be The Next In Line | Reprise 0366 |
| 08/01/66 | 13 | Kinks | A Well Respected Man | Reprise 0420 |
| 18/06/66 | 36 | Kinks | Dedicated Follower Of Fashion | Reprise 0471 |
| 27/08/66 | 14 | Kinks | Sunny Afternoon | Reprise 0497 |
| 15/10/66 | 5 | Herman's Hermit's | Dandy | MGM 13603 |

maintained a consistent level of success during 1965 and 1966, writing a further seven Top 40 hits for the group, as well as one ('Dandy') for Herman's Hermits (Table 4.5)

## COMPARATIVE ANALYSIS OF SONGWRITING STYLE

This section provides a comparative analysis of all of the songs listed in the preceding tables[3] and focuses on a number of components: lyrics, melody, rhythm, harmony, form and production.[4]

### Lyrics

Lyrics relating to aspects of relationships are a feature of more than four in five of the songs by Lennon–McCartney and Clark (Table 4.6). Most of Lennon–McCartney's songs from 1964 offer a simple, positive, optimistic view of relationships, evident in titles such as 'I Want To Hold Your Hand', 'She Loves You', 'I Saw Her Standing There', 'Thank You Girl', 'Love Me Do', 'P.S. I Love You'. These songs tend to use very simple language and rhyme schemes:

- 'Love, love me do. You know I love you. I'll always be true, so please love me do' ('Love Me Do')
- 'Oh yeah, I'll tell you something I think you'll understand. When I say that something, I wanna hold your hand' ('I Want To Hold Your Hand')
- 'You be good to me, you make me glad when I was blue. And eternally I'll always be in love with you' ('Thank You Girl')

*Table* 4.6   Lyrics

| | Lennon–McCartney (%) | Jagger–Richards (%) | Clark (%) | Davies (%) |
|---|---|---|---|---|
| *Relationships overall* | | | | |
| positive | 55 | 18 | 45 | 22 |
| ambivalent | 3 | 0 | 9 | 11 |
| negative | 27 | 45 | 27 | 22 |
| *Other elements* | | | | |
| social comment | 15 | 55 | 0 | 44 |
| teen interests† | 6 | 0 | 9 | 0 |
| poetic devices§ | 30 | 64 | 9 | 56 |
| direct address | 48 | 45 | 73 | 67 |

*Notes:*

\* Figures represent the percentage of songs by each writer which contain the particular attribute, and are rounded off to the nearest whole number. This applies to all analytical tables.

† Surfing, cars/bikes, going out/parties, dancing, and so on

§ Simile, metaphor, satire, and so on

Clark's lyrics in songs like 'Glad All Over', 'Can't You See That She's Mine and 'Because', parallel those by Lennon–McCartney in their focus on straightforward and positive relationships.

The songs by Jagger–Richards deal less with relationships overall (approximately two in three songs) and often express negative sentiments, dealing with topics such as the ending of relationships ('Tell Me', 'Paint It Black'). In addition a number of their songs ('Heart Of Stone', 'The Last Time') portray an uncaring, disdainful masculinity. Almost half their songs comment on aspects of society – often by satirizing certain types of people and/or social situations. Their first two US Number One hits – 'Satisfaction' and 'Get Off Of My Cloud' – express a personal sense of frustration with contemporary society, and rebellion against some of its norms, while 'Mother's Little Helper' satirizes the older generation's reliance on tranquilizers.

As well as employing satire, Jagger–Richards use the poetic device of metaphor in approximately one in three songs, and four song titles ('Heart Of Stone', 'Get Off Of My Cloud', 'Mother's Little Helper' and 'Have You Seen Your Mother, Baby, Standing In The Shadow'). An additional lyric technique involves the use of extended repetition to increase dramatic effect, either by reinforcing the lyric hook ('Satisfaction' and 'Get Off Of My Cloud') or by heightening the impact of a prehook ('Heart Of Stone' and '19th Nervous Breakdown').

Although the songs of Ray Davies from 1964 and 1965 all deal with relationships, his Top 40 hits of 1966 all involve social comment. Like Jagger–Richards, he makes pointed satirical observations about contemporary British society, but unlike them, Davies invariably takes the role of detached observer ('Well Respected Man', 'Dedicated Follower Of Fashion').

It should be noted that the Lennon–McCartney songs tend to move away from simple, optimistic love themes after 1964. With the exception of 'Eight Days A Week', all their 1965 hits refer to the ending of relationships or problems within relationships. In addition, although social comment is present in only a small overall proportion of their songs (approximately one in seven), it is more common in the latter part of this period: of the three songs containing the most overt social observations, all of which were hits in 1966, two make general observations about social apathy:

- 'Doesn't have a point of view, knows not where he's going to. Isn't he a bit like you and me?' ('Nowhere Man')
- 'When the rain comes, they run and hide their heads. They might as well be dead, when the rain comes' ('Rain')

and one deals with the plight of social misfits:

- 'Father Mackenzie, writing the words of a sermon that no-one will hear. No-one comes near ... All the lonely people, where do they all come from? All the lonely people, where do they all belong?' ('Eleanor Rigby')

## Melody

The songs by Lennon–McCartney, Jagger–Richards and Davies all use a median vocal range of between an octave and a tenth, while Clark's vocal melodies are mostly within an octave range (Table 4.7).

*Table 4.7*  Melody

|  | Lennon–McCartney (%) | Jagger–Richards (%) | Clark (%) | Davies (%) |
|---|---|---|---|---|
| *Vocal range* | | | | |
| less than octave | 21 | 9 | 73 | 33 |
| octave to tenth | 61 | 73 | 18 | 67 |
| > tenth | 18 | 18 | 9 | 0 |

| *Mode types* | | | | |
|---|---|---|---|---|
| major pentatonic | 0 | 0 | 9 | 0 |
| major hexatonic | 18 | 9 | 9 | 0 |
| major (ionian) | 58 | 45 | 55 | 33 |
| minor pentatonic | 3 | 0 | 0 | 22 |
| mixolydian | 9 | 18 | 9 | 22 |
| blues inflections | 21 | 9 | 18 | 11 |
| *Disjunct* | | | | |
| 0–5 | 82 | 91 | 91 | 78 |
| *Intervals\** | | | | |
| 6–10 | 18 | 9 | 9 | 11 |
| *Within phrases* | | | | |
| >10 | 0 | 0 | 0 | 11 |
| *Overall contour†* | | | | |
| rising | 48 | 36 | 18 | 33 |
| falling | 36 | 9 | 27 | 22 |
| flat | 15 | 27 | 55 | 33 |
| *Melodic riffs* | | | | |
| overall | 18 | 55 | 0 | 11 |

\* Defined for the purposes of this study as leaps of a perfect fourth or more.
† The pattern of overall pitch placement of different song sections (that is, 'rising' contour means that the chorus or bridge is set higher than the verse)

*Vocal Range*
The songs by all writers tend to be highly conjunct, but although Lennon–McCartney do not utilize a large overall amount of disjunct melodic movement, they often feature leaps in prominent ways. Many songs include large leaps which contrast markedly with the predominantly conjunct surrounding melodic movement, and which function as a strong melodic hook.

*(a) Leap of an Octave*

'Eleanor Rigby'

### (b) Leap of a Major Sixth

'Rain'

### (c) Leap of a Minor Sixth

'Day Tripper'

'She's A Woman'

Many other songs feature smaller leaps as song hooks. Fifth leaps occur in 'Yellow Submarine', 'We Can Work It Out', 'Can't Buy Me Love', 'Thank You Girl' and 'I Want To Hold Your Hand' and leaps of a fourth are prominent melodic hooks in 'Nowhere Man', 'I Feel Fine', 'Please Please Me', 'And I Love Her' and 'I'll Keep You Satisfied'.

Songs by Jagger–Richards rarely feature such devices (the ballad-style 'Lady Jane' is an exception). Instead they regularly employ the repetition of simple, mostly conjunct melodic phrases ('The Last Time') or they may focus attention on a particular pitch in more freely-articulated, chant-style melodies typical of the blues ('Satisfaction').

And in two songs – 'Satisfaction' and 'Heart Of Stone' – repeating melodic phrases are used to create a dramatic rising prehook.

*Scale Usage*

The songs by Lennon–McCartney, Jagger–Richards and Clark employ a very similar profile of scale usage. These writers clearly favour complete major scales over major pentatonics and hexatonics, and they use blues-inflections and/or mixolydian scales in approximately one in three songs. Jagger–Richards are more inclined towards melodies which incorporate the flattened seventh but not the flattened third. On the other hand Davies favours both the flattened seventh and third scale degrees; more than half his songs involve either mixolydian, minor pentatonic or blues scales, and only one in three features complete major scales.

In a number of their songs ('A Hard Day's Night', 'P.S. I Love You', 'Ticket To Ride') Lennon–McCartney achieve contrasts between the A and B sections of AABA songs by employing different modes. In 'A Hard Day's Night', for example, the verse (or A section) prominently features the flattened seventh degree, while the B section features the major seventh degree:

*(i) A section melody*

*(ii) B section melody*

Another device which is employed to achieve contrast between the A and B sections of the typical AABA songs involves varying the pitch placement of song sections: the number of AABA songs with the B section melody set at a higher pitch than the A section exactly equals the number of songs in which the B melody is set at a lower pitch level (Table 4.8).

*Table* 4.8    Pitch placement of melodies in Lennon–McCartney
AABA songs

| B section melody lower than A section melody | B section melody higher than A section melody |
|---|---|
| I Want To Hold Your Hand | I Saw Her Standing There |
| Please Please Me | Can't Buy Me Love |
| Thank You Girl | Do You Want To Know A Secret |
| Love Me Do | P.S. I Love You |
| A World Without Love | Nobody I know |
| And I Love Her | A Hard Day's Night |
| I'll Keep You Satisfied | I'll Cry Instead |
| I Feel Fine | From A Window |
| She's A Woman | I Don't Want To See You Again |
| Eight Days A Week | I Don't Want To Spoil The Party |
| Ticket To Ride | We Can Work It Out |

Other techniques, most notably those relating to melodic rhythms and aspects of harmony, also assist in creating the notable sectional variety in the Lennon–McCartney songs. Although Clark, like Lennon–McCartney, favours the AABA song form, he does not introduce the same sectional contrasts. Of Clark's six AABA songs, four maintain the same pitch between A and B sections. In addition, two in five songs have flat or irregular verse contours, compared with one in four of the Lennon–McCartney songs.

Jagger–Richards employ similar sectional AABA pitch contrasts only on rare occasions, such as 'Have You Seen Your Mother, Baby, Standing In The Shadow'. They sometimes contrast long, free-flowing, chant style verse melodies with shorter repetitive chorus melodies, as in 'Satisfaction' and 'Get Off Of My Cloud'. Both they and Lennon–McCartney use arch-contoured verse melodies for around half their songs, but Jagger–Richards are much more inclined towards flat or irregular contours.

Jagger–Richards also make greater use of melodic riffs, utilizing them in more than half their songs (compared with one in five Lennon–McCartney songs). These frequently take the form of guitar riffs which employ the dominant seventh 'flavour' commonly associated with the blues ('Satisfaction', 'The Last Time' and Lennon–McCartney's 'I Feel Fine').

When present, a guitar riff normally plays an important role in song structure, its presence or absence often helping to define song sections, and sometimes acting in tandem with the vocal melody to create call-response patterns. For example, a notable feature of Davies's 'All Day And All Of The Night' and 'You Really Got Me' is the close connection between the melody and the prevailing rhythmic-chordal guitar riff, which helps to give the riff an added aural prominence and structural importance.

## Rhythm

Lennon–McCartney employ a wide variety of tempos overall, but make no use of very slow tempos (below 100 bpm). Jagger–Richards favour fast tempos, with almost half their songs employing 160 or more bpm, while the songs by Clark and Davies mostly fall within the 120–140 bpm range. Lennon–McCartney, Jagger–Richards and Clark clearly favour eighth subdivisions over shuffles, while Davies uses a more even balance of the two (Table 4.9). Jagger–Richards use shuffles mainly in their faster songs such as '19th Nervous Breakdown', 'The Last Time' and 'Mother's Little Helper'.

*Table* 4.9    Rhythm

|  | Lennon–McCartney (%) | Jagger–Richards (%) | Clark (%) | Davies (%) |
|---|---|---|---|---|
| *Tempo* | | | | |
| <100bpm* | 0 | 9 | 9 | 0 |
| 100–119 | 15 | 18 | 9 | 0 |
| 120–139 | 39 | 18 | 36 | 33 |
| 140–159 | 18 | 9 | 36 | 33 |
| 160– | 27 | 45 | 9 | 33 |
| *Beat subdivision* | | | | |
| shuffle/triplet | 21 | 36 | 36 | 44 |
| eighth | 73 | 64 | 64 | 56 |
| sixteenth | 3 | 0 | 0 | 0 |
| changing subdivision | 3 | 0 | 0 | 0 |
| *Specific features* | | | | |
| distinct harmonic rhythm† | 9 | 27 | 18 | 44 |
| sectional rhythm changes§ | 6 | 0 | 9 | 0 |
| *Riffs overall* | 6 | 27 | 18 | 33 |
| rhythmic-chordal | 3 | 27 | 18 | 33 |
| rhythmic | 3 | 9 | 0 | 0 |

* Beats per minute
† Chord changes are associated with a prominent rhythmic pattern
§ Significant rhythmic changes between different song sec⁺ions (for example: subdivision change; presence/absence of a distinctive  ythmic motif/riff and so on)

Several ballads by Lennon–McCartney ('Yesterday', 'Eleanor Rigby') and Jagger–Richards ('Lady Jane', 'As Tears Go By') avoid the use of the drum kit, and instead employ strings and/or acoustic guitars to create a more subdued atmosphere.

Jagger–Richards attach distinct rhythmic patterns to chord changes in several songs ('Get Off Of My Cloud', 'Have You Seen Your Mother, Baby, Standing In The Shadow', 'Satisfaction', 'The Last Time') to form recurring rhythmic-chordal riffs. Davies also employs prominent rhythmic-chordal guitar riffs in the first three of his Top 40 hits ('You Really Got Me', 'All Day And All Of The Night', 'Tired Of Waiting For You'). These riffs consist of major chord sequences with root movements outlining notes of the blues scale (the flattened seventh and minor third), which are attached to prominent rhythmic figures.

Although Lennon–McCartney make little use of distinct harmonic rhythms, sectional rhythm changes, or rhythmic/rhythmic-chordal riffs, rhythm does play a significant role in their melodic style. They create a variety of easily-recognized melodic rhythms, and often establish distinctive patterns in the opening bars of the vocal melody.

'Do You Want To Know A Secret'

'Love Me Do'

'And I Love Her'

Bright   are the   stars   that   shine

'From A Window'

Late        yes - ter - day night        I saw a light

'Yellow Submarine'

In      the town        .        where I        was born

In addition, they employ changes in melodic rhythm to achieve variety and contrast between the A and B sections of AABA songs. Typically, a contrasting bridge melody involves a significant increase or decrease in rhythmic activity:

'Please Please Me'

'Thank You Girl'

♩=132

You be good to me you make me glad when I was blue

Thank you girl for lov - in' me the way that you do

'She's A Woman'

♩=170

My love don't give me pres - ents

She's a wo - man who un - der - stands

'We Can Work It Out'

♩=107

Try to see it my way Do I have to keep on talk - ing

Life is ve - ry short and there's no time

## Harmony

Most of the songs by Lennon–McCartney, Jagger–Richards and Clark arc either completely or predominantly diatonic (Table 4.10). Clark's harmonic language is extremely simple. Four in five songs are either completely or predominantly diatonic. The only secondary dominant used is the II7 chord, and bVII chords and chord colourations are used infrequently (one in five songs). Only the occasional use of borrowed chords, such as the iv chord, adds some harmonic interest to the songs. Four songs employ repeated two-chord sequences: 'Anyway You Want It' (I vi); 'Bits And Pieces' and 'Glad All Over' (I IV); 'Try Too Hard' (I bVII).

*Table* 4.10   Harmony

| | Lennon–McCartney (%) | Jagger–Richards (%) | Clark (%) | Davies (%) |
|---|---|---|---|---|
| *General* | | | | |
| exclusively diatonic | 24 | 18 | 18 | 0 |
| predominantly diatonic | 48 | 82 | 55 | 56 |
| complex | 27 | 0 | 27 | 45 |
| *Special features* | | | | |
| blues-based | 15 | 9 | 0 | 0 |
| repeated short chord cycle | 12 | 36 | 45 | 56 |
| modulating section(s) | 6 | 0 | 0 | 11 |
| ambiguous keys | 3 | 0 | 0 | 0 |
| Secondary dominant progressions | 39 | 27 | 55 | 67 |
| use of bVII | 27 | 27 | 18 | 56 |
| use of borrowed/unusual chords* | 42 | 36 | 36 | 45 |
| chord colourations† | 12 | 0 | 27 | 22 |

*Notes:*
\* It is difficult to find an appropriate term for this type of chord, which might at times be considered to be 'borrowed' from a different mode (such as a 'dorian' major IV chord employed in a minor key), and/or occur as an unusual/unexpected non-diatonic harmonic element.
† Additions or alterations to the basic major or minor triad, such as a 6th, major 7th, major 9th and so on. Minor 7th chords were not included, given their widespread use within the song field as a substitute for a minor triad, particularly in ii V progressions.

Although Lennon–McCartney's songs are mostly diatonic, their harmony is notable for the variety of chord types and progressions employed (Table 4.11). This variety is evident in the range of diatonic progressions, secondary dominant progressions, and borrowed chords which provide these songs with an unusual degree of harmonic interest. Several incorporate very unusual diatonic progressions and some utilize less common secondary dominant sequences (VI7 ii: 'Bad To Me', 'From A Window').

*Table* 4.11   Unusual diatonic progressions employed in
Lennon–McCartney Songs

| Progression | Song title |
| --- | --- |
| I vi iii V | She Loves You (verse) |
| I vi iii ii | Do You Want To Know A Secret (B section)* |
| I V vi iii | I Want To Hold Your Hand (A section) |
| I ii I V vi V | P.S. I Love You (A section) |
| vi V vi iii vi ii V | And I Love Her (B section) |

* The B section moves to the IV as the new key centre. The quoted
progression refers to this new key centre.

Similarly, while Lennon–McCartney's favoured borrowed chord is
the iv (used in seven songs) they import a wide range of different
borrowed/unusual chords into many of their songs (Table 4.12).

They also employ a wide range of chords to commence the B
section of AABA songs, adding an extra element of variety and
unpredictability (Table 4.13).

By contrast, the harmonic language employed by Jagger–Richards
is much simpler: all their songs are completely or predominantly
diatonic, and regularly incorporate repeated short chord cycles based
on simple harmonic formulae. Examples include 'Have You Seen
Your Mother, Baby, Standing In The Shadow' (I IV); 'Get Off Of My
Cloud' (I IV V IV); 'The Last Time' and 'Satisfaction' (I bVII IV).
Their favoured diatonic sequences are (I) IV V I and I IV, and the use
of secondary dominant chords is infrequent, and mostly limited to the
II7 chord. They demonstrate a liking for minor keys ('Paint It Black'
and 'Mother's Little Helper') and in 'Heart Of Stone' they exploit the
ambiguity between major and relative minor by alternately ending the
lyric-melodic hook in A minor and C major.

Davies's songs from 1964 and 1965 mostly involve major chords
and tend to favour root notes such as the flattened seventh and flattened third scale degree. The guitar facilitates this type of chord
movement by sliding chord shapes up and down the fretboard.[5] It is
possible to move a complete chord progression up or down in pitch
without altering the fingering pattern of the chords (or to avoid the
upper reaches of the fretboard by making one fingering alteration).
This procedure can lead the tonality into non-diatonic areas. 'You
Really Got Me' shows the clearest evidence of this technique, with

*Table* 4.12    Borrowed/unusual chords in songs by
Lennon–McCartney

| Chord | Song title |
|-------|-----------|
| iv | She Loves You |
|  | I Saw Her Standing There |
|  | Do You Want To Know A Secret |
|  | A World Without Love |
|  | I'll Keep You Satisfied |
|  | I Don't Want To See You Again |
|  | Nowhere Man |
| vii | Yesterday |
| bVI | P.S. I Love You |
|  | Nobody I Know |
|  | A World Without Love |
| II | Eight Days A Week |
|  | Yesterday |
|  | Day Tripper |
|  | She Loves You |
| chromatic passing chord | Do You Want To Know A Secret |
|  | Bad To Me |
| VI | She's A Woman |
| bIII | Please Please Me |

the descending tone movement between the opening two chords (G
F) repeated a tone higher (A G) and then a further fourth higher
(D C) for the 'chorus', which consists of several repetitions of the
main lyric hook.

*Table* 4.13    Chords used to commence the B section in
Lennon–McCartney AABA songs

| Chord | Song title |
|-------|-----------|
| I | I Don't Want To Spoil The Party |
|  | I Feel Fine |
| ii | I Want To Hold Your Hand |
|  | Help* |

| iii | Can't Buy Me Love* |
| | A Hard Day's Night |
| | I'll Cry Instead |
| | She's A Woman |
| | Nowhere Man |
| iv | A World Without Love |
| IV | I Saw Her Standing There |
| | Please Please Me |
| | Do You Want To Know A Secret |
| | P.S. I Love You* |
| | Bad To Me |
| | From A Window |
| | I Don't Want To See You Again |
| | Ticket To Ride |
| V | Love Me Do |
| | I'll Keep You Satisfied |
| | Eight Days A Week |
| vi | Thank You Girl |
| | Nobody I Know |
| | And I Love Her |
| | We Can Work It Out |
| vii | Yesterday† |

*Notes:*
\* These songs are AABA forms with an introductory section.
† The vii chord actually functions as a ii in a ii V I in A minor.

**Form**

Songs by Lennon–McCartney and Clark tend to be shorter than those by Jagger–Richards and Davies (Table 4.14). Two-thirds of Lennon–McCartney's songs are less than two and a half minutes, and four ('Please Please Me', 'I'll Cry Instead', 'I Don't Want To See You Again', 'From A Window') are, unusually, less than two minutes. The median duration of songs by Jagger–Richards is between two and a half and three minutes. Four ('Paint It Black', 'The Last Time', '19th Nervous Breakdown', 'Satisfaction') are, equally unusually, more than three and a half minutes.

Lennon–McCartney and Clark use very simple and regular forms[6] and clearly prefer the AABA scheme. Several of Lennon–McCartney's AABA songs ('Love Me Do', 'A Hard Day's Night', 'I

*Table* 4.14   Form

|  | Lennon–McCartney (%) | Jagger–Richards (%) | Clark (%) | Davies (%) |
|---|---|---|---|---|
| *Duration* | | | | |
| <2mins | 12 | 0 | 45 | 11 |
| 2mins–2mins 30secs | 55 | 9 | 45 | 44 |
| 2mins 31secs–3mins | 27 | 45 | 9 | 33 |
| 3mins 01secs–3mins 30secs | 6 | 9 | 0 | 11 |
| >3mins 30secs | 0 | 36 | 0 | 0 |
| *General form type* | | | | |
| verse–chorus | 24 | 45 | 27 | 33 |
| verse–chorus–bridge | 0 | 9 | 9 | 11 |
| AABA | 76 | 18 | 67 | 44 |
| AAA | 0 | 27 | 0 | 11 |
| *Special features* | | | | |
| irregularity | 12 | 18 | 9 | 22 |
| prominent pre-hook | 0 | 27 | 0 | 11 |
| chorus first | 6 | 0 | 0 | 11 |
| step modulation* | 3 | 0 | 9 | 0 |
| *Riffs* | | | | |
| overall | 21 | 64 | 18 | 44 |
| melodic | 18 | 55 | 0 | 11 |
| rhythmic-chordal | 0 | 18 | 18 | 33 |
| *Instrumental solo* | | | | |
| overall | 48 | 45 | 27 | 22 |

\*  An upwards key shift of a semitone or tone occurring towards the end of a song (usually for a final verse or chorus).

Don't Want To Spoil The Party') involve an immediate statement of the lyric hook, rather than placing it (as is more common) at the end of the A section. However, they generate a surprising amount of variety and interest within the simple song forms employed, by incorporating the previously-discussed melodic, rhythmic and harmonic contrasts between song sections.

Jagger–Richards seem to prefer song forms involving a verse and chorus (with or without bridge). This form occurs in more than half their songs, compared with only one in four songs by Lennon–

McCartney and Clark). They employ the AAA form in three songs ('Lady Jane', 'Paint It Black', 'As Tears Go By') and they occasionally use pre-hooks (involving the extensive repetition of short lyric and melodic ideas) to create a build-up to a lyric-melodic climax.

Melodic guitar riffs appear in more than half the Jagger–Richards songs and one in five of the Lennon–McCartney songs. As previously noted, these riffs normally play an important role in song structure. The use of the well-known riff in 'Satisfaction' provides an excellent illustration of this process; here, the riff functions as the introduction, but does not continue during the opening chorus. Rather, it is introduced to support the emphatic lyric statement 'I can't get no', at which point it operates in a call–response pattern with the vocal melody for several bars. After this, the riff continues underneath the verse melody. Jagger–Richards also use rhythmic-chordal riffs to help define sections in songs such as 'Get Off Of My Cloud', 'The Last Time' and 'Satisfaction' by employing the riff during the verse, but not during the chorus.

Although they do not employ riffs in as great a proportion of songs as do Jagger–Richards, Lennon–McCartney also tend to associate riffs with particular song sections. In 'Day Tripper' the riff provides the introduction, and then continues over the first 16 bars of what appears to be a 24 bar blues. When the chord pattern deviates from the anticipated blues chord sequence (at the point where the listener would expect the V chord), the melodic guitar riff stops simultaneously.

Davies writes an even number of AABA forms and verse–chorus–(bridge) forms and, as already noted, several of his early songs involve guitar riffs, which feature prominent melodic, rhythmic and harmonic elements. These riffs also play an important role in song structure; in 'You Really Got Me' and 'All Day And All Of The Night' the riff is present throughout (apart from the pre-hook of the latter song), and the riff's upward movement in pitch is the main element providing a sense of melodic/lyric climax.

**Production**

Both John Lennon and Paul McCartney were inexperienced recording artists when they commenced their recording careers. Consequently, they relied on producer George Martin to create a studio sound appropriate to their songs. His aim during the recording of the group's first album, *Please Please Me*, was to:

reproduce the Cavern performance in the relative calm of the studio ... we started at ten that morning ... and recorded straight on to twin-track mono. By eleven o'clock at night we had recorded the lot, thirteen new tracks, to which we added the existing recording of 'Please Please Me'. (Martin 1979: 131)

In order to approximate the Beatles' live sound, the choice of instrumentation was that of the group itself – guitars, bass, and drums. Any substantial addition of other instruments would have meant a departure from their live sound, and made it difficult for them to reproduce their studio sound on tour. Consequently, studio augmentation is minimal, and involves instruments such as tambourine (36 per cent of songs) and piano (15 per cent), which are normally placed low in the mix. Voices are very prominent in the mix, and a second lead vocal track is often overdubbed to reinforce the melody line.

The involvement of the songwriters (particularly McCartney) in the production process increased over time, culminating in *Sgt Pepper's Lonely Hearts Club Band* in 1967. It seems clear, however, that Lennon–McCartney were providing production suggestions for Martin to realize from the start.[7] In tandem with this increasingly collaborative production was a trend towards increasingly complex production and the inclusion of orchestral instruments such as strings.

Like Lennon and McCartney, Mick Jagger and Keith Richards lacked recording studio experience when they commenced their recording careers. Andrew Loog Oldham, their manager and nominal producer, was equally inexperienced, but insisted that their records' 'raw, uncluttered production [was] ... precisely what the kids wanted' (Rogan 1988: 164). As in the early songs of the Beatles, production is generally designed to capture the essence of the group's live sound, although several ballads, including 'As Tears Go By', receive a lighter treatment, with instruments such as acoustic guitars and strings featured.

Dave Clark was both writer and producer for the Dave Clark Five, who, like the other British groups, were active on the live music circuit;[8] and for whom it was also desirable that hit recordings should allow a reasonable live reproduction. The group featured organ and saxophone in addition to guitars, bass and drums, and these are the instruments on most of the recordings; acoustic piano is also featured occasionally ('Try Too Hard', 'Please Tell Me Why'). Other prominent aspects of Clark's production style include the use of exaggerated echo effects, and the placement of drums prominently in the final mix.[9]

Most of the Kinks' songs were produced by American Shel Talmy, who initially favoured a raw, studio sound dominated by distorted guitar and well-suited to the riff-based songs written by Davies. Like Lennon–McCartney, Davies gradually became more involved in production, and his input is apparent in the later satirical songs, which are characterized by a cleaner sound featuring both acoustic and undistorted electric guitars.

Backing vocals are present in most of the songs by all writers. In the songs of Lennon–McCartney and Jagger–Richards they most commonly involve a male voice singing a third or sixth harmony to the lead melody. Lennon–McCartney achieve some distinctive sounds by regularly incorporating fourth and fifth intervals into the vocal harmony:

'Eight Days A Week'

They also occasionally rely on a technique which involves a repeated harmony note sung against a moving melody, as in the opening of 'Please Please Me'.

In addition to third and sixth harmonies, Jagger–Richards regularly use unison/octave backing vocals (approximately one in three songs) to help to emphasize a particular melodic and/or lyric hook by doubling it, as in the case of the emphatic statement 'I can't get no' in 'Satisfaction'. Clark makes extensive use of backing vocals to harmonize melody lines, and, like Lennon–McCartney, employs the sound of fourth and fifth intervals in a number of songs. In 'Any Way You Want It' harmony parts continue throughout almost all the song and voices are mixed so evenly that it is difficult to discern a predominant melody line.

Davies also uses harmony-style backing vocals but, unlike Clark, he does not employ the sound of the fourth or fifth interval; his unison/octave parts tend to provide a sustained string-line style backing, rather than melody reinforcement.

## SUMMARY AND DISCUSSION

### The First Phase of the British Invasion

The British Invasion began in early 1964, and the most successful writers during the initial stages were Lennon–McCartney and Clark, whose songs share a number of common features, including happy, romance-based lyrics and a simple musical language.

The songs tend to be short, and utilize AABA forms which allow for the early statement of the song hook. Vocal range is limited, melodies tend to be very conjunct, and the harmonic language is predominantly diatonic. Studio production is orientated towards capturing the essence of the group's live sound, and normally involves minimal augmentation of instruments beyond their usual resources. Certain sound-enhancing techniques, such as echo, are sometimes employed to add a brightness and fullness to the sound, particularly in recordings by the Dave Clark Five.

Blues elements – melodic guitar riffs, chord progressions showing the influence of the 12 or 24-bar sequence, flattened third and seventh scale degrees – are present in several Lennon–McCartney songs. Rather than dominating the musical language, however, they constitute one of many elements borrowed from earlier songwriters. Lennon–McCartney's liking for songs by a diverse group of other songwriters is well-documented. For example, Lennon has defined 'Please Please Me' as 'my attempt at writing a Roy Orbison song' (Clayson 1990: 113). The Beatles included five American girl-group songs on their first two albums (Betrock 1982: 49); 'P.S. I Love You' was 'written in the style of one of their favourite girl groups, The Shirelles' (Elson 1986: 56); and there are demonstrable stylistic connections between the songs which ushered in the British Invasion and the pre-existing and co-existing teen-orientated songs written by established professional songwriters such as New York's Brill Building songwriters (Fitzgerald 1995).[10] It is also clear that Lennon–McCartney saw little difference between their role and that of the established professional writers. Lennon has remarked: 'I had a sort of professional songwriter's attitude to writing pop songs ... I was already a stylized songwriter on the first album' (Wenner 1980: 126); and McCartney later admitted: 'We wrote for our market. We knew that if we wrote a song called "Thank You Girl" that a lot of the girls who wrote us fan letters would take it as a genuine thank you. So a lot of our songs ... were addressed to the fans' (Lewisohn 1988: 9). And Smokey Robinson has claimed that the Beatles were 'not only respectful of us, they were downright worshipful. Whenever reporters asked them about their influences, they'd go into euphoria about Motown' (Robinson and Ritz 1989: 136). George Martin maintains that 'a lot of the things the boys did were dead copies of things they'd heard' (Smith 1990: 203), while Clayson notes that in their early live performances the Beatles included 'a perverse choice of non-originals ... from the jokey "Sheik Of Araby" to a rocking "Hully Gully"' (1985: 25).

However, despite the derivative nature of their early compositions, and the simplicity of the musical language they employed, Lennon–McCartney undoubtedly had a rare ability to create distinctive pop songs, incorporating memorable hooks and a great deal of musical variety. Their melodies frequently feature very large and prominent leaps, which contrast markedly with the surrounding conjunct movement: in 'I Want To Hold Your Hand', O'Grady describes how 'the melody moves mostly by step in a narrow range, but uses its few leaps effectively' (1983: 41).

Other melodic features include changing modes for different song sections, and B section melodies (in the AABA form) which are evenly divided between those involving a move up in pitch from the A section, and those involving a move down in pitch. Melodies regularly incorporate strong rhythmic hooks, as well as prominent rhythmic contrasts between the melodies of the A and B sections.

Similar contrasts between the A and B sections exist in relation to harmony. The notable range of chords used to commence B sections contributes significantly to the varied and unpredictable nature of the bridges. O'Grady has pointed to the unusual effect of the minor chord (iii) used at the opening of the bridge (or B) section in 'Can't Buy Me Love' which strongly contrasts with the traditional blues major chord sequence employed in the A section (Ibid.: 45). He also observes the use of distinctive vocal parts in the bridge of 'Eight Days A Week' which he describes as 'notable for its use of perfect fourths in the [vocal] harmony' (Ibid.: 59).

Given the range of melodic, rhythmic and harmonic elements, it is not surprising that the bridges often become a major part of the song's overall appeal. In some situations, the hook potential of the B section is sufficient for its elevation to a place of primary prominence, as in 'Can't Buy Me Love' where the beginning of the B section became (upon George Martin's suggestion) the introduction. In considering the effectiveness of the Lennon–McCartney bridge (or middle eight) sections, it is important to note that the collaboration between the two writers often consisted of a contribution to this part of the song.[11] In the light of the much discussed differences between the two writers,[12] this type of collaboration can be seen as a particularly effective way of introducing interest at an important point in the song.[13]

In addition to sectional contrasts, the Lennon–McCartney songs introduce other elements to the simple pop song format, including a wide range of tempi, distinctive vocal harmonies (often involving intervals of a perfect fourth and fifth), borrowed chords and unusual diatonic progressions. In addition, certain songs involve interesting interplay between riffs and vocal melodies, or provide clever adaptations of blues chord sequences.

## The Second Phase of the British Invasion

It was not until 1965 that Jagger–Richards and Davies began to achieve consistent pop chart success within the USA, and their songs reveal a number of stylistic contrasts to those by Lennon–McCartney and Clark. Many of the songs by Jagger–Richards and Davies feature social commentary and/or satire. While Davies assumes the role of detached observer, several of the Jagger–Richards songs express a sense of personal frustration or rebellion.

The Jagger–Richards songs also typically adopt a negative, often disdainful tone when dealing with relationships. Whiteley describes 'The Last Time' as 'a taunting slogan [which] … projects an anti-woman, anti-love attitude [and] … aggressive and uncaring masculinity' (unpublished: 7). And noting the appeal of the Rolling Stones to male audiences, she suggests:

> With publicity confirming the image of the dominant male, submissive female, and songs expressing a defiant sense of speaking out and self-assertion, there was a positive affirmation of hegemonic masculinity. (Whiteley, unpublished: 12)

The group's live performances tended to reinforce this image. Frith and McRobbie include Mick Jagger in the category of 'cock rock performers … aggressive, dominating and boastful' (1978: 375).[14]

Davies's early songs, and many of the songs by Jagger–Richards, utilize repeated rhythmic-chordal riffs as a primary structuring device – a device which is virtually absent in songs by Lennon–McCartney and Clark. These riffs are often specific to the guitar, with the instrument's idiomatic playing technique asserting an important role in the creation of particular chord progressions.[15] Keith Richards acknowledges: 'I can write a song out of a chord sequence, a riff, and eventually come up with lyrics to fit onto it, but the other way, no way' (Pollock 1986: 9). Some of Davies's songs (most notably 'You Really Got Me') feature vocal melodies which are inextricably tied to the riff – doubling the melodic pattern created by the root movement of the riff chords. As well as rhythmic-chordal riffs, the Jagger–Richards songs regularly feature the type of single-line melodic riffs used by Lennon–McCartney. Davies, however, makes little use of this type of riff. In addition to riffs, many songs feature short, repeated melodic motifs as part of the vocal melody. Normally, these motifs are built from a small range of pitches, and involve predominantly conjunct motion. Lyric repetition often complements the melodic repetition, and assists in the creation of lyric/melodic climaxes.

It should be noted that repetitive elements, such as those discussed above, are an important part of African–American musical traditions (Fitzgerald 1996: 168–75; Middleton 1983). The early songs by Davies, and many of the songs by Jagger–Richards, can therefore be seen to be more closely related to these traditions than are those by Lennon–McCartney and Clark. Other elements in the Jagger–Richards songs support this conclusion. Many melodies involve the type of irregular, free-sounding[16] rhythmic articulation of melodies (particularly in verses) associated with such genres as blues and gospel. Gospel-style vocal hook reinforcement, and blues-style call–response patterns between instrument and voice, form part of the musical language. In the early songs, Jagger–Richards and Davies feature prominent electric guitars and 'raw' vocal delivery, bearing a strong relationship to the Chicago blues sound associated with artists such as Muddy Waters, whom the Rolling Stones greatly admired.

In addition, Davies and Jagger–Richards wrote several ballad-style songs which feature longer, more contoured melodies, an absence of elements such as rhythmic-chordal riffs, and a lighter studio production involving instruments such as acoustic guitars. Davies's satirical songs of 1966 ('A Well Respected Man', 'Dedicated Follower Of Fashion') are of this type, and represent a complete departure form the riff-based songs which preceded them. In contrast to Jagger–Richards (who employ the ballad for more wistful lyrics), Davies attaches his satirical lyrics to incongruously sweet ballad-style melodies and production.

The second phase of the British Invasion also involved some significant changes in Lennon–McCartney's songwriting style. Lennon has recognized that the impact of Bob Dylan's songs resulted in his own adoption of a more subjective, personal approach to lyric writing (Wenner 1980: 126) and has described 'Help!' and 'Strawberry Fields Forever' as 'my best songs ... they were the ones I really wrote from experience and not just projecting myself into a situation and writing a nice story about it' (Bronson 1985:182).

From 'Help!' (August 1965) onwards, the Lennon–McCartney songs increasingly involve a more personal, serious and philosophical approach to relationships ('We Can Work It Out') and observations about society ('Nowhere Man'). One element involved in this changing approach to lyric writing was the consumption of drugs.[17] When asked about the musical contrast between 'Can't Buy Me Love' and 'We Can Work It Out', Lennon responded: 'I suppose it was pot then' (Wenner 1980: 82).

Certain other changes are also evident as the period progresses. O'Grady notes the decreasing occurrence of blues-influenced melodies from 1965 (1983: 111); while McCartney recalls a new, more melodic bass style and increase in bass presence in recordings from 1966 (Lewisohn 1988: 12). Other studio developments during 1965–6 resulted from the continuing collaboration with George Martin, and included the use of orchestral instruments and special recording effects.

The significance of George Martin's involvement with the Beatles should not be underestimated. After some initial hesitation,[18] he strongly supported the recording of Lennon–McCartney's original songs, at a time when 'it was unheard of for an unknown group to insist on recording their own songs' (Elson 1986: 57). Martin was able to create the bright, live sound which proved so successful on early recordings, and then adapt his talents to the creation of more varied studio productions associated with the later songs, as well as write specific arrangements, such as that for the string quartet on 'Yesterday'.[19]

Oldham, who encouraged the raw, live style of production evident in many of the Jagger–Richards songs, also played an important role in the creation of the Rolling Stones' image, which 'stood for everything bad' in contrast to the Beatles' image as the 'happy-go-lucky good guys of pop music' (Rogan 1988: 64). He maintains that after seeing an early performance by the Beatles 'from that night on it registered subconsciously that when they made it, another section of the public were gonna want an opposite. The Stones were gonna be that opposite' (Dalton 1981: 27). Associated with their rougher image (and consistent with Jagger–Richards' liking for the US blues repertoire) was a more obviously rhythm and blues-influenced style, whose deliberate cultivation has been verified by Keith Richards: 'At the time the Rolling Stones started off in England, rock and roll had degenerated to where it meant, like, Fabian and Frankie Avalon ... Hence we stressed the rhythm and blues end of it' (White 1990: 188). This was despite the fact that the earliest Jagger–Richards songs were ballads, 'sweetened with lush string arrangements and optimistic back-up vocals' (Dalton 1981, p.35),[20] and despite the fact that the Rolling Stones did not consider themselves to be blues purists. Jagger has recalled: 'We said, "Well, we like rock 'n' roll as much as we like rhythm and blues ... we'll do anything from Elvis Presley to Buddy Holly and Ritchie Valens"' (Smith 1990: 206).

Finally, it should be noted that the invasion of the US pop charts initiated by the Beatles did not only benefit writer-performers. In fact the Broadway tradition of complex, highly-arranged popular songs was well represented within the British Invasion by Tony Hatch's songs for Petula Clark.[21] Instead of posing a threat to his sophisticated, adult-oriented style of songwriting, the success of the Beatles' guitar-based pop actually assisted Hatch in attaining US chart success by creating a fashion for British music in general, as he himself has explained:

> The great thing that the Beatles did, and it was mainly the Beatles, was to open the doors for us to America. We couldn't – nobody could – get into America. If you got a hit on the British charts, it did not mean automatically that you'd get that record released in America. What you'd probably get was an American cover, and that would be it. But when the Beatles started seriously exporting their music, then the record companies in America started coming to the UK and saying 'What've you got?', and they started releasing things that weren't even hits in the UK. (Hatch: 1991)

His songs, which feature complicated orchestral arrangements and demonstrate an understanding of (and liking for) complex harmony, more closely resemble those of Bacharach–David than those of the British group songwriters (Fitzgerald 1996: 240). His success indicates that, despite the prominence of the writer-performers, the non-performing professional songwriter still had a place in the British Invasion.[22]

Further evidence of this is provided by the fact that not all British guitar bands chose to write their own songs; many still elected to record songs by professional writers. Peter Noone of Herman's

Hermits has admitted: 'We didn't write songs. I didn't even want to write songs. I figured, let Carole King or Neil Diamond write me a song. Even their demos sounded like Number One songs!" (Smith 1990: 12).

## NOTES

1.  The term has been used to describe a number of highly successful song-writers (Gerry Goffin–Carole King, Jeff Barry–Ellie Greenwich) who worked from a small section of Manhattan in the late 1950s and early 1960s, and were often involved in writing songs about teen romance for young soloists and girl groups. The actual Brill Building is situated at 1619 Broadway, and was named after the Brill Brothers, who originally ran a clothing store at street level, and later purchased the building. Space in the building was first rented to music publishers soon after its completion in 1931 (Betrock 1982: 38).
2.  The pop chart analysis is based on *The Billboard Book of Top 40 Hits* (Whitburn 1987).
3.  It should be noted that two Jagger–Richards songs ('As Tears Go By' and 'Satisfaction') were recorded by the Rolling Stones, and also covered by other artists (Marianne Faithfull and Otis Redding, respec-tively). The analytical information is based on the versions by the Rolling Stones.
4.  Popular music analysts have examined a wide range of specific musical parameters, but there appears to be a broad general consensus regarding more generic analytical categories. For example, Tagg's (1979: 69–70) 'check list of musical considerations' for the analysis of popular music includes aspects relating to time, melody, instrumenta-tion, tonality and texture, dynamics, acoustics and studio recording. Burns's (1987) 'typology of hooks' includes reference to rhythm, melody, harmony, lyrics, instrumentation, tempo, dynamics, improviza-tion, sound effects and technology of production. Friedlander's (1987) 'rock window' considers lyrics, ensemble, rhythmic emphasis, vocal style, instrumental solo and harmonic progression. Bjornberg's (1990) analysis of mainstream popular songs considers musical form, melody, harmonic language and instrumentation/accompaniment.
5.  The instrument utilizes a 'barre' effect, involving the placement of the left index finger over all the strings. This enables the same fingering pattern to slide up and down the neck of the instrument.
6.  Some songs (such as 'Can't Buy Me Love') add an introductory section to an otherwise AABA form, but even these introductions do not appear to have always been Lennon–McCartney ideas. George Martin has claimed credit for the use of part of the B section in 'Can't Buy Me Love' as an introduction to the song (Smith 1990: 204).

7. John Lennon commented of his use of a reverse-tape effect: 'It was the first time I'd discovered it [the reverse-tape effect]. On the end of "Rain" you hear me singing it backwards. We'd done the main song at E.M.I. and the habit was then to take the tapes home and see what you thought a little extra gimmick or what the guitar piece should be' (O'Grady 1983: 93). George Martin has recalled that 'as the boys got to know the studio better, because they were very canny boys, it became much more of a democratic team' (Smith 1990: 204).

8. Dave Clark has explained: 'The Dave Clark Five was basically a live band ... but we still needed a record. I thought "Well, why not go out and make ourselves one?"' (Smith 1990: 205).

9. This was presumably related to Clark's role as drummer for the group.

10. The Brill Building songs also tend to be of a short duration, deal predominantly with positive aspects of romantic relationships, and rarely incorporate social comment. Melodies utilize a small vocal range and are highly conjunct, with a notable predominance of major scales and arch verse contours. The songs are very similar to those of the early British Invasion in terms of their use of melodic and rhythmic riffs, harmonic rhythms and instrumental solo sections, and they utilize an almost identical spread of tempi.

11. John Lennon stated: 'In a lot of the songs, my stuff is the "middle eight", the bridge' (Bronson 1985:191). Compton (1988: 99–131) offers a comprehensive analysis of the specific contributions of each writer to particular songs; 'She's A Woman' provides a good illustration of a song written in this way, resulting in a striking contrast between the musical elements of verse and bridge.

12. Compton describes McCartney as 'always more interested in music' and Lennon as 'always more interested in lyrics' (1988: 123). McCartney himself has said: 'John brought a biting wit. I brought commerciality and harmony' (Smith 1990: 200).

13. The typical AABA form employs the B section after two verses, at which time further immediate repetition of the A section potentially runs the risk of overstatement.

14. Hellmann (1973: 370) notes the influence upon the Rolling Stones of aspects of blues lyrics – in particular, their often direct, anti-romantic language and sexual boasting.

15. Moore believes that one aspect which is always overlooked in any discussion of rock harmonies is 'whether songs have been written "at the fretboard" or "at the keyboard"' (1993: 54).

16. Actual improvisation is very limited.

17. O'Grady has noted the Beatles' early involvement with pep pills, introduction to marijuana (allegedly by Bob Dylan) in 1964, and first experiences with LSD in 1965. It is not often easy, however, to draw connections between drug use and specific aspects of particular songs, and he makes only cautious and general observations: 'It is probable that this involvement [with marijuana and LSD] and Lennon's desire to appear "experienced" had some influence on the lyrics he (and the other Beatles) wrote in 1966' (1983: 90). Of course, many other artists experimented with drugs at this time: in his autobiography (Wilson and

Gold 1993), Brian Wilson chronicles a prolonged involvement with a wide variety of drugs.

18. George Martin has said of the Beatles' recording test: 'Frankly, the material didn't impress me, least of all their own songs. I felt I was going to have to find suitable material for them' (1979: 123).

19. See Bronson (1985: 185).

20. Gene Pitney, the US pop ballad performer, recorded one of these songs – 'That Girl Belongs To Yesterday' – as well as being involved, along with Phil Spector, in the studio recording of 'Not Fade Away' (Dalton 1981: 35–6).

21. Hatch wrote 11 US Top 40 hits between 1965 and 1966, but since this chapter focuses on the work of writer-performers, his work is not considered in detail.

22. It should be noted that despite the observation from Ellie Greenwich in the introduction to this chapter, US professional songwriters were not all equally affected by the British Invasion; writers such as Barry Mann–Cynthia Weil and Burt Bacharach–Hal David were able to maintain previous levels of chart success (Fitzgerald 1995).

## REFERENCES

Betrock, Alan (1982) *Girl Groups: the Story of a Sound*. NewYork: Delilah.

Bjornberg, Alf (1990) 'Sounding the Mainstream: an Analysis of the Songs Performed in the Swedish Eurovision Song Contest Semi-Finals 1959–1983', in K. Roe and U. Carlsson (eds), *Popular Music Research*. Goteborg: Nordicom–Sweden.

Bronson, Fred (1985) *The Billboard Book of Number One Hits*. New York: American Photographic Books.

Burns, Gary (1987) 'A Typology of "Hooks" in Popular Records', *Popular Music*, **6**: 1–20.

Clayson, Alan (1985) *Call up the Groups: the Golden Age of British Beat, 1962–1967*. London: Blandford.

Clayson, Alan (1990) *Only the Lonely: the Life and Artistic Legacy of Roy Orbison*. London: Pan.

Coleman, Ray (1989) *Brian Epstein*. London: Viking.

Compton, Todd (1988) 'McCartney or Lennon? Beatle Myths and the Composing of the Lennon–McCartney Songs', *Journal of Popular Culture*, **22**(2): 99–131.

Dalton, David (1981) *The Rolling Stones: the First Twenty Years*. London: Thames & Hudson.

Elson, Howard (1986) *McCartney: Songwriter*. London: W.H. Allen.

Fitzgerald, Jon (1995) 'When the Brill Building Met Lennon–McCartney: Continuity and Change in the Early Evolution of the Mainstream Pop Song', *Popular Music and Society*, **19**(1): 59–78.

Fitzgerald, Jon (1996) *Popular Songwriting 1963–1966: Stylistic Comparisons and Trends within the U.S. Top Forty*. Unpublished PhD thesis, Southern Cross University.

Friedlander, Paul (1987) *A Characteristics Profile of Eight 'Classic Rock and Roll' Artists, 1954–1959: as Measured by the 'Rock Window'*. Unpublished PhD thesis, University of Oregon.

Frith, Simon and Angela McRobbie (1978) 'Rock and Sexuality', in Simon Frith and Andrew Goodwin (eds) *On Record*. London: Routledge.

Hatch, Tony (1991) Personal interview with the author: Sydney, Australia, 3 December.

Hellmann, John M. (1973) 'I'm a Monkey', *Journal of American Folklore*, **86**: 367–73.

Lewisohn, Mark (1988) *The Complete Beatles Recording Sessions: the Official Story of the Abbey Road Years*. London: Hamlyn.

Martin, George (1979) *All You Need Is Ears*. London: Macmillan.

Middleton, Richard (1983) 'Play It Again, Sam: Some Notes on the Productivity of Repetition in Popular Music' *Popular Music*, **3**: 241–61.

Moore, Alan (1993) *Rock: the Primary Text: Developing a Musicology of Rock*. Buckingham: Open University Press.

O'Grady, Terence (1983) *The Beatles: a Musical Evolution*. Boston: Twayne.

Pollock, Bruce (1986) *Interviews with Contemporary Songwriters*. New York: Cherry Lane.

Robinson, Smokey and David Ritz (1989) *Smokey: Inside My Life*. London: Headline.

Rogan, Johnny (1988) *Starmakers and Svengalis: the History of British Pop Management*. London: MacDonald Queen Anne Press.

Smith, Joe (1990) *Off the Record: an Oral History of Popular Music*. London: Pan.

Tagg, Philip (1979) *Kojak: 50 Seconds of Television Music: Towards the Analysis of Effect in Popular Music*. PhD thesis, Goteborg University.

Wenner, Jann (1971) *Lennon Remembers*. London: Penguin.

Whitburn, Joel (1987) *The Billboard Book of Top 40 Hits*. New York: American Photographic Books.

White, Timothy (1990) *Rock Lives: Profiles and Interviews*. New York: Henry Holt.

Whiteley, Sheila (undated) *Mick Jagger: an Analysis of Sexuality and Style*. Unpublished manuscript.

Wilson, Brian and Todd Gold (1991) *Wouldn't It Be Nice: My Own Story*. New York: HarperCollins.

# 5 From Me to You: Austerity to Profligacy in the Language of the Beatles

Guy Cook and Neil Mercer

Imagine that it is 1962, you are in the Cavern, the Beatles are playing and you are hearing – for the first time – 'Love Me Do'. The quality of the group's PA system means that the only words you are sure you understand are those in the title. But that doesn't matter; the song has an overall effect on you as a performance, in which lyrical detail is not important. Later that year, you buy the single and soon you can sing all the words along with the group. But you don't give the words any close, reflective consideration, because it's not that kind of song. Jump now to 1967, where you and your friends have been listening to 'A Day In The Life'. Like everyone else, you have only heard it on disc, because the song is never performed live. Not only are the words clearer, they are also printed out for you to follow on the record cover. As the song finishes, someone says, 'What do you think it's about?'and everyone has an opinion.

Anyone who has followed the Beatles' career knows that the style of their songs changed over the years they were together – but exactly how did the language of the songs change? In this chapter, we shall seek to answer this question by analysing the lyrics of those songs written by John Lennon and Paul McCartney, or occasionally George Harrison, and recorded by the Beatles. The methods we shall use are of the kind known as 'discourse analysis'. By 'discourse', we mean language as it occurs in social context; and by 'analysis', we mean the careful consideration of the meanings which forms of words take on in context, and the relationship between choices of words and the overall structure of the texts they compose (see Cook 1992, 1994). We shall offer some explanations of the changes which come to light, although we shall certainly not be attempting to say what any of the songs are 'really about'. One of the principles of discourse analysis is that the meaning of any text (and perhaps especially any song) varies, depending on who is listening to it, the circumstances in which they hear it, and the way in which they relate it to their own ideas and concerns. We also recognize that lyrics can only be fully appreciated in the company of rhythm and melody. Unlike a poem or a novel, a popular song depends for its existence upon some kind of performance – whether on stage or in the recording studio.

Nevertheless, songwriters are people working inside cultures and social contexts, and like anyone else the ways in which they use language are bound to reflect their conscious and unconscious responses to the lives they are living and the goals they are pursuing. Lennon, McCartney and Harrison wrote songs of immense popularity in a period of significant cultural change, a period in which each of them also made the personal transition from struggling club musician to member of the world's most popular and influential group. It is for these reasons that we feel it is justifiable and interesting to take their lyrics out of their musical context and consider them simply as words. As the publication of the words on record sleeves and inserts seems to indicate, together with a growing market for books of lyrics, this focus also reflects a change in attitude to pop lyrics in exactly the period we are considering.

## THE 'EARLY' AND 'LATER' SONGS

As others (for example, Inglis 1997) have suggested, the songs written and recorded by the Beatles can be divided into two periods: 'early' (1962–5) and 'later' (1966–70). The songs of each period differ in their suitability for performance, the instruments used, the nature of the music, and the range of subject matter. In the early period the songs could be – and were – performed live by the four Beatles with three guitars and a drum kit. A vocal melody with intermittent sung harmonies was imposed over a steady rhythm, usually prefaced, punctuated and rounded off with a lead guitar riff. The subject matter was *always* romantic love. In the second period the majority of songs could not be easily performed live, and consequently never were. The original guitars and drums were augmented or replaced, not only by familiar pop instruments such as the harmonica, piano or organ, but also – adventurously and experimentally – by sitars, full orchestras, brass sections, barrel organs, recorders. The music became more complex and eclectic, and the words dealt unpredictably with a much wider variety of topics: taxation, pulp fiction, circus acts, traffic

wardens, family arguments, places in Liverpool, revolutionary politics, cowboy shoot-outs, car accidents, 64-year-olds. Although the
topic of love still figures, it comes in more varieties than the stereotypical teenage crush (Inglis 1997).

The transition happened rapidly, but was not clear cut. On *Help!*
(1965), there were already hints of change: the title song 'Help!' is not
necessarily about romantic love; 'You've Got To Hide Your Love
Away' has a folk-influenced, Dylan-like quality; 'Yesterday' has a
poignant orchestral and acoustic guitar backing. And *Rubber Soul*
(1965), with its new instruments, musical experimentation and
broader themes (as dealt with in 'Nowhere Man'), seems to face in
both directions.

For our analysis, we selected some albums from the complete
Beatles catalogue (as listed in Robertson 1994) for reasons that we
will explain later. Those we have used have been assigned to the two
periods as follows.

**The Early Period**

1. A Hard Day's Night (1964)
2. Beatles For Sale (1964)
3. Help! (1965)
4. Rubber Soul (1965)

**The Later Period**

5. Revolver (1966)
6. Sgt Pepper's Lonely Hearts Club Band (1967)
7. The Beatles (The White Album) (1968)
8. Abbey Road (1969)
9. Let It Be (1970)

Our aim is to show that it is not just performance, instruments,
music, and subject matter which make the songs of these two periods
so distinct, but also their language. This is not just a question of some
vague general increase in linguistic 'richness'. There are also subtle
but specific changes in the grammar and vocabulary of the songs, and
these affect their nature as discourse. Whereas the communicative
contexts evoked by the earlier songs tend to be conversation, argument, gossip or soliloquy, the later songs are often concerned with
storytelling and with philosophizing, and they draw upon a much

wider range of genres of communication – such as narra
joke, satire, religious text, advertisement. These chan
language and discourse seem to reflect not only the life
the songwriters, but also the cultural passage from austerity to
permissiveness which characterized the 1960s.

## PRONOUNS AND NAMES

All the Beatles' songs are about human situations. There is a basic but
indicative fact about the way language is used to refer to the characters in these situations, which concerns the use of pronouns and
names. In the songs of 1964, everyone is referred to by a pronoun,
nobody is ever named. People are only *I* (the male lover); *you* (the
female loved one, or a confidant(e) as in 'She Loves You' or 'You're
Going To Lose That Girl'); *she* (the female loved one); or *he* (the
male rival as in 'Baby's In Black', 'No Reply', 'You Can't Do That'
and 'This Boy'). The first character ever to be named in a Beatles
song – significantly on *Rubber Soul* – is Michelle. In the songs of the
later period, however, there is a positive infatuation with naming. It
grows on *Revolver* in 1966 with Eleanor Rigby, Father McKenzie and
Doctor Robert; and then, in 1967 and 1968, explodes with Lucy, Rita,
Mr Kite (together with the Hendersons, Pablo Fanques and Henry
the Horse), Vera, Chuck and Dave, Prudence, Desmond and Molly,
Bungalow Bill, Martha, Rocky Racoon, Julia and Sexy Sadie. *Sgt
Pepper's Lonely Hearts Club Band* even gives the group itself a new
and extravagant name, and the first singer a new persona: 'the one
and only Billy Shears'. Places are named too. On *Sgt Pepper* we have
Bishopsgate, the Isle of Wight, Blackburn, the House of Lords, the
Albert Hall; and, in the singles of this period, Strawberry Fields and
Penny Lane. The unspecified pronouns remain, but often with a new
meanings. *They* may now mean people in general; and *he* and *she* are
more often characters in a story than the rival or loved one of the
singer (for example, 'she's leaving home' and 'he was from the House
of Lords').

This change in the way people and places are named is significant.
It may help us understand the sense of drama and immediacy which
characterizes the early songs, and the amused detachment which
characterizes the later ones. We use pronouns rather than names to
refer to people who are present or whose identity is clear. Thus, in
conversation, *I* is the speaker, *you* is the person (or people) the

speaker is addressing; *he* and *she* refer either to someone who has already been named, or to someone who is present. On some occasions, the pronouns *he* and *she* can be used to refer to someone who is so prominent in the speakers' thoughts that they do not need to be named. Parents, for example, can successfully refer to a son or daughter in this way ('Isn't she home yet?') or employees to a domineering boss ('Guess what he wants now'). This is very similar to the way that the omnipresent *she* is used in the early Beatles songs.

In these early songs, the use of pronouns without names echoes immediate conversational interaction about known characters. It creates the urgent tone of a close-quarters conversation about shared mutual concerns. We seem to be listening to intense face-to-face exchanges in which the participants are either discussing each other (*you* and *I*), or someone who is in their sight or very much on their minds (*I* and *you* talking about *him* or *her*). No explanation of identity is offered to us the audience; it is as though we are eavesdropping on a fragment of someone else's life:

- 'You think you've lost your love, well I saw her yesterday' ('She Loves You')
- 'I think I'll take a walk and look for her' ('I Don't Want To Spoil The Party')
- 'Well it's the second time I've caught you talking to him' ('You Can't Do That').

Alternatively, in some of the songs addressed to *you* or referring to *her*, it seems the singer is alone, singing – as it were – to himself. Indeed in some songs this *must* be the case, for although the words are addressed to you, they are specifically about the fact that *you* are not here:

- 'This happened once before, when I came to your door, no reply' ('No Reply')
- 'When I call you up, your line's engaged' ('You Won't See Me').

Some songs mix the two, both talking to the loved one as *you* and about her as *she*:

> The kiss my lover brings
> She brings to me
> And I love her.
> A love like ours
> Could never die

As long as I
Have you near me ('And I Love Her').

I've got every reason on earth to be mad
'Cos I've lost the only girl I had ...
If I could see you now,
I'd try to make you say it somehow ('I'll Cry Instead').

In such songs as these, which mix pronouns, the only viable situation seems to be one in which the singer is alone, sometimes imagining himself talking *to* his loved one, and sometimes talking to himself *about* her. There are also many songs using pronouns more consistently which, although they might be addressed to a third party, are equally interpretable as soliloquies:

- 'You know if you break my heart, I'll go but I'll be back again' ('I'll Be Back')
- 'Oh dear, what can I do? Baby's in black and I'm feeling blue' ('Baby's In Black').

Whether the interlocutors are present or imagined, in the early songs three combinations of pronouns are ubiquitous: *I* talking to *you*; *I* talking to *you* about *her*; *I* talking about *her*. Of the 13 songs on *A Hard Day's Night*, for example, 10 are addressed by *I* to *you*, one is *I* talking about *her*, and two mix the two. On *Beatles For Sale*, of the eight songs by Lennon–McCartney, four are *I* addressing *you*, three are *I* talking about *her* (*she*) and the remaining one ('I Don't Want To Spoil The Party') is *I* talking to *you* (a friend or perhaps himself) about *her*.

The very indeterminacy of these pronouns, however, while it gives a sense of access into the thoughts, emotions and interaction of an individual, also simultaneously allows the reference to be generalized to any male or female enmeshed in the pairings and triangles of romantic heterosexual relationships. Hence their appeal to a teenage audience who – fancying themselves in love – could easily identify with any song. Precisely because they are unnamed, the *I* and the *you* could be appropriated by the listeners to refer to themselves: the boys presumably identifying with the male *I*, and the girls imagining the song addressed to them (either by the singer or some other such as their own boyfriend).

In many of the later songs, in contrast, this opportunity for easy identification is often denied. References to characters are more specific, achieved either by naming or by precise details in the narrative. This specificity creates a distance both between singer and character, and between listener and character. Many people fall in and out of love; far fewer are 'meeting a man from the motor trade'. Songs like 'She's Leaving Home' or 'Lovely Rita' are about someone else, not about ourselves – a change which reflects the passage, perhaps, during this period, of a sizeable proportion of Beatles fans from the self-obsession of adolescence to the greater objectivity of adulthood.

In the early songs, then, the exclusive use of pronouns without names is a linguistic detail which creates both a sense of specific immediacy and of general applicability. This does not mean, of course, that the songwriters were consciously aware of this choice, or used it deliberately, any more than we make a conscious decision to refer to ourselves as *I* in conversation, but by name when filling in a form. We all have an automatic sense of the linguistic choices appropriate to particular 'genres'. In their early songs, the Beatles created a very distinctive genre with its own linguistic characteristics. Like gossip and argument, it uses pronouns in a way which creates a sense of immediacy and drama.

There are other linguistic factors which have a similar effect, and lend the songs the air of intimate conversation. One is a general lack of specificity and explicitness. Playwrights sometimes compensate for the absence of a narrator by having characters tell each other more about people and events than real conversationalists would need to do. In real conversation, when both situation and a frame of reference are shared, many things can be left unspecified. Time and place can both be referred to *deictically* – that is to say by reference to a shared and mutual known point of reference. We say 'yesterday', 'today' and 'tomorrow', rather than naming the day, date and year. We can say 'here' or 'there', or 'in' or 'out', rather than naming the place. Similarly we do not need (unless it is the topic of conversation) to describe the age, appearance, clothes, nationality – or any other personal details – of the person we are talking to, or of third parties who are well known to both of us. There is a simple conversational principle in operation here (of the kind identified by Grice 1975): do not tell people facts they already know or which are evident from the situation. Only when telling a story about previously unknown characters and events are specific details needed. The early Beatles songs adhere with absolute rigour to the principle of never giving superfluous situational information. Times and places are referred to only deictically, as though their precise reference were already quite clear to those involved:

'your door'; 'the party'; 'home'; 'here'; 'there'; 'places I remember all my life'; 'call me tonight'; 'things we said today'; 'I saw her yesterday'; 'tomorrow may rain'; 'though you've gone away this morning, you'll be back again tonight'.

In these early songs, no information is ever given about the immediate characters other than their sex, their role in the relationship (rival, friend, lover) and some evaluation of them (as cruel, hurting, loveable). About their age, appearance, occupation, health, wealth, nationality, we are told nothing (with the exception of 'I Saw Her Standing There' which tells us 'she was just seventeen'). Other people are similarly general or unnamed: 'they'; 'everybody'; 'people that I meet'; 'that boy'; 'another man'; 'a girl'; 'all the girls'; 'I've just seen a face'. Of course, the subject matter suggests that the songs are about teenagers and young adults, and we may well imagine faces and scenes as we listen to the songs – but this is not because of anything we are told in the songs. Any such precise details – like the identities of people referred to only by pronouns – must be being supplied by the listener. Can this be one of the factors which helped to make these songs so popular with so many different people at so many different times and in so many different places?

In many of the later songs this general applicability has gone. While there are still some of this kind ('Today's your birthday, we're going to have a party'), many of the later songs are far more specific about people, places, even times ('It's five o'clock, everywhere in town is getting dark'). Consequently – and ironically – although they came later and marked an original and distinctive break with the past, they can now seem more dated ('keeps a ten bob note up his nose'). And they are narrated, told to us by the singer who is often not one of the people involved.

Yet while there is sparseness of situational detail and precise reference in the early songs, and a conversation-like reluctance to say more than is already known, this economy is by no means extended to the inner landscape of the characters' emotions or the singer's assessment of the relationships between them. Here there is superfluity and repetitiveness rather than economy. The early songs are about emotion and the expressions of emotion: happiness, sadness, feeling, hurting, crying, saying 'I love you', kissing, holding hands. They are also relentlessly about one person's perception of another person's perception: what I think you think, what I think you think I think, or – when a friend is involved – what he or she thinks you think I think.

This obsession is reflected in the high frequency of a particular grammatical construction: the reporting clause, used to embed one person's opinion or words within the opinion or words of another. In the following examples, the square brackets mark off the clauses, showing how one is embedded inside another.

> [Can't you see [that when I tell you [that I love you
> You're gonna say [you love me too]]]
> [I must be sure from the very start [that you would love me more
>     than her]]
> [And now she says [she knows [ you're not the hurting kind]]]
> I think [I'll let you down]
> [I've told you before [you can't do that]]
> [I thought [that you would realise [that [if I ran away from you] you
>     would want me too]]]
> [I tried to telephone] [They said [you were not home]]
> [[If I were you] I'd realise [that I love you more than any other guy]]
> [[When I'm with her]] I'm happy [just to know [that she loves me]]]
> [Yes I know [that she loves me now]]
> [I've been waiting here for you, wondering [what you're going to
>     do]]

There is nothing surprising about the obvious appeal of this recursive preoccupation with words, thoughts and feelings *about* words, thoughts and feelings. The early Beatles songs are primarily reflections upon, or conversations about, three subjects of perennial interest to all of us:

- our own emotional states and self-esteem
- our success and failure in sexual relationships
- our ability to predict the behaviour of others, especially regarding loyalty and betrayal.

The songs are a kind of fictional gossip, and as such they exert the same kind of appeal as do other gossip-like genres such as 'human interest' journalism, soap operas and psychological novels. In Britain, the TV soap opera *EastEnders* is watched by one-third of the population, the main tabloid newspapers may be read by half the population, and sales of 'blockbuster' novels such as those by Jackie Collins or Jeffrey Archer regularly exceed one million. The early Beatles songs also sold in millions. The appeal of stories about the psychological permutations of sexual relationships appears to be inexhaustible. Some evolutionary psychologists (Carroll 1995;

Dunbar 1996) have suggested that the human obsession
dramatical dynamics of relationships has its origin in the
of life in expanding prehistoric hunter–gatherer communiti
other animals, humans are motivated by the desire to perpetuate
their own genes, and, like other intelligent animals, individuals are
in competition with each other and may make alliances against
enemies to further their own ends. But much more than other
animals, humans have the capacity to dissemble and deceive, to be
faithful, and also to be unfaithful. As the early hominid communities grew in size, it became more and more imperative to understand
the psychology of others, and to make correct predictions about how
others will behave, and about who can be trusted and who cannot.
The appeal of fiction and gossip is that they may help us develop
that ability, and provide vicarious models for the contemplation of
our own lives. A common experience in the breakdown of a marriage
or similar relationship is that the words of popular songs take on a
special, personal significance (which justifies them being played
repeatedly, late at night.) Like the characters in the Beatles songs,
we need to think very carefully about what others think and feel
about us. The cost of mistakes is too high:

> I thought that you would realise
> That if I ran away from you
> You would want me too
> But I got a big surprise. ('I'll Be Back')

In this light, all the early Beatles songs may be seen as permutations
on a single but endlessly fascinating theme. Sometimes the variations
are subtle and – within the limits of the genre – highly original. Indeed
to have written, in the early period alone, more than 70 songs, *all*
about conventional romantic relationships, but all slightly different, is
a feat of considerable creative ingenuity. Yet this narrow focus also
means that the words and subject matter of the songs are in a general
sense predictable, and although the variations may be subtle, it is also
possible to relate to them quite superficially. Each one is essentially
about either success or failure in love and the resulting happiness or
despair. In addition, words, lines and whole stanzas are often
repeated many times. All this can help to draw attention away from
the songs as texts and towards their music and their performance.

In the later period, this predictability has gone. 'Taxman', the
opening song on the first album of the later period – *Revolver* – is a
good example. By broaching a totally unexpected and original subject

for a pop song (can you think of any other songs about tax?) it demands attention to the words. And they are absolutely specific, not just about tax in general, but about a very specific tax bracket for high earners (95 per cent) in one country's period under two successive prime ministers. They even make reference to the pre-decimal British currency, with its idiosyncratic 20 shillings to the pound:

> There's one for you, nineteen for me …
> Should five per cent appear too small
> Be thankful I don't take it all …
> Taxman Mr Wilson
> Taxman Mr Heath. ('Taxman')

## LIVE PERFORMANCE VERSUS THE PRODUCTION OF RECORDS

There is an additional possible reason why the lyrics of the later songs became more salient and complex. In their early days as performing musicians, the Beatles emulated, and in many ways still belonged to, a rhythm and blues tradition in which songs were created for live performance and dancing. (The words of many early Beatles songs, like those of their influential predecessors Chuck Berry or Eddie Cochran, either refer to dancing, or to a possible dialogue between a couple on or near the dance floor). In this oral tradition, the words of songs were inextricably linked to the music, and audiences only heard them as part of their experience of a specific event. On such occasions, words were often hard to distinguish and easy to misunderstand in the sound and the movement. Performing musicians could not expect complex lyrics to be given close attention or critical appreciation.

However, the new availability of the record player and the wider distribution of records were to change the nature of the relationship of audiences to both music and words. Of course, records were being made long before the success of the Beatles in the 1960s. But with the appearance of any new technology there may be some delay before its full impact is felt, and there is often a transitional period when it seems to support the old ways it will shortly supplant. In the 1950s and early 1960s, the record was in many ways still regarded as a substitute for hearing the music live, and a way of imagining oneself at a dance or a performance. (Many listeners would dance or mime to the records as they listened.) The song could thus remain a social phenomenon even when listened to in solitude, evoking a performance in which the audience would be actively involved in dancing, clapping and applauding. In the 1960s, however, there emerged a kind of pop song which focused attention upon words, encouraging listeners to assess song as text. In some early performances, singers such as Bob Dylan and Leonard Cohen (and their many imitators) downplayed both musical accompaniment and visual presentation, thus foregrounding the potential literary quality of their lyrics. Delivered by a casually dressed, static figure on stage, singing in a hoarse (and to many, unmusical) voice with resonances somewhere between speech and song, the performance inevitably emphasized the words of the song – with the result that (even when the musical accompaniment was polished and intricate) the fashion of the time was to reflect upon and discuss the song as text. In addition, the growing acceptance, distribution and improvement of recordings meant that songwriters could use words which did not have to be absorbed on first hearing; the words of their songs took on some of the permanence of written genres. Records could be taken home and played in solitude, replayed when words were missed, repeated as often as desired, stacked on shelves, handled, and generally treated – in many ways – like books. Significantly, many songwriters of this period, such as Leonard Cohen, Bob Dylan and John Lennon, published poems and fictional prose in addition to their songs.

## A COMPUTER-BASED TEXT ANALYSIS

So far we have been arguing impressionistically, selecting examples to illustrate the changing quality of Beatles songs from the early to the later period. In what follows, we shall use computer-based methods of text analysis to provide a more systematic account of change. Linguistic research has recently been revolutionized by the development of software for analysing texts. There now exist packages known as 'concordancers' which enable any file of written language (known as a 'corpus') to be scanned easily for all instances of particular words, showing their frequency, and the words which occur together with them. Words which commonly occur together are known as *collocations*. The results of such searches can be presented as *concordances*.

These software packages are readily available: the one we used (Conc 1.71, 1992), was downloaded from the Internet. (We acquired the electronic text version of the song lyrics needed for computer analysis in the same way.) A concordancer allows a researcher to move almost instantly between words and texts, thus dramatically speeding up searches, and making it much easier for qualitative and quantitative analysis to be combined (Wegerif and Mercer 1997). Initial exploratory work on particular short texts (or text extracts) can be used to generate hypotheses which can then be tested systematically on a large text or series of related texts. Concordances can reveal some of the more subtle meanings that words have gathered in use, meanings which are not captured by literal definitions. For example, by analysing all the occurrences of the phrase 'days are' in an 18 million-word corpus of English texts, Louw (1993) found that over two-thirds of them were collocated with words like 'past', 'over' and 'gone', so that the meaning was commonly one of nostalgia or lost time. However, such collocations were not found for 'day is' in the singular, nor for other time words in the plural, such as 'weeks are'. Louw argues that although this kind of subtle connotation of a word like 'days' is not one that most of us would be conscious of, it is an effective resource for creative writing (as in the Ray Davies song 'Days' – although Louw does not make this connection).

In our own analysis, we begin by looking at the occurrence of certain words and expressions in particular Beatles songs, and in so doing set out our hypotheses about how their relative occurrence is an important aspect of the difference between the lyrics of the early (1962–5) and later (1966–70) periods. We shall then show what the results of a computer-based concordance analysis reveal about the lyrics of a selection of representative records.

## A CONCORDANCE ANALYSIS OF SELECTED EARLY AND LATER ALBUMS

Table 5.1 below gives concordance statistics for a selection of early and later albums. We have omitted *Please Please Me* and *With The Beatles* because they include too many songs by other songwriters to provide suitable corpuses for analysis. *Magical Mystery Tour* and *Yellow Submarine*, which are film soundtracks rather than albums, have also been excluded.

One column of figures in Table 5.1 includes what we have called the 'type/token ratio' for each album. 'Type' refers to the incidence of particular words in a text; 'token' refers to the number of word items which make up the text. For example, the lines

If you don't take her out tonight, she's going to change her mind,
and I will take her out tonight, and I will treat her kind

consist of 26 tokens but (because some words like 'her' occur more
than once) only 18 types. The figures in the type/token ratio column
have been calculated by dividing the total number of word items
which make up the whole set of lyrics of an album (the 'token' count,
as given in Column 1) by the number of different words found in the
lyrics (the 'type' count, as given in Column 3). The type/token ratio
figure is thus a measure of the range of vocabulary used: the *lower* the
figure for any album, the *more varied* are the words making up its
songs. The figures in parentheses in the 'I', 'you' and 'love' frequency
columns are the decimal fractions of the whole lyrics of an album
constituted by those target words (number of target words divided by
number of total words multiplied by 100). *Smaller* figures mean that
the target words occur relatively *less* in the lyrics as a whole.

*Table* 5.1    Concordance analyses for selected early and later albums

| Album title | Year of release | Total of words in lyrics | type/ token ratio | No. of different words | No. of 'I' | No. of 'You' | No. of 'love' |
|---|---|---|---|---|---|---|---|
| A Hard Day's Night | 1964 | 2004 | 4.8 | 420 | 184 (9.2) | 130 (6.5) | 53 (2.6) |
| Beatles For Sale | 1964 | 1228 | 4.2 | 293 | 131(10.7) | 43 (3.7) | 25 (2.0) |
| Help! | 1965 | 2131 | 5.1 | 420 | 154 (7.2) | 131 (6.2) | 15 (0.7) |
| Rubber Soul | 1965 | 2518 | 4.8 | 528 | 183 (7.3) | 168 (6.7) | 25 (1.0) |
| Revolver | 1966 | 2114 | 3.9 | 542 | 119 (5.6) | 99 (4.6) | 21 (1.0) |
| Sgt Pepper | 1967 | 2257 | 3.0 | 743 | 82 (3.6) | 73 (3.2) | 13 (0.6) |
| The Beatles | 1968 | 2857 | 3.9 | 982 | 131 (3.4) | 209 (5.4) | 23 (0.6) |
| Abbey Road | 1969 | 1644 | 3.0 | 545 | 53 (3.2) | 58 (3.5) | 8 (0.5) |
| Let It Be | 1970 | 1643 | 3.6 | 452 | 98 (6.0) | 74 (4.5) | 7 (0.4) |

*Note:*
The figures in parentheses in the 'I', 'you' and 'love' frequency columns are
the decimal fractions of the whole lyrics of an album constituted by those
target words (number of target words divided by number of total words
multiplied by 100). *Smaller* figures mean that the target words occur relatively
*less* in the lyrics as a whole.

Table 5.1 shows some interesting linguistic features of the shift from
early to later lyrics. First, the type/token ratios for later albums are
much lower, with the strongest contrast being between *A Hard Day's
Night/Rubber Soul* on the one hand and *Sgt Pepper/Abbey Road* on the
other. That is, the computer analysis demonstrates that the later

songs use a much wider range of vocabulary. This reflects the fact that the writers were dealing with more varied topics and moving beyond the conventional vocabulary of rock and roll.

We can also see that the extent to which the songwriters use 'I' is proportionally much lower on the five later albums (a mean decimal fraction of 4.4 compared with a mean of 8.6 for the four early albums). The sudden rise in the incidence of 'I' in the songs on *Let It Be* is perhaps an exception which proves the rule. 'I' appears there with its highest incidence (30 times) in Harrison's 'I Me Mine', which is not a conventional, autobiographical love song but a rather abstract commentary on life; and 16 times in 'One After 909', which is in fact a song from the group's early period, written by John Lennon in 1959 (Robertson 1994). The use of 'you' shows a less consistent shift, but there is an obvious proportional reduction in explicit references to 'love' on the later albums (the mean fraction falling from 1.58 to 0.64). These shifts support our claim that the later songs deal less with autobiographical-style love issues, and more with observed events, named characters and non-romantic themes. Figures 5.1 to 5.3 give graphical representations of the proportional occurrence of the same target words on the various albums.

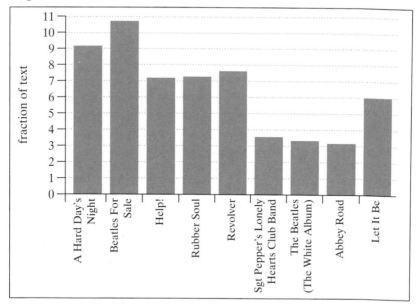

*Figure* 5.1    Fractional incidence of 'I' in lyrics of albums

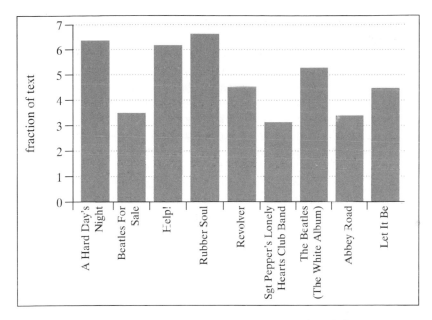

*Figure* 5.2    Fractional incidence of 'you' in lyrics of albums

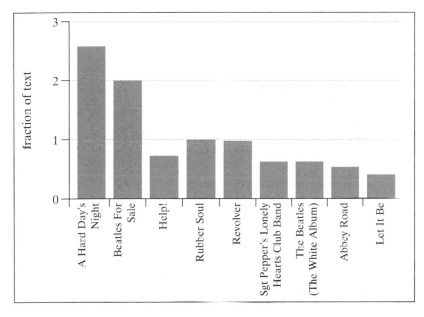

*Figure* 5.3    Fractional incidence of 'love' in lyrics of albums

## COLLOCATIONS AND CONTRASTS: 'SHE' AND 'GIRL'

As explained earlier, 'collocation' means the association words have with each other. A collocation analysis enables us to see how target words gain meanings from the company of other words. We have suggested that the transition from the early lyrics to the later lyrics is characterized by a change of perspective on the part of the song-writer: from involvement and immediacy to observation and detach-ment. One way that this can be seen is by comparing the collocations of certain words on the archetypal early and later albums *A Hard Day's Night* and *Sgt Pepper* (Tables 5.2 and 5.3 below). As is normal with collocation analysis, we have presented the target words in each occurrence in its context of 4–5 preceding and succeeding words. The first word is the pronoun 'she'. The relative incidence of 'she' does not

*Table 5.2*  Collocations of 'she' on two selected albums

|  | A Hard Day's Night | |
|---|---|---|
| 1 | to love you And that | she will cry When she learns we are |
| 2 | she will cry When | she learns we are two If I fell in |
| 3 | her too I love her | She gives me ev'rything And tenderly |
| 4 | kiss my lover brings | She brings to me And I love her A |

|  | Sgt Pepper's Lonely Hearts Club Band | |
|---|---|---|
| 1 | from the things that | she loved Man I was mean but I'm |
| 2 | Leaving the note that | she hoped would say more She goes |
| 3 | key Stepping outside | she is free. She (We gave her most of |
| 4 | gone. Why would | she treat us so thoughtlessly How |
| 5 | thoughtlessly How could | she do this to me. She (We never |
| 6 | at nine o'clock | she is far away Waiting to keep the |
| 7 | keep the appointment | she made Meeting a man from the |
| 8 | white book. In a cap | she looked much older, And the bag |
| 9 | Go to a show you hope | she goes. I've got nothing to say but |
| 10 | hoped would say more | She goes downstairs to the kitchen |
| 11 | outside she is free. | She (We gave her most of our lives) |
| 12 | the top of the stairs | She breaks down and cries to her |
| 13 | she do this to me. | She (We never thought of ourselves) |
| 14 | from the motor trade. | She What did we do that was wrong |
| 15 | sun in her eyes, And | she's gone. Lucy in the sky with |
| 16 | money could buy) | She's leaving home after living alone |
| 17 | our lives to get by) | She's leaving home after living alone |
| 18 | many years. Bye, Bye | She's leaving home bye bye For the |

show any striking or consistent pattern of change between the early and later periods (which is why we did not include it in Table 5.1), but there *is* a change in the *way* it is used.

It can be seen that on *A Hard Day's Night*, 'she' is only used to refer a former or current lover. On *Sgt Pepper*, only one collocation (Number 1) represents this kind of meaning; in all other instances 'she' is an observed person or character in a narrative.

Another interesting comparison is for collocations of 'girl' on the same two albums, as set out in Table 5.3.

*Table 5.3*   Collocations of 'girl' on two selected albums

| A Hard Day's Night | | |
|---|---|---|
| 1 | known better with a | **girl** like you, that I Would love |
| 2 | I've just Lost the only | **girl** I had. If I could get my way, I'd |
| 3 | say you'll be mine, | **girl**, Until the end of time. These |
| 4 | days such a kind | **girl** Seems so hard to find. Someday |
| 5 | To make you mine, | **girl**, Be the only one. Love me all the |
| 6 | Love me all the time, | **girl**. We'll go on and on. Someday |
| 7 | Love me all the time, | **girl**. We'll go on and on. Someday |
| 8 | trivialities, I've got a | **girl** who's waiting home for me |
| 9 | better hide all the | **girls**, I'm gonna Break their hearts |

| Sgt Pepper's Lonely Hearts Club Band | | |
|---|---|---|
| 1 | quite slowly, A | **girl** with kaleidoscope eyes. |
| 2 | head. Look for the | **girl** with the sun in her eyes, And |
| 3 | at the turnstile, The | **girl** with the kaleidoscope eyes. It's |

On the early album, 'girl' is a sexual partner, won, lost or desired by 'I/me' the singer ('I' appears seven times in the words close to 'girl', 'me' four times; in a number of collocations, 'girl' is even used as a direct form of address). On the later album, 'girl' is a named character ('Lucy In The Sky With Diamonds'), observed with apparent detachment by the writer, who tells 'you' to look at her. The singer does not appear in this song, and this is reflected by the fact that in it, 'girl' does not collocate at all with 'I' or 'me'.

## CONCLUSION

Our methods of discourse analysis have revealed clear patterns of change in the language of Beatles songs, with some striking variations between the early and later periods. Shifts from generality to specificity, and from romantic involvement to detached commentary are accomplished in the songs by a broadening of vocabulary, increased use of names, changes in pronoun use and words being set in different connotational contexts. Language use inevitably reflects speakers' concerns and preoccupations, whether or not they are consciously aware of the particular words they choose to use, and that is why we suggest that the patterns of change in the words of the songs represent the personal and social changes experienced by the songwriters between 1964 and 1970. This linguistic sensitivity to social change may be one of the reasons why the songs of Lennon, McCartney and Harrison were (and continue to be) so successful.

## REFERENCES

Carroll, Joseph (1995) *Evolution and Literary Theory*. Columbia: University of Missouri Press.

Cook, Guy (1992) *The Discourse of Advertising*. London: Routledge.

Cook, Guy (1994) *Discourse and Literature*. Oxford University Press.

Dunbar, Robin (1996) *Grooming, Gossip and the Evolution of Language*. London: Faber.

Grice, H. Paul (1975) 'Logic and Conversation' in P. Cole and J. L. Morgan (eds), *Syntax and Semantics, Volume 3: Speech Acts*. New York: Academic Press.

Inglis, Ian (1997) 'Variations on a Theme: the Love Songs of the Beatles', *International Review of the Aesthetics and Sociology of Music*, **28**(1): 37–62.

Louw, Bill (1993) 'Irony in the Text or Insincerity in the Writer? The Diagnostic Potential of Semantic Prosodies' in M. Baker, G. Francis and E. Tognini-Bonelli (eds), *Text and Technology: In Honour of John Sinclair*. Philadelphia: John Benjamins.

Robertson, John (1994) *The Complete Guide to the Music of the Beatles*. London: Omnibus.

Conc 1.71 (1992) *Concordance Generating Program Version 1.71 Beta*. Dallas: Summer Institute of Linguistics.

Wegerif, Rupert and Neil Mercer (1997) 'Using Computer-Based Text Analysis to Integrate Qualitative and Quantitative Methods in Research on Collaborative Learning', *Language and Education*, **11**(3): 271–86.

# 6 The Postmodern White Album

## Ed Whitley

Since the release in 1968 of the double album *The Beatles* (immediately and persistently referred to as the *White Album*), fans and critics have tended to regard it as something of a failure, lacking as it does the cohesion and unity that characterize *Sgt Pepper* and other of the group's albums. Many lament what the album could have been had the Beatles worked a structure into it. Doney believes: 'It could have been a great record ... It was tragic ... but it *could* have worked had the Beatles been able to blend as a unit ... all these [songs] are fragments. The album was a collection of bits and pieces' (1981: 88–9); Robertson claims: 'It lacks the formal unity of *Sgt Pepper* and *Abbey Road*' (1990: 91); O'Grady complains that 'there is little in this collection of songs to suggest either literary or musical unity ... the album fails to demonstrate any particular theme or conceptual reference point' (1983: 150); Salewicz calls the *White Album* 'something of a failure. In the main, it consisted of rough sketches of songs that sounded as though they had been conceived for separate solo records' (1986: 204); and Coleman concludes: 'The impression of all the songs on the album is that they are fragments which developed into finished songs at the last moment ... the songs are scraps of paper ... sometimes throwaway and disposable' (1984: 450).

When viewed within conventional aesthetic boundaries, these critiques are wholly justified. But seen through the theoretical lens of postmodernism, it becomes clearer that the *White Album depends* on these 'failings' to be an effective postmodern text. The *White Album* uses fragmentation, genre mixing, and other postmodern aesthetic techniques which, instead of spelling out what the album should mean, create a zone where meaning can be opened and where readers can participate in the discussion of what this album – and by extension all pop music – does in contemporary society.

The ideas and theories grouped under the heading of 'postmodernism' all have in common a tendency to re-evaluate the modern desires for unity, objectivity, enlightenment and progress, and the associated modernist theories which assume a single, unified direction towards emancipation, salvation, and the liberation of the human race – what Lyotard calls a *master narrative*: 'This idea of a possible, probable, or necessary progress is rooted in the belief that developments made in the arts, technology, knowledge, and freedoms would benefit humanity as a whole' (1992b: 77). The modern ideal, Lyotard explains, is 'the progressive realization of social and individual emancipation encompassing all humanity' (Ibid.: 76). But the postmodern complaint is that 'no single theory or paradigm can encompass the whole of human experience' (Arnowitz 1994: 41). In place of the monolithic, totalizing instinct of modernism, the paradigm of postmodernism contains 'a multiplicity of arguments never arriving at agreement' (Docker 1994: 109); postmodern theories thus organize the world according to plural perspectives, based on multiple narratives which are often contradictory and paradoxical.

For Lyotard, the postmodern 'abandon[s] a global reconstruction of the space of human habitation' in favour of a de-centred, contradictory worldview with 'no ... horizon of universality' (1992b: 76). Within the world of cultural theory, the shift from modernism to postmodernism involves the privileging of 'margins versus centres, circularity versus linearity, fragments versus wholes, decentred verses stable selves, subjectivity versus objectivity, the reflexive versus the referential' (Wilde 1989: 137). Postmodernism questions and re-examines traditional ideas, and then critiques those very doubting conclusions:

> Postmodernism cannot be an affirmative culture. It is condemned to subvert traditions, to recast their forms, to decentre and recombine art, politics, and theory in ways that defile their pristine expression ... Its primary activity is to delegitimate the norms and values of the prevailing order by showing that they are the ideology of a particular group, rather than objective 'truth'. (Arnowitz 1994: 42–3)

As an aesthetic of disturbance which seeks to disrupt the presupposed expectations between reader and text, postmodern art requires us to re-examine our assumptions about art and its role in society. Postmodern art causes this disruption in order to generate discourse between the reader and the text, because when a text does not explicitly spell out its meaning, a place develops for the reader to contribute to the production of meaning. The goal of postmodern art is not to resolve those issues, but to clear a space where that discourse between reader and text can exist; this is precisely what the *White Album* accomplishes for discussions about the nature and place of pop music.

*[marginal handwritten note: Relate to Serialism of Modernist music (eg) Schoenberg etc.]*

As an artistic movement, postmodernism 'starts roughly in 1960 after the High Modernism of the 1920s lost its direction' (Jencks 1996: 35). Best has described the period as 'less serious and moralistic than modernism', a time when 'artists in many fields began mixing media and incorporating *kitsch* and popular culture into their aesthetic' (1991: 10). Postmodernism was a part of the intellectual and artistic Zeitgeist of the late 1960s that also included the Beatles – especially John Lennon, who had recently become involved with Yoko Ono and the artistic culture of New York and London. Some of its principal ideas, which directly influenced artists and writers during this period, can be recognized in the music on the *White Album* and usefully assembled for analysis.[1]

## ANTI-REPRESENTATION

Postmodern artists reject representational art for its attempt to present the unpresentable. Lyotard contends that the goal of postmodern art should be to ' "present" something though negatively ... [to] enable us to see only by making it impossible to see' (1992a: 122). In these terms, 'the postmodern would be that which ... denies itself the solace of good forms ... in order to impart a stronger sense of the unpresentable' (Ibid.: 124). Postmodern artists do not create because there is something to say, but because there is something which cannot be said:

> The postmodern would be that which ... invokes the unpresentable in presentation itself, that which refuses the consolation of correct forms, refuses the consensus of taste permitting a common experience of nostalgia for the impossible, and inquires into new presentations – not to take pleasure in them, but to produce the feeling that there is something unpresentable. (Lyotard 1992b: 15)

Lyotard argues that the traditional techniques of realism and accurate representation are ultimately incapable of presenting the Real, and thus encourages artists to exaggerate this inability by abandoning all such techniques. Similarly, Hoover believes that the postmodern poet 'in saying nothing ... says everything' (1994: xxxi); and Barthes asserts that art in the postmodern era 'has reached in our time a last metamorphosis, absence' because it 'could no longer find purity anywhere but in the absence of all signs' (Ibid.: xxxvii).

On the album cover of *Yellow Submarine* are the words 'nothing is real' – from 'Strawberry Fields Forever' – which seem to convey the anti-representational aspect of postmodernism, but via the aesthetic of representation. Using psychedelia to show that 'nothing is real' fails, however, because if a text relies on 'correct forms', it can do no other than fail. For the Beatles to be successful in their attempts to convey anti-representation, they had to jettison the expectations of conventional aesthetics; in order to present the message that 'nothing is real', they had to do everything but say 'nothing is real'. What they needed was an album that could present something though negatively, '[something] "white" like one of Malevitch's squares ... [something that] enable[s] us to see only by making it impossible to see' (Lyotard 1992a: 122).

The all-white cover of the *White Album* is the antithesis of the psychedelic and intricate covers of albums like *Magical Mystery Tour* and *Sgt Pepper*. Where *Sgt Pepper*, with its 'who's who' of pop icons, begs to be read, the *White Album* is decidedly non-representational. Okun reminds us that 'With the *White Album* ... The Beatles set out to create a work as unlike *Sgt Pepper* as possible. (Its whiteness is significant in view of *Sgt Pepper*'s elaborate and expensive album jacket.) And they succeed' (1986: 142). Instead of showing readers what rock and roll is, the *White Album*'s blank, nameless cover presents readers with a *tabula rasa* that shifts the centre of meaning from the text itself and onto the readers, who are then given a share of the responsibility for creating meaning. And once inside the cover, the album itself continues to resist a solid and unifying theme through its combination of disparate musical styles and in its fragmentation of structure.


## BRICOLAGE

Lyotard defines bricolage as 'the multiple quotation of elements taken from earlier styles or periods, classical and modern; disregard for the environment; and so on' (1992b: 76); it is an important element of postmodern art because, as De La Croix suggests, this mixture of styles within a single work provides postmodern artists the opportunity to 'analyze the operation of all art styles and the place of art in culture' (1991: 968). Juxtaposing high and low art makes each style a comment on the other and a commentary on art in general. Gitlin has explained:

> Postmodernism is completely indifferent to the questions of consistency and continuity. It self-consciously splices genres, attitudes,

styles. It relishes the blurring or juxtaposition of forms (fiction-nonfiction), stances (straight-ironic), moods (violent-comic), cultural levels (high-low) ... It neither embraces nor criticizes, but beholds the world blankly, with a knowingness that dissolves feeling and commitment into irony ... It takes pleasure in the play of surfaces, and derides the search for depth as mere nostalgia. (Kene 1991: 110)

Barthes also stresses that a text is a 'multi-dimensional space in which a variety of writings, none of them original, blend and crash' (1992: 116). The only power possessed by the creators of such texts is the power 'to mix writings, to counter the ones with the others, in such a way as to never rest on any one of them' (Ibid.: 117).

Following these observations, Perloff adds that 'postmodernism in art is the appropriation of other genres, both high and popular' (1988: viii) and, very significantly, that postmodern art seeks a *both/and inclusion* of plural styles, not an *either/or exclusion* (Ibid.: viii). Ralph Cohen urges that instead of looking at what are and what are not postmodern genres, theorists should look at how postmodern texts navigate the space *between* the multiple genres they appropriate, and how this appropriation of multiple genres in a single work produces an area of discourse in the gaps between styles (1988: 18). A genre is a set of expectations, a contract between reader and text. A postmodern text disrupts an audience's expectations – it breaks this contract – by mixing 'high' genres with 'low' genres. Whereas readers can go into a conventional text knowing what to expect, looking for the conventions and codes with which they are comfortable, postmodern texts violate contracts and expectations, either by calling into question the binaries in a hierarchy ('low' art becomes 'high' art) or by calling attention to the marginal material and gaps of the text, making margins as important as the centre and gaps as important as the substance. 'Thus the issue is not a matter of multiple subjects or discontinuous narration, but of the shift in the kinds of "transgressions" and in the implications of the revised combinations' (Ibid.: 16).

Some have suggested that the Beatles should have taken the 'best' songs recorded during the *White Album* sessions to make one solid album instead of a disjointed, fragmentary double album. But, as Riley has recognized, 'the options for making a satisfying single record from this compilation seem limited' (1988: 260) since there is no group of songs on this album that seems to go together any better than any other random grouping. The album consists of 30 incongruous, thematically unrelated songs which appear in many ways to be arranged according to the laws of chance. In the *Beatles Anthology* television documentary series, Ringo Starr, asked whether or not the Beatles should have reduced the album down to one record, (jokingly) replied that they should have made two albums out of it: 'a *White Album* and a *Whiter Album*' (1996). The truth behind Ringo's response is that the *White Album* loudly proclaims its irreducible plurality in such a way that it is impossible to extract any sort of definable theme from it. Paul McCartney, speaking in the same film, commented: 'It's a fine little album and the fact that it's got so much on it is one of the things that's cool about it … they're very varied stuff'; he then fumbled around for a moment, weighing the pros and cons of making a double album with so many disparate songs on it, before proclaiming: 'It's the bloody Beatles' *White Album*! Shut up!' (1996). The album's bricolage of styles and fragmented nature seem to make it 'unreadable' (anti-representational) to one of its key contributors; even after McCartney had helped to make the album, he was unable to make sense of it, label it, totalize it, or reduce it to a cohesive whole.

Many Beatles critics have repeatedly emphasized that bricolage is one of the most salient features of the *White Album*. Schaffner concludes that 'the *White Album* includes pastiches of so many different styles of music that it virtually amounts to an irreverent encyclopedia of pop' (1977: 113). Okun describes it as 'a helter-skelter of cross-references, and a Monty Python's Flying Circus of bizarre inventiveness' (1986: 142–3); and Kozzin sees in it 'a fascinating compendium of compositional and performance styles … there are some marvelous parodies and tributes here' (1995: 180).

One of the factors which adds to the bricolage of the album are the out-of-place, non-rock songs which sever the traditional reader–text contract. Rock and roll fans had come to expect albums to contain either rock songs or love ballads and, in the case of projects like *Sgt Pepper*, a consistent musical and lyrical theme. The effect of making an album with so many different musical styles, especially styles found outside pop music, is to make readers stop to reconsider the question of what does, and does not, constitute rock and roll. Mixing styles in the manner of the *White Album* obliges readers to move from the passive consumption of music to an active discussion of the function and role of art.

Thus, songs such as 'Back in the USSR' and 'Helter Skelter' violate some of the (stereo)typical expectations of Beatles music – one with its seemingly pro-communist lyrics, the other with its hard-driving, never-ending noise. 'Ob-La-Di, Ob-La-Da' is a calypso, West Indies-style song which sounds like a children's sing-along. 'The Continuing Story of Bungalow Bill' recalls and is performed in 'the mode of the Saturday afternoon kiddie shows' (Wenner 1968: 11), a view reinforced by Robertson's comment that 'with its musical simplicity and singalong chorus [it] ... works well as a children's song' (1990: 84). The same insight has been applied to 'Rocky Raccoon': '[it] is more a zany children's song rather than anything one would expect to find on a straight ahead Beatles album' (Giuliano 1985: 126). 'Cry Baby Cry' recalls an infant's bedtime song, with lyrics reminiscent of Lewis Carroll's *Alice In Wonderland* and any number of nursery rhymes.

'Good Night' was quite literally a children's song, written by Lennon for his five-year-old son, Julian (Taylor 1996: 11); it employs the narrative language of a nursery rhyme – 'Now the sun turns out his light' – as well as the personal address from singing parent to sleeping child – 'Dream sweet dreams for me/Dream sweet dreams for you'. Also at work in 'Good Night' is the bricolage effect of situating old or traditional forms inside new frameworks. As a result, '[it] sounded like a standard the first time you heard it; Bing Crosby might have sung it back in the thirties' (Robertson 1990: 93). Kozzin agrees that the song 'could easily pass as something from the Bing Crosby or Frank Sinatra songbooks' (1995: 181); William Mann, writing in the week the album was released, suspected that '[the song] will be a regular request for *The Jimmy Young Show* – it is as well constructed a ballad as any that won Sinatra or Humperdinck a golden disc' (1988: 153). And Mellers reported that singer Vera Lynn (the 'Forces Sweetheart' of the Second World War) admired and wished to include 'Good Night' in her repertoire because it reminded her of so many of the songs from that previous generation (1973: 135).

There are other songs too which hark back to older music styles. In 'Honey Pie', McCartney takes a 1930s-style song and repositions it in the new environment of 1960s rock and roll – he even includes old 78 scratches on the recording in order to age it. 'Martha My Dear' is a song with a 'music hall ambience' (Fricke 1986: 48) that 'has its roots in the turn-of-the-century salon song' (Kozzin 1995: 180), and 'Rocky Raccoon' is reminiscent of songs from the era of the storytelling ballads of the American West. Just as Vera Lynn chose to include 'Good Night' in her repertoire, years later Bob Hope would sing 'Rocky Raccoon' on television (Giuliano 1985: 126). As the Beatles were appropriating the style of older musicians, so they themselves were later appropriated by musicians from outside their musical circles. Hope and Lynn's exploitation of Beatles' songs is a fitting continuation of the postmodern project started by the *White Album* where the appropriation and re-appropriation of styles is taken to such an extent that any sense of origin becomes lost. Even though Lennon disparaged 'Honey Pie', 'Rocky Raccoon' and 'Martha My Dear' as part of McCartney's 'f——ing Cole Porter routine' (Giuliano 1985: 125), he too contributed a music hall-style song in 'Sexy Sadie', whose piano part and backup singers sound as antique as anything McCartney did. And George Harrison borrows from a musical style hundreds of years old with the pseudo-baroque harpsichord sound on 'Piggies'.

There has been a temptation to see these songs as nothing more than kitsch and to criticize the Beatles for including 'low' art on the *White Album*. But, as Arnowitz points out, this kind of thinking tends to

> confuse postmodern art and kitsch. Kitsch is not a pastiche of exhausted forms; [kitsch] takes these forms seriously and imitates them without irony. Postmodernism is nothing if not ironic; its entire enterprise is to deconstruct the solemnity of high modernism ... it challenges the idea of a single art, and presents its politics as molecular, the alliance of otherwise disparate groups for specific and perhaps temporary goals. (1994: 40)

Situating these older-sounding songs within the framework of a rock album turns them into a postmodern comment on the conventions and cultural constructions of pop music. Aside from challenging the notion of what is and what is not 'acceptable' pop music, they seem to ask: if these types of songs were popular then, but are laughable now, how will the pop songs we produce today be received in 50 years?

The Beatles also borrow from the older styles of contemporary artists in different fields. 'Blackbird' and 'Mother Nature's Son' imitated the folk sound that Bob Dylan and Joan Baez had initially popularized in the 1960s. Ringo Starr wrote a country and western piece 'Don't Pass Me By', said by O'Grady to be 'like so many others on the *White Album* ... perfectly idiomatic and representative of its style' (1983: 154). 'Yer Blues' and 'Why Don't We Do It In The Road' are basic 12–bar blues with the standard lyric pattern of AABA that many blues musicians had been using for decades. Lennon's 'Revolution 9' borrows from the avant-garde *musique concrète* sound, which while familiar in avant-garde circles, was a shock for rock and roll readers, and added another in a long series of incongruous pieces to the album's bricolage.

Other styles from the past adopted and adapted by the group include the doo-wop sound of 1950s and early 1960s rock and roll and references to their own earlier music. 'Back In The USSR' is a play-off of Chuck Berry's 'Back In The USA' and also borrows from the Beach Boys' 'California Girls'. But instead of the sandy-haired beach bum going for a cruise with his girlfriend in a red convertible, as the cliché became for Beach Boys' songs, here the invitation is to 'show me round your snow peaked mountains way down south and come and keep your comrade warm'. Whereas 'California Girls', in the spirit of the male gaze, sings the praises of the well-tanned, blonde-haired, blue-eyed, West Coast girl, 'Back In The USSR' cele-brates girls from the Ukraine, Moscow, and the Republic of Georgia. Its reference to 'Georgia On My Mind', an old blues standard chiefly associated with Ray Charles, is also significant, as rock and roll, blues, and (misdirected) social commentary come together in a disjointed collection. The song simultaneously pays tribute to early rock and roll while parodying those contemporary rock groups, including the Beatles themselves, who had appropriated that sound. Wenner notes that it 'is not just an imitation ... of the Beach Boys, but an imitation of the Beach Boys imitating Chuck Berry' (1968: 10), which reinforces the idea of an appropriation and reappropria-tion of styles that undermines a single origin. The opening cadences of 'Back In The USSR' also borrow from the Isley Brothers' 'Twist and Shout', a song the Beatles had previously, and triumphantly, performed on *Please Please Me*, allowing McCartney to mimic not just 'the perpetually sunny Beach Boys, but also himself' (Giuliano 1985: 124), thus illustrating the the practice of postmodern texts to parody conventionality as they parody themselves and their own claim to truth (Docker 1994: 143).

In fact, parody is of course an important part of postmodernism for artists and theorists who challenge the modern claim to objectivity (the ability to critique a system from outside that system) and argue that the only way to critique a system is by using its very language (Cowles 1994: 112–20). Waugh has suggested that there can only be disruptions from within, including 'parody, dissensual language games, metafiction, varieties of aesthetic play' (1992: 8); these are the *only* way for a postmodern critique to exist. Parody not only exposes art for its limitations, but it also '"replenishes" through a self-conscious recognition that implication in a prior discourse does not entail exhaustion and inert imitation' (Ibid.: 2). Parody subverts the pretentiousness of a system by taking it to its illogical extremes and revealing its limitations, thus commenting on the system while using the very modes and techniques of that system.

The doo-wop techniques of 'Back In The USSR' are also found in 'Happiness Is A Warm Gun' and 'Revolution 1'. In the final part of 'Happiness Is A Warm Gun' Lennon borrowed the I VI IV V chord progression that was standard for love ballads in the 1950s, such as Ritchie Valens's 'Donna'. Juxtaposing these 1950s-style chords with a commentary on the politics of gun control (Lennon sings 'Happiness is a warm gun' while the back-up singers echo 'Bang bang, shoot shoot') is as incongruous as postmodern art gets. 'Revolution 1' combines doo-wop and social commentary in a way that Robertson describes as 'wonderfully inappropriate, full of joyous harmonies that sound like a celebration rather than a warning' (1990: 86). Just as the placement of an older style in a different environment transforms the impetus of 'Honey Pie' and 'Martha My Dear', the musical styles borrowed for 'Back In The USSR', 'Happiness Is A Warm Gun' and 'Revolution 1' have a different effect from that on the records of Ritchie Valens, the Beach Boys, and Chuck Berry. In addition, the subject matter of the songs – 'Back In The USSR' and 'Revolution 1' are observations on East–West political relationships; 'Happiness Is A Warm Gun' critically challenges gun-lovers and sexual deviants – shows how the world (of popular music) had changed since the 1950s. The juxtaposition of 1950s rock with 1960s social commentary simultaneously undercuts the innocence of the 1950s and the pretentiousness of the 1960s.


## FRAGMENTATION

A close reading of *any* text, postmodern theory argues, will reveal that it is fragmented, paradoxical, and contradictory. Postmodern artists do not set out to make fragmented texts just because there have never been anything like them; rather, their intentionally fragmented texts show that fragmentation is present in *every* text and that unity is a myth, a constructed code.

Inside the jacket of the *White Album* is a huge fold-out poster which on one side has four professional portraits of the individual band members and on the other side a collage of all sorts of unprofessional, casual photographs of the band (including an unflattering shot of McCartney in the bathtub, and Ringo Starr dancing with Elizabeth Taylor). One side of the poster has the Beatles as the studio would package them and present them: The Fab Four, Our Boys from Liverpool; the other side presents them as irreducibly plural selves. Included in the photo spread are old publicity photographs, negatives, black-and-white and colour photographs, photographs of their younger selves, a shot of McCartney in horn-rimmed glasses and slicked back hair, a rough pencil sketch of a nude Lennon and Yoko Ono, shots of the Beatles playing music, laughing, talking, eating, and so on. In this fragmentary, disjointed photo spread, the Beatles challenge whoever looks at them to totalize them, to fix them, to stabilize them. *A Hard Day's Night*, the Beatles' first movie, presented them as four distinct personality types, caricatures even, which persist(ed) in the public mind as being an accurate depiction of the real Beatles: Clever Boy John, Heartthrob Paul, Straight Man George, and Goofy Ringo. A few years later, *Sgt Pepper* presented them in the disguise of the perfect pop band. The photo spread and musical content of the *White Album*, however, resist any totalizing definition of the self, and revel in the plurality of personality. Wenner observes in his *Rolling Stone* review of the album:

> There is not the dissemblance of being 'our boys' from *A Hard Day's Night* nor the disguise of Sgt Pepper's band ... There is almost no attempt in this new set to be anything but what the Beatles actually are: John, Paul, George, and Ringo. Four different people, each with songs and styles and abilities. They are no longer Sgt Pepper's Lonely Hearts Club Band, and *it is possible that they are no longer the Beatles*. (1968: 10, 12; emphasis added)

The photo spread reflects the infinite nature of the self to the extent that the individuals are greater than the whole they add up to. Postmodern thought teaches that no master narrative, including even the powerful force of Beatlemania, can totalize the irreducibly plural self.

The *White Album* exaggerates the fragmentary nature of texts by placing unrelated songs next to each other, which eliminates a stable centre from which to explain the album and clears a space for discourse about the place of art in society. Thus, the immediate transition between 'Back In The USSR' which parodies 1950s rock and roll and 'Dear Prudence' which is a sincere song of innocent love, is an illustration of what Riley calls 'the journey from parody to purity' (1988: 261), 'from the ridiculous to the sublime' (Ibid.: 24). Following the sincerity of 'Dear Prudence' is the accusatory tone of 'Glass Onion', whose intense interpretation-defying message is in turn disrupted by the surface simplicity of 'Ob-La-Di, Ob-La-Da'. After this light-hearted piece is 'Wild Honey Pie', one of the most bizarre tracks the Beatles ever recorded. Its cacophony is interrupted by a five-second virtuoso Spanish guitar solo which also ends abruptly and gives way to 'The Continuing Story Of Bungalow Bill', another disruption in a series of already unrelated material. The (at best goofy, at worst bitingly sarcastic) track is followed by Harrison's 'While My Guitar Gently Weeps', arguably the most well-produced, well-crafted song on the album. Its supple guitar work is then attacked by the disjointed 'Happiness Is A Warm Gun', which Lennon described as 'three bits strung together' (Schaffner 1977: 114) and which O'Grady calls 'one of Lennon's most fragmented and discontinuous songs' (1983: 152). Not only does the *White Album* have an *overall* sense of fragmentation, but there are also individual songs like 'Happiness Is A Warm Gun' which are *internally* fragmented and songs like 'Wild Honey Pie' that are nothing *but* song fragments.

'Happiness Is A Warm Gun' ends side one, and side two opens up with the happy and peppy 'Martha My Dear', which is then countered by the dragging and pathetic 'I'm So Tired' before 'Blackbird' comes on and clears out the pathos of the previous track with its simple acoustic sound. 'Piggies' has been described as 'an amazing choice to follow "Blackbird" with such an opposite mood and meaning, "Blackbird" so encouraging, "Piggies" so smug' (Wenner 1968: 12). 'Rocky Raccoon', 'Don't Pass Me By', and the bluesy 'Why Don't We Do It In The Road' continue to shift and disrupt the flow of the album, denying any cohesive direction. Particularly jarring is the transition between 'Why Don't We Do It in The Road' and 'I Will', which O'Grady calls 'an unusually graphic contrast' (1983: 151). By now the second side of the first record is almost over and readers might be coming to think of this as 'the parody album' and seeing a comical theme to the arrangement and placement of songs; indeed, Okun entitles his chapter on the *White Album* 'The Wit Of White' (1986). As this theme of parody seems to emerge, however, 'Julia' confronts the text's readers with Lennon's sincere and painful meditation on his mother's death, ending the second side of the first record on a sombre and melancholy note.

The first side of the second record starts with some sturdy rock and roll in 'Birthday' and 'Yer Blues' which is then interrupted by the acoustic pastoral 'Mother Nature's Son', which provides a contrasting depiction of solitude and isolation to the track that precedes it. Whereas the loneliness in 'Yer Blues' is unbearable, even suicidal,

'Mother Nature's Son' revels in the delights of rural sec\
contemplative mood is quickly undercut by the off-balanc\
'Everybody's Got Something To Hide Except Me And My\
whose intro in 4/4 time with a 3/4 feel halts the even flow of ~~~~~
Nature's Son'. 'Sexy Sadie' provides a respite before the hard-hitting
'Helter Skelter', which is in turn undercut by 'Long Long Long', a
gentle ballad in waltz time which completes the first side of the
second record.

Side two opens with 'Revolution 1', an ironic and cynical song
about political upheaval whose message is not 'Workers of the world,
unite', but 'It's gonna be alright', and is followed by the sappy and
parodic 'Honey Pie'. The beefy rocker 'Savoy Truffle' and the cryptic
'Cry Baby Cry' are incongruous with the first two songs on the side, as
well as with each other, and are followed by a simple acoustic number
'Can You Take Me Back', a 30-second song fragment not listed on the
album, which precedes the experimental collage of 'Revolution 9', a
song that would be difficult to place thematically on any kind of rock
album. 'Good Night' ends the album on a final, incongruous note; an
incongruity which calls attention *away* from the work of art itself and
directs it at the way art is constructed and interpreted, and its overall
social function.

## PLURAL TONE

Postmodern texts encourage readers actively to create meaning in a
text by deferring meaning rather than spelling it out:

> The Text is plural. Which is not simply to say that it has several
> meanings, but that it accomplishes the very plural of meaning: an
> *irreducible* (and not merely an acceptable) plural. The Text ...
> answers not to an interpretation, even a liberal one, but to an
> explosion, a dissemination. (Barthes 1989: 1007)

Postmodern texts strive for this irreducible plurality, through which
they can create a zone where negotiation between reader and text
may take place. A postmodern text (which, in the case of popular
music, may be an album or an individual song within that album)
offers itself to be interpreted an infinite number of ways. Best
explains: 'Since the world has no single meaning, but rather countless
meanings, a [postmodernist] seeks multiple interpretations of
phenomena and insists there is "no limit to the ways in which the

world can be interpreted"' (1991: 39). Open texts that infinitely defer the signified in a playful field of signifiers follow Lyotard's injunction, paraphrased by Godzich, that since there can be no single meaning, 'the only option that remains is that of an indefinite experimenting with language games' (1992: 127). The image of the 'Glass Onion', whose infinite layers defer meaning indefinitely, illustrates this postmodern experimentation. As readers peel away at layer after layer trying to get to the centre of a text, they realize that ultimately there *is* no centre, just a periphery that constantly postpones meaning in an infinity of outside layers. Barthes rejoices in 'the infinite deferment of the signified' (1989: 1007) – the postmodern shift away from the centre (the meaning of a text, the *signified*) to the margins (the gaps in a text, the *signifier*). Jencks's reference to a postmodern art which opens itself to multiple interpretations by having a dual or plural tone calls attention to its 'radical schizophrenia [and] … hybrid language [which] … affirms and subverts simultaneously [and] … sends a mixed message of acceptance and critique' (1996: 30).

'Dear Prudence' refuses to be confined to any single interpretation. Lennon wrote it for Mia Farrow's sister, who had accompanied the Beatles to Rishikesh, India to study transcendental meditation with the Maharishi Mahesh Yogi. She had remained in her cabin meditating for days, and people were beginning to worry about her physical and mental health (Coleman 1984: 447–8). The song works on a very literal level as an invitation to come back to the world, showing sincere concern and love in the invitation that Prudence experience the beauty of life. Both the gentle, simple lyrics and the picking pattern on the guitar suggest what Robertson calls a 'childlike appreciation of the natural world' (1990: 85). The bridge, where Lennon, McCartney, and Harrison chant 'look around', becomes a new mantra of wonder at the outside world which replaces the inward mantra of meditation. However, Riley reads 'Dear Prudence' as 'a song about sexual awakening, the heady euphoria of natural pleasures wooed by a sublime musical arc' (1988: 265), whose invitation to partake of nature is more a sexual proposition than a call to spiritual awakening. The music itself refuses to employ just one tone, as the gentle string plucking of the verses is overtaken by the momentum of the bridge, which includes some of the most enthusiastic drumming of Ringo's career. Russell has noted that 'the song could almost be made up of two songs joined together, rock song and ballad' (1989: 98). Even the section which sounds like a string ensemble swelling in orchestral majesty is an aural trick: 'they got that electric string ensemble sound

by over dubbing half a dozen guitars' (Fricke 1986: 51). Okun reads
'Dear Prudence' in yet another way; he sees it as evidence of intra-
group parody, claiming that the song 'seems very like Lennon
mocking McCartney' (1986: 142). The Beatles' appropriation of other
musical styles does include intra-group parody – Lennon speaking in
McCartney's voice on gentle love songs like 'Dear Prudence' and
'Julia'; McCartney speaking with Lennon's voice on 'Why Don't We
Do It In The Road' and 'Helter Skelter'. This parody is so well-
crafted and carries with it the plural tone of acceptance and critique
that Mann mistakenly labels 'Why Don't We Do It In The Road' and
'Helter Skelter' as Lennon pieces (1988: 153).

Another song with a decidedly plural tone is 'I'm So Tired', which
at first seems to be the cry of a frustrated lover asking for 'a little
peace of mind' from the woman who keeps him up at night thinking
about her. But with the knowledge that Lennon wrote this song while
in India with the Maharishi, the plea 'I'd give you everything I've got/
for a little piece of mind' in this context seems more like the yearning
of the disenchanted transcendentalist rather than the complaining of
a forlorn lover. Or, as the song was written during the time of
Lennon's divorce, soon after the death of Brian Epstein, and at the
time when the Beatles were starting to sow the seeds of a break-up,
the lyrics might equally reflect the condition of a man whose personal
life is endlessly frustrating. The last verse of the song complicates the
tone even more when Lennon blames Sir Walter Raleigh, 'the stupid
get', for his own smoking habit. What once could have been a sincere
song expressing genuine anguish now becomes laughable as the frustrated lover/disenchanted transcendentalist/distressed Beatle curses
the man who centuries earlier had brought tobacco back from the
New World, and blames him for his own addiction to cigarettes. The
humorous aside to colonial American history in this last verse gives
way to the song's final chorus, which is followed by a few seconds of
undecipherable studio blather from Lennon, suggesting that the song
works as a less serious piece than it first may have appeared.

At first, 'Helter Skelter' sounds like a rebellious rock and roll song
with its loud, out of tune guitars and distorted feedback. McCartney
has said that he wrote the song in order to show the Who, who had
recently claimed to be the hardest rocking band around, that the
Beatles could still out-rock anyone else (Garbarini 1986: 57). Also, the
onomatopoeia of the title suggests all hell breaking loose. In reality, a
'helter skelter' is the British term for a fairground slide (Dowlding
1989: 243). One look at the lyrics challenges the weighty sound of the

screaming guitars, thumping drums and shouting vocals: 'When I get to the bottom I go back to the top of the slide/Where I stop and I turn and I go for a ride/Till I get to the bottom and I see you again'. The song then becomes utterly simple and childish; it *is* about a slide. The hardest rocking song on the album – designed to impress the group's rivals – is also most obviously a children's song. It has the dual tone of serious/ironic postmodern art in that it is a solid rocker which simultaneously undercuts the bad boy attitude of rock and roll.

'Happiness Is A Warm Gun' is also characterized by confusing and complex tensions. Okun sees it as 'a gorgeous bit of self mockery by Lennon' (1986: 142) who loved 1950s rock and roll, but chose here to lampoon it with what Fricke calls a 'sinister doo-wop chorus' (1986: 51); it operates equally as a serious song about sexual violence and as an anti-gun tract. 'Martha My Dear' is a charming love song and a parody of such songs, which 'works on the level of a send-up [and] as an inherently good song, standing fully on its own merits' (Wenner 1968: 11). 'Cry Baby Cry' may be perceived lyrically as a children's song, but there is a maturity in the delivery of the lyrics which makes it much more adult than 'Ob-La-Di, Ob-La-Da' or 'The Continuing Story Of Bungalow Bill'. It is a song whose content is taken from every unwritten nursery rhyme, but which exceeds the innocence of the nursery rhyme ('she's old enough to know better'). George Harrison's 'Long Long Long' is also 'ambiguous in that he could be singing either to his lady or to his Lord' (Schaffner 1977: 115). Lyrically, it is hard to tell where Lennon stands on radical political action in 'Revolution 1' as he simultaneously announces that he may be counted out *and* in, when it comes to destruction. 'The Continuing Story Of Bungalow Bill' can be read as a children's song and as a social commentary on everything from American imperialism to animal rights. 'Rocky Raccoon' maintains its plurality of tone by relating the story of a fatally wounded cowboy to the accompaniment of a peppy upright piano.

'Don't Pass Me By' works as a country song and a parody of the genre, just as 'Yer Blues' exemplifies and parodies contemporary blues rock; while groups like Cream and the Jeff Beck Group were writing blues rock songs with virtuoso guitar solos, one of the solos on 'Yer Blues' consists almost entirely of just one note. Lennon later revealed:

The Beatles were super self-conscious people about parody of Americans which we do and have done. I know we developed our own style, but we still in a way parodied American music ... There was a self-consciousness about singing blues ... Paul was saying, 'Don't call it "Yer Blues", just say it straight.' But I was self-conscious and I went for 'Yer Blues'. (Wenner 1981: 131)

Despite its self-conscious tone, which characterizes much postmodern art's recognition that it 'can only imitate a gesture that is always anterior, never original' (Barthes 1992: 117), 'Yer Blues' also remains a solid blues rock piece. This dual tone, which Riley calls the ability to 'walk the tight rope between respectful emulation and high musical satire' (1988: 259), is a part of the integral tendency of postmodern art to 'affirm and subvert simultaneously' (Jencks 1996: 30), as is the ability to engage simultaneously in parody (of conventionality) and self parody (Docker 1994: 143). The parody in the *White Album* increases its overall plural tone since so many of its songs are simultaneously a homage to and a parody of a certain style. The plurality of the individual songs is, concludes Okun, 'brilliant, devastating, affectionate and weird, all at once' (1986: 142–3).

## META-ART

Postmodern art is aware of its own conventions and constructed codes. By 'laying bare the device' (showing that artistic techniques are constructed conventions), postmodern texts self-consciously reveal to readers how they are produced and provide a commentary about the production of art. Postmodern architecture, for example, frequently displays heating vents, plumbing, and other internal workings on the outside of buildings. Postmodern writers, notes McCaffery, 'lay bare the artifice of their work, comment on the processes involved, [and] refuse the realist illusion that the work mimics operations outside itself' (Wilde 1989: 135). Postmodern art goes so far as 'to show the sutures in its wounds' (Arnowitz 1994: 40), proudly proclaiming to viewers and readers that it is a constructed artifice, not a natural artifact. While other artistic traditions attempt through realism, mimesis, and other conventions to hide the fact of their art, postmodern art revels in its own self-conscious realization. The postmodern texts of author John Barth often remind readers, 'Don't forget I'm an artifice!' (1988: 28).

One such traditional convention challenged by the *White Album* is the notion of closure. 'Helter Skelter', for example, fades in and out three times before ending and only comes to a halt when Ringo screams, 'I've got blisters on my fingers!' Ringo's announcement 'lays bare the device' and demonstrates to readers that endings are forced. All texts end because of human limitation, but conventional texts attempt to conceal that fact by presenting endings as natural; here, Ringo reveals the real reason that songs/texts come to an end – after a while we get blisters on our fingers and are forced to stop. Endings, postmodern theory argues, are enforced through an unnatural, constructed code which exists only in texts. No matter how many cadences there may be or how complete the last chord of a song (such as the final chord of *Sgt Pepper*'s 'A Day in the Life') may appear, closure is not a natural occurrence, but a convention required by artistic tradition; postmodern texts refuse to deceive readers and make explicit this refusal to their readers. The Beatles reject closure in 'Helter Skelter' by leaving the studio microphone running and encouraging readers to eavesdrop on why a song really comes to an end.

In the same vein, 'Good Night', the last song on the album, comments on the conventions of closure through its self-presentation as the grand finale to the album. The sweeping orchestration throughout the song recalls the triumphant conclusion to a musical or a concerto, and the gently whispered 'good night everybody' at the end seals the finality of the song. But the tone is wonderfully ironic. Lennon, who composed the song, insists that it was intended to be insincere: 'I just said to George Martin, "Arrange it like Hollywood. Yeah, corny"' (Schaffner 1977: 115). The song mimics the closure of a modern text, but greatly exaggerates it in order to show how such attempts at closure are always constructed.


## CONCLUSION: WHAT DOES THE WHITE ALBUM DO?

By employing the disruptive aesthetics of postmodern art, the *White Album* calls attention away from itself as a source of meaning and instead clears a space where readers can engage the issues of what popular music is and what role it plays. It does not hold up a unified, understandable, interpretable theme, but blurs any possible theme, making it impossible to grasp its essential motivation. 'The *White Album* defies structure. Where *Revolver* and *Sgt Pepper* had ... beginnings and endings, the compilation of songs here is less formally arranged; its totality is not as central as the idea of any given track' (Riley 1988: 287). Its tendency to call attention to its own limitations takes the locus of meaning away from the text itself and makes the production of meaning the responsibility of its readers.

Thus is revealed the total existence of writing: a text is made of multiple writings, drawn from many cultures and entering into mutual relations of dialogue, parody, contestation, but there is one place where this multiplicity is focused and that place is the reader. (Barthes 1992: 118)

The album deconstructs itself, pop music, the Beatles themselves, and their own musical history. By not *meaning anything*, the *White Album* is then able to *do something*; and what it does is to clear a space in which the reader is able to participate in a negotiated discourse about the role(s) of popular music within Western culture.

## NOTE

1. Whether or not the Beatles intended this album to be a postmodern text would be a moot point for many postmodern critics who proclaim the 'Death Of The Author' and focus only on the effects of the text itself. Is there actually any postmodernism 'in' the *White Album*? Or am I imposing this reading strategy onto the text? The reader should bear in mind that such questions are current points of debate in critical circles; much ink has been spilt over whether critics find or impose meaning. My purpose in presenting a postmodern analysis of the *White Album* is to argue that there are things it does which today we call 'postmodern', and that recognizing those things provides for a much richer reading of the album.

## REFERENCES

Arnowitz, Stanley (1994) *Dead Artists, Live Theories, and other Cultural Problems*. New York: Routledge.

Barth, John (1988) 'Life Story', in R. V. Cassill (ed.), *The Norton Anthology of Contemporary Fiction*. New York: W.W. Norton & Co.

Barthes, Roland (1989) 'From Work to Text', in David H. Richter (ed.), *The Critical Tradition: Classic Texts and Contemporary Trends*. New York: St Martin's.

Barthes, Roland (1992) 'The Death of the Author', in Philip Rice and Patricia Waugh (eds), *Modern Literary Theory: a Reader* (2nd edn). London: Edward Arnold.

*Beatles Anthology No. 8.* (1996) Executive Producer, Neil Aspinall. Director, Geoff Wonfor. Capitol Video, Turner Home Entertainment.

Best, Steven (1991) *Postmodern Theories: Critical Interrogations*. New York: Guilford Press.

Cohen, Ralph (1988) 'Do Postmodern Genres Exist?', in Marjorie Perloff (ed.), *Postmodern Genres*. Norman, OK: University of Oklahoma Press.

Coleman, Ray (1984) *Lennon*. New York: McGraw-Hill.

Cowles, David (1994) 'Deconstruction and Poststructuralism', in David Cowles (ed.), *The Critical Experience* (2nd edn). Dubuque, Iowa: Kendall Hunt.

De La Croix, Horst, *et al.* (1991) *Art through the Ages* (9th edn). New York: Harcourt Brace Jovanovich.

Docker, John (1994) *Postmodernism and Popular Culture: a Cultural History*. Cambridge University Press.

Doney Malcolm (1981) *Lennon and McCartney*. New York: Hippocrene.

Dowlding, William J. (1989) *Beatlesongs*. New York: Fireside.

Fricke, David (1986) 'A Musical History (1962–1970)', in *The Beatles Book*. Chicago: Omnibus Press.

Garbarini, Vic (1986) 'Paul McCartney Interview', in *The Beatles Book*. Chicago: Omnibus Press.

Giuliano, Geoffrey (1985) *Blackbird: the Life and Times of Paul McCartney*. Harmondsworth: Penguin.

Godzich, Wlad (1992) 'Afterword: Reading against Literacy', in Jean-Francois Lyotard, *The Postmodern Explained*. Minneapolis: University Of Minnesota Press.

Hoover, Paul (1994) *Postmodern American Poetry: a Norton Anthology*. New York: Norton.

Jencks, Charles (1996) *What is Post-Modernism?* (4th edn). Singapore: Academy Editions.

Kene, Sam (1991) *Fire in the Belly*. New York: Bantam.

Kozzin, Allan (1995) *The Beatles*. Singapore: Phaidon.

Lyotard, Jean-Francois (1992a) 'Answering the Question: What is Postmodernism?' in Patricia Waugh (ed.), *Postmodernism: a Reader*. London: Edward Arnold.

Lyotard, Jean-Francois (1992b) *The Postmodern Explained*. Minneapolis: University of Minnesota Press.

Mann, William (1988) 'The New Beatles Album', in *The Lennon Companion: Twenty-Five Years of Comment*. New York: Macmillan.

Mellers, Wilfrid (1973) *Twilight of the Gods: the Music of the Beatles*. New York: Viking.

O'Grady, Terence J. (1983) *The Beatles: a Musical Evolution*. Boston: Twane.

Okun, Milton (1986) 'To (Be)atles Or Not To (Be)atle', in *The Beatles Book*. Chicago: Omnibus Press.

Perloff, Marjorie (ed.) (1988) *Postmodern Genres*. Norman, OK: University of Oklahoma Press.

Robertson, John (1990) *The Art and Music of John Lennon*. New York: Birch Lane Press.

Riley, Tim (1988) *Tell Me Why: a Beatles Commentary*. New York: Vintage.

Russell, Jeff (1989) *The Beatles Album File and Complete Discography*. New York: Blandford.

Salewicz, Chris (1986) *McCartney*. New York: St Martin's.
Schaffner, Nicholas (1977) *The Beatles Forever*. Harrisburg, PA: Cameron House.
Taylor, Derek (1996) *The Beatles Anthology 3* (CD). Capitol Records.
Waugh, Patricia (ed.) (1992) *Postmodernism: a Reader*. London: Edward Arnold.
Wenner, Jann (1968) 'Beatles', *Rolling Stone*, 21 December : 10–13.
Wenner, Jann (1981) 'John Lennon' in Peter Herbst (ed.), *The Rolling Stone Interviews*. New York: St Martin's.
Wilde, Alan (1989) 'Postmodernism from A to Z', *Contemporary Literature*, **30**: 133–41.

# 7 You Can't Do That: The Beatles, Artistic Freedom And Censorship

## Martin Cloonan

At the end of the twentieth century, the Beatles' position as the most important popular music group of all time is virtually unchallenged. Critics seem to argue only about the relative merit of early and later works, rather than their overall importance. In Britain the country's most successful band, Oasis, constantly cite the Beatles and proudly carry the group's imprint in their work. Their former rivals, Blur, sought to distance themselves from Oasis via an eponymously-titled album whose debt to the Beatles is almost painfully obvious. Meanwhile, the Beatles themselves continue to earn vast sums of money each year from their back catalogue and seem to have found a new generation of fans with the *Anthology* albums.[1] In sum, the Beatles' legacy is almost undisputed.

Faced with such euphoria, it is hard to recall that the group was often opposed by various and powerful forces throughout its career. They were censored, saw their artistic freedom constrained, and were accused of being everything from capitalist dupes through satanists to communist conspirators. Universal acclaim was a long time coming. Thus, to explore their legacy fully it is necessary to look at those who came to bury the Beatles, as well as those who came to praise them.

This chapter explores that other side of the Beatles' legacy. It examines their struggle for artistic freedom; the attempts to censor them; and some of the accusations levelled against them. In doing so, it draws upon some of my earlier work,[2] and shows that the Beatles' story is in many ways a familiar one, in that the group was subject to censorship throughout the popular music-making process. However, it also argues that they simultaneously achieved greater artistic freedom than any previous British pop act. The chapter concentrates on censorship of the group, rather than of its individual members in their post-Beatle years.[3] It leans heavily on material from Britain and the United States, although other countries are not excluded.

The chapter falls into three sections. First, the Beatles' struggle for artistic freedom within the music industry is examined. The second part considers censorship outside the industry, but within the pop process. The third part identifies the various opponents and censors the group encountered.

## THE MUSIC BUSINESS AND ARTISTIC CONTROL

As I have noted before,[4] one of the most common, but least reported, occurrences of censorship comes at the point of production, when record companies decide not to release certain tracks. Such decisions can be taken for reasons ranging from alleged obscenity to lack of commercial potential. This form of censorship does not deny artists the opportunity to make music, but it does limit artistic freedom by ensuring that only certain types of music reach the public.

The struggle between label and artist for control of what is recorded and released is as old as the industry itself.[5] Control is censorship's alter-ego, and the battle for control over the destiny of their work certainly played an important role in the Beatles' story. In many ways their career trajectory – from a position of acting under orders (such as being told what clothes to wear by their manager) to one of near-total artistic control (such as spending hours in the studio at their employers' expense) is a considerable journey.

Even being initially signed to a label was a triumph; as Gillett notes, at the time it was rare for groups outside London to be offered a contract (1971: 262). Indeed, they had been turned down by Decca partly because the label thought it unlikely that any group from Liverpool could be successful nationally (MacDonald 1995: 38).

When the Beatles signed to EMI in 1962, it is fair to say that the industry was one in which artistic freedom was severely stifled. Singers typically sang songs written for them by others, and groups normally consisted of a leader and his backing group. Singles were regarded as the key to the market; albums contained merely the relevant singles and 'filler' material, and were made approximately every six months. Tours were a necessary duty, and a career as a pop star was almost unthinkable as there was such a rapid turnover of stars. Generally, pop stardom was seen as a temporary phase, after which came either a return to obscurity (as in the case of Terry Dene) or a step on the road to a career in showbiz (as exemplified by Cliff Richard).

But the Beatles were different. One of the pioneering aspects of their career was the way in which they managed to negotiate and overcome many of the obstacles to artistic freedom which characterized the industry at this point. They were unusual in having two songwriters within the group, which freed them from a reliance upon outside songwriters and simultaneously undermined EMI's control over them. They also played their own instruments and were thus less reliant on producers (Gillett 1983: 264):

> The Beatles' music was created under conditions that gave them a degree of artistic autonomy rare in the world of pop music. Because they wrote their own songs, they were free from the grip of hack songwriters and A&R men of the publishing industry. Because they accompanied themselves, producers had less power over how they sounded. Because they had served a long apprenticeship, and because they had tried out their songs in front of the audiences before recording them, they knew what made their music work better than producers and executives did. (Weiner 1985: 50)

The Beatles also knew what they wanted. Hardened by their Hamburg experiences, they would play the game only to a certain point. Thus they won producer George Martin over to the choice of 'Love Me Do' as their first single, from his preferred choice, Mitch Murray's 'How Do You Do It'.[6] The fact that both sides of that first single were self-composed emphasized from the beginning that there was something unusual about the group.[7] From this point on, there was a slow increase in the amount of control they were able to exert. Doubtless, the fact that their second single, 'Please Please Me', was a UK Number One[8] would have made EMI more confident in allowing the group increased freedom. This was reflected on their first album, *Please Please Me*, which contained an unprecedented eight self-composed songs. By their third album, *A Hard Day's Night*, they were writing the whole thing themselves.

Of course, this hardly meant total artistic control. Carr and Tyler report that in mid-1964 the Beatles often found themselves in the studio recording cover versions of US rock and roll songs as EMI was worried that they would either split or find their creativity drying up (1975: 29). The British EPs and the films *Help!* and *A Hard Days Night* can also generally be seen as attempts to milk a market, rather than to expand artistic endeavour.

The group was also constantly on the road in the early years;[9] subsequently they had limited time in the studio, with the result that tracks were issued which, under more ideal conditions, would have been re-recorded. There were also financial constraints. MacDonald asserts that 'Ask Me Why' is played too fast, but notes that 'at this stage the Beatles' production budget was too tight to allow for second thoughts' (1995: 47).

In August 1966 touring was abandoned and the group became studio musicians. By this point EMI was very aware of the huge sums of money the Beatles could make, and recording budgets were effectively ignored as the group was allowed as much time as it wanted to produce new material. The first album, *Please Please Me*, took 10 hours to record (MacDonald 1995: 47);[10] four years later, the song 'Strawberry Fields Forever' took 'an unprecedented 55 hours' (Ibid. 1995: 175). *Sgt Pepper's Lonely Hearts Club Band* took four months (Harker 1980: 35); 'A Day In The Life' alone accounted for 34 hours (MacDonald 1995: 183) and a George Harrison guitar solo which had taken seven hours to record was simply discarded (MacDonald 1995: 185). By the recording of *The Beatles*, studio time appeared to be of even less concern. Several tracks – 'Revolution 1' (40 hours), 'Revolution 9' (two days *prior* to studio recording), 'Ob-La-Di, Ob-La-Da' (42 hours), 'Sexy Sadie' (35 hours), 'While My Guitar Gently Weeps' (37 hours) – took perhaps unwarranted lengths of time to be completed.[11]

To some extent, the increased time can be accounted for by the drugs – LSD and cannabis[12] – the group was using in this period, and by the fact that the Beatles were becoming ever more interested in the possibilities that studio technology offered. However, that they were able to pay such attention to detail also shows how they were gaining control over the creative process. Of course, artistic freedom does not necessarily equate with artistic success. For this listener the undisciplined approach from *Sgt Pepper* onwards resulted in their later work being inferior to earlier work which had been produced under much stricter conditions.

Nevertheless, the Beatles did make important strides in the relative power that musicians had over the recording process. This raises the question of what such power actually meant. Chapple and Garofalo have been dismissive of the notion of artistic freedom, arguing that

> The amount of artistic control given to acts does not change [the] ... process of commoditization ... all that happens is that the artist has been integrated into the selling process in a more complete way. The fact that rock acts in the sixties received large advances and lucrative

contracts in comparison to a few years before did not change the industry in any fundamental way. (1977: 306)

They suggest that as one of the main concerns for a record company is the maintenance of a steady flow of material, it is quite willing to allow artistic freedom if this means that the products keep coming (Ibid.: 307).

Perhaps more damningly, Harker argues that the Beatles simply knuckled down to the demands of the industry – they wore the clothes they were told to, they diluted their music and they became thoroughly respectable in order to appeal to mums and dads and thus increase their earnings potential (1980: 84). He cites 'I Want To Hold Your Hand' as an example of their 'crassness' and return to 1950s morality, and concludes that the Beatles career does not illustrate the industry's ability to turn 'revolt into style' (Melly 1970), but rather 'the transition from amateur style to commercially successful style' (Harker 1980: 86). But while it is true that the Beatles did engage in the activity of money-making, this in itself did not conflict with their pursuit of artistic freedom. That they did not change the capitalist nature of the business is, in terms of pop, beside the point.[13] The Beatles' commercial success earned them unprecedented artistic freedom.[14]

But not total. As the group fell apart later, EMI sought to ensure that its most marketable commodity did not simply disappear. Thus the *Let It Be* album, a collection of old material, semi-finished songs, and out-takes was released in a format which pleased none of its contributors. Its most notorious example was McCartney's 'The Long And Winding Road' to which Phil Spector, as producer, added an orchestra and female choir without the consent of the song's writer. Nearly 30 years later, this still rankled McCartney.[15] George Harrison also found that a 30–piece orchestra had been added to his 'I Me Mine' without his knowledge. Thus the Beatles' artistic control, while greater than that of most of their contemporaries, was, to EMI, still very much secondary to its drive for profits.

But before this, perhaps the most obvious area in which the Beatles lacked control was over their US output. In the early days the problem was getting any output; their US label, the EMI subsidiary Capitol,[16] was reluctant to release anything, believing that the group appealed only to British audiences. Not until the fifth single, 'I Want To Hold Your Hand', did the label actively promote the Beatles. Its success encouraged Capitol then to release as much Beatles material as possible, and several albums appeared on the US market which were shorter versions of their British equivalents and/or compilations. Some of these albums barely stretched over 30 minutes. The Beatles had little, if any, say in this.

Another measure of the group's inability to control their output came with the cover of the US album, *The Beatles: Yesterday ... And Today*, a compilation of leftovers from *Rubber Soul* and earlier tracks, which was released in June 1966. Its original cover pictured the group dressed in butchers' aprons, holding pieces of meat and headless dolls. Initially Capitol accepted the cover, but the hostile reaction to preview copies from disc jockeys and others led the label to recall all the albums. Capitol employees then spent the weekend stripping 750 000 copies of the offending cover from the records and replacing them with an innocuous picture of the group posing around a trunk.[17]

*Time* called the cover 'a serious lapse in taste' (Weiner 1985: 17), while the British press blamed the joke on a temporary lapse following the group's visit to the USA (Stallings 1984: 150). Capitol hurriedly issued a statement apologizing for what it described as an 'attempt at pop satire', and in its defence, John Lennon maintained that the cover was as relevant as US involvement in Vietnam (Weiner 1985: 17). Evidence suggests that it was Lennon who was behind the 'butchers' cover (Stallings 1984: 150), and another of his ideas was also vetoed – that of having Adolf Hitler among the crowd on *Sgt Pepper* (MacDonald 1995: 250). The suggestion to similarly include Gandhi was overruled for fear of upsetting the Indian market (Martin and Segrave 1988: 187).

These disputes over covers show that the Beatles' artistic control was far from total, and provide examples of the various forms of self-censorship which the group exercised, such as the woman who was actually a 'prick teaser' in 'Day Tripper' becoming a 'big teaser' for the single's release (Miles 1997a: 20).

The group also sought to preserve its image as rockers, if not actual rebels. Plans for the release of 'Yesterday' as a single in the UK were abandoned on the grounds that it would harm their rock and roll image and that it would focus on McCartney at the expense of the others (Miles 1997a: 19). McCartney was anxious not to be seen as too political and so he vetoed Lennon's plan to release 'Revolution 1' as a single (MacDonald 1995: 229). These releases were self-censored in order to protect a certain image. A similar example was provided by 'Get Back'. An earlier version of this song exists on bootlegs where it is entitled 'The Commonwealth Song'. It was written as Ugandan Asians, expelled from that country by Idi Amin, began to arrive in

Britain. Apparently satirical, the lyrics refer to Pakistanis taking all the people's jobs and being told to get back to where they once belonged. Perhaps advisedly, by the time the single came to be released these lines had been replaced by references to dope-smokers and transexuals (MacDonald, 1995: 267).

Artistic control was more important to some Beatles than it was to others. Marcus has suggested that while McCartney was the pop craftsman, it was Lennon who was always more interested in using the music for genuine self-expression (Riley 1987: 262). This was not always welcome, especially in such cases as Lennon's insistence on singing 'Baby, you're a rich fag Jew', in apparent reference to Brian Epstein, on the track 'Baby, You're A Rich Man' (MacDonald 1995: 206). From an early stage, McCartney seemed more ready to play the game. On the group's 1963 Christmas Fan Club record, he announced that: 'We'll try to do everything we can to please you with the type of songs we write and record next year' (Riley 1987: 262). By the end of their career, however, it is clear that group members were less concerned about what the fans wanted. So in contrast to their earlier caution, they seemed willing to stretch the boundaries by, for example, including references to drugs, which they knew George Martin would not recognise. McCartney has suggested that this was a piecemeal process, saying of 'Day Tripper':

> This was getting towards the psychedelic period when we were interested in winking to our friends and comrades in arms, putting in references that we knew our friends would get but that the great British Public might not ... The mums and dads didn't get it but the kids did. 'Day Tripper' was to do with tripping ... that was one of the great things about collaboration, you could nudge-nudge, wink-wink a bit. (Miles 1997a: 20)

By nudge-nudging, the Beatles were able to talk about subjects generally considered inappropriate for popular music.[18] Again, this was not a total artistic freedom, but it did amount to some pushing back of boundaries. For example, while there is no swearing on Beatles' albums, Lennon was soon to make free use of expletives in his solo work; arguably, it was the Beatles who had laid the ground for such forms of expression by gently pushing against what were increasingly open doors. Thus the tendency for more open attitudes to sex and drugs within their songs not only engendered greater creative freedom for the group members themselves, but also for those who followed in their wake.

The desire for greater control can be seen at its most convincing in the Apple project. The Beatles' financial wrangles are not my concern here, but the various exploitations suffered by the group certainly form a backdrop to their decision to establish Apple in 1968. Apple had five divisions, including records, music publishing, films, electronics and retailing, and was intended as a benevolent enterprise to which those with ideas could apply for funding; thus, at the very heart of the project there were notions of greater artistic control. Idealistic and chaotic, within a year Apple was bleeding the Beatles dry financially. Their altruistic exercise to secure artistic autonomy for others went badly wrong as funds and equipment disappeared. Apple was subsequently slimmed down and reorganized, and by the late 1990s it was one of the most ruthlessly efficient record labels of all, jealously guarding the Beatles' legacy.[19] Apple is now a far cry from the original design, but it still signifies an attempt to seek artistic freedom and to escape from the business pressures which caused so much bitterness;[20] and it was, at the time, a giant step from the days when they obeyed Brian Epstein's orders about their appearance and behaviour on stage.

It was such restraints as these from which the Beatles ultimately managed to escape. Gaining greater control over the recording process, deciding not to tour, and gradually broadening their lyrical frontiers, allowed the group at least to present itself in ways which the Beatles themselves, rather than their label or manager, saw fit. This makes it hard to accept MacDonald's prognosis that

> The only significant aspect of pop the Beatles failed to change was the business itself. Acquiring possibly the only honest manager in Britain at the time (certainly the only one to vote Labour), they nevertheless ended their career together on the time-honoured killing-field of the contractual dispute. Twenty-five years after them, the commerce in this area continues to move in the traditional direction: into the bank accounts of the money men. (1995: 23)

This rather naïve 1960s-based critique of 'bread-heads' belies a more ambiguous result. It is true that the group saw little of the money they earned and that businessmen who write nothing continue to make more money out of popular music than many of its stars. Nevertheless McCartney remains one of the world's richest musicians, Yoko Ono collects Lennon's royalties, and Harrison and Starr are far from poor.

Furthermore the Beatles' achievement in terms of artistic freedom is considerable. They managed to change the *relative* power in the relationship between artist and industry. In their daily praxis most popular musicians relish artistic freedom above political clout, and it is such freedom which the Beatles constantly sought. Most musicians do not want to change the world beyond their own relatively narrow field, and it is within that field that the Beatles made their impact. Their pioneering work here should not be forgotten, regardless of the fact that it was based upon (unprecedented ) sales of popular music. The Beatles' commercial successes underpinned their artistic freedom, but they were at least *relatively* free. As their career progressed, they were able to exert ever greater control over the type of product which they released. However, as with all popular musicians (and other sellers), they had no control over what happened to their products once they reached the market. This forms the next part of the story.

## CENSORSHIP IN THE MARKETPLACE

Censorship can occur at any of the various stages after a record's release. The first step from the record company, after distribution, is to the retailers, who can decide not to stock selected records, but I am unaware of any examples of Beatles' records being boycotted by retailers.

The next step in the pop process is to the radio airplay, which is often crucial to a record's success; here, the group was certainly censored. The best-documented case in the UK is that of 'A Day In The Life', banned by the BBC in 1967 because of its references to drugs.[21] MacDonald (1995) refers to radio bans of 'Lucy In The Sky With Diamonds', 'Happiness Is A Warm Gun' and 'I Am The Walrus', but offers no evidence, and as the BBC does not release internal documents for 30 years, these alleged bannings are yet to be confirmed.[22] Thus, as far as I am aware, 'A Day In The Life' is the only Beatles' track to be banned by the BBC during the group's lifetime.

They faced greater problems on US radio, especially after remarks made by John Lennon in early 1966. In an interview to the journalist Maureen Cleave, he said: 'Christianity will go ... we're more popular than Jesus now ... Jesus was alright, but his disciples were thick and ordinary' (Sullivan 1987: 313). The remarks were initially printed in London's *Evening Standard* on 4 March 1966 as part of Cleave's article 'How Does A Beatle Live', where they provoked little comment. When reprinted in the US teen magazine *Datebook* in the summer, however, they caused outrage, particularly in the Bible Belt of the southern states.

I deal with this incident at greater length in the next section, and it is enough to note here that among the actions taken against the Beatles were radio bans by several US stations. The first organized protest took place in Birmingham, Alabama, where local disc jockey Tommy Charles encouraged protestors to throw Beatles' records into a giant tree-grinding machine; soon, 30 US radio stations had banned all Beatles records (Weiner 1985: 14). They were mainly in the southern states, but included stations in Boston, and New York's WABC, which had previously promoted the group strenuously. In Longview, Texas, KLUE organized a bonfire of Beatles records (Ibid.: 14), as did WAYX in Waycross, Georgia (Sullivan 1987: 313). Bans were also implemented in apartheid South Africa and Franco's Spain (Ibid.), some of which were lifted following an apology by Lennon in August.

Another US radio ban came in 1967 when Gordon McLendon, owner of 13 stations across the country, banned 'Penny Lane' from six of his stations. McLendon was at the time campaigning against 'raunchy lyrics' after one of his employees had complained that his nine-year-old daughter had been listening to the Rolling Stones' 'Let's Spend The Night Together'.

The group's use of religious imagery caused further problems in 1968, when the repeated use of the interjection 'Christ!' in 'The Ballad Of John And Yoko' offended some US radio stations, several of whom, including WABC and WMCA in New York, immediately banned the track.[23] So did WABI in Bangor, Maine, because, announced its operations chief, the record 'violates every rule of fair play and decency' (Martin and Segrave 1988: 181).

Bans continued long after the group's career had ended. In 1991 'Back In The USSR' was on BBC Local Radio's list of records to be excluded or treated with extreme caution for the duration of the Gulf War.[24] The following year, the *Liverpool Echo* (10 December 1992) reported that an unnamed Canadian oldies station had banned 'Run For Your Life' following complaints from women listeners that it incited violence against women.

The group's 'comeback' in 1995 also caused some controversy. At this point, BBC Radio 1 was restructuring in an attempt to attract a younger, hipper audience. However, it was also seeking to distinguish itself from commercial radio stations by treating pop as a cultural artefact. These two agendas did not always coincide and problems occurred with the Beatles' second 'new' single, 'Real Love'. Initially it appeared that Radio 1 would not include the track in its weekly playlist. This did not imply censorship – despite some press stories to that effect – but rather a view that the record was considered unworthy of extensive plays, which produced some outrage from Beatles' fans before the record was eventually playlisted.[25]

What the various bans show is that censorship is often tied to contemporary events. In 1967 there was a moral panic in Britain about the recreational use of soft drugs – hence the BBC's sensitivity to drug references and its decision to ban 'A Day In The Life'. Similarly, Lennon's remarks about Christ caused outrage in the Bible Belt because of the social and religious traditions there. The ban on 'Back in The USSR' was again influenced by contemporary events (the Gulf War), while the ban on 'Run For Your Life' perhaps reflected a new 'politically correct' atmosphere. Radio 1's reluctance to playlist 'Real Love' showed how time had moved on, and that even the Beatles could not assume automatic airplay for inferior product.

'Real Love' was tied in with the *Anthology* television series and it is television which provides the next stage for potential censorship in the pop process. Television also played an important part in the Beatles' career. In Britain, the group's appearance on ITV's prestigious *Sunday Night At The London Palladium* on 13 October 1963 was the 'official' start of Beatlemania (MacDonald, 1995: 62). Their appearance in the televised *Royal Variety Performance* on 4 December 1963 was another significant step in their career. In addition to publicly confirming their all-round appeal, it provided an example of a little self-censorship, as John Lennon eventually refrained from using the word 'fucking' in his exhortation that those in the expensive seats rattle their jewellery in time to the music (Lawton 1992: 109).

As the Beatles sought more control over their art, this was to include television projects. They were given free reign over the *Magical Mystery Tour* project by the BBC. Unfortunately, this was not their best work and was poorly received. It was to prove controversial in another way after Lennon's 'I Am The Walrus'[26] attracted the attention of moralist campaigner Mary Whitehouse, President of the National Viewers And Listeners' Association (NVALA), established by herself and others in 1965 to campaign for higher moral standards on television. Whitehouse was upset by the implications of the reference to knickers and was particularly concerned that *Magical Mystery Tour* was scheduled for broadcast on Boxing Day (26 December) 1967 by BBC1 during the early evening family viewing time. She urged the BBC's Chairman, Lord Hill, to agree with her that the song 'was most unsuitable for children's viewing' (Whitehouse 1977: 101) and to cancel the film. Hill, however, eventually backed a decision by the BBC's Director General, Sir Hugh Greene, to broadcast the programme as planned.

But although the Beatles survived the attempted censorship, the incident apparently caused a rift between Hill and Greene; the latter was to depart the BBC the following year with a feeling that his editorial independence was being undermined by such incidents. Whitehouse later claimed that the controversy over the song was the defining moment which led to Greene's resignation (1982: 65). Thus, an attempt to censor the Beatles may have played a significant role in the history of British television. In the US the group's success was specifically assisted by appearances on such programmes as the *Ed Sullivan Show*, and generally, television was more of a help than a hindrance to their career.

The next part of the pop process is the live arena; here the experiences of the Beatles were more ambiguous. Certainly their visits to Hamburg played a key role in making them the tight musical unit which they became, but the visits themselves also involved a kind of censorship, resulting from concerns over volume levels;[27] for this reason, in November 1960, they were banned from playing in the Indra Club and moved to the Kaiserkeller (MacDonald 1996: 303).

The group limited the amount of original material which it played in its early sets; indeed, the majority of the group's live act between 1957 and 1963 was cover versions. However, such gigs did give them chances to express themselves more freely than the tighter constraints of the recording studio provided. MacDonald reports that 'I Saw Her Standing There' would often last more than ten minutes when performed live, whereas the studio version had to be much reduced in order to fit the demands of radio-play (1995: 49).

Once Beatlemania took hold, any Beatles performance became the subject of concerns about public safety. The Beatles were never barred from performing in Britain, but after a 1963 gig at Glasgow Concert Hall resulted in damage to a number of chairs, the City treasurer, Richard Buchanan commented: 'This type of semi-savage conduct cannot be tolerated. There were one hundred seats damaged after the show, and it took 50 stewards and 40 policemen to keep the audience under control' (Martin and Segrave 1988: 130). City councillors then decided to cancel a forthcoming Gerry And The Pacemakers concert, and closely monitored all subsequent concert licence applications. By 1965, groups with a 'large and disorderly' following were banned from civic-owned halls in Glasgow (Ibid.: 130) – as a direct result of Beatlemania.

As noted earlier, touring demonstrated the lack of control over their career practised by the Beatles in their early days. However, the live shows were important in furthering that career, as was shown by the huge symbolic significance attached to their appearance at New York's Shea Stadium on 15 August 1965, which was to Beatlemania in the United States what the London Palladium performance was to Beatlemania in Britain.

But by 1966, it was clear to the Beatles that the endless touring had to end. They were becoming more aware of the possibilities which an improved technology and their own increased knowledge had created in the recording studio, but they were denied the time to explore these avenues. Moreover, much of the new music they were producing was impossible to perform live. Rather than permitting self- expression, live performances became a process of self-denial. Thus, although it involved no forms of censorship *per se*, the Beatles found the process of touring to be a severe form of restraint.

While it is true that the Beatles suffered less overt censorship during the pop process than some of their peers, such as the Rolling Stones and Frank Zappa, the occasions on which they were censored provide valuable insights into the era within which they worked. Likewise, the activities of those who opposed the group provide insights into the ideology of censorship.


THE CENSORS

In this section I examine various potential censors of popular music, and the role they played in the career of the Beatles. A recurring theme will be that those who attacked the Beatles often did so not on musical grounds, but because they believed the group to be represen- tatives of something else.[28] This echoes a familiar theme in the history of popular music, in which factors outside the music itself are often the cause for censorship.[29] The Beatles' critics did not generally want to ban the group, merely for their fans to come to their senses.

I have illustrated elsewhere[30] that organized pressure groups offer one of the most frequent opponents of popular music, but this was not always so for the Beatles. In Britain, it appears that the NVALA's opposition to 'I Am The Walrus' was the only example of opposition from a pressure group. However, in the USA there was organized opposition to Lennon's 'Christ' remarks from the Ku Klux Klan who picketed their Memphis show in August 1966. In South Carolina a Klan Grand Duke nailed Beatles' records to a cross (Martin and Segrave 1988: 179), and the journal of the far-right John Birch Society, *American Opinion*, frequently accused the Beatles of being communists (Sullivan 1987: 314, 323). In 1966 the same society sponsored a recorded telephone message in Indiana which railed against the 'potentially destructive process, harmonic dissonance and discord in the form of Beatle-type music' (Martin and Segrave 1988: 157–8), and warned that the communists had discovered how to use music for their own ends. One of the censors' tools is aesthetic critique[31] and this too was employed here, as the Beatles were denounced as 'musical trash ... inanity ... long-haired slobs who twang, screech and thump in a mixture of unrelated noise that would insult the ear of any self-respecting orangutan' (Ibid.: 158).

The group's main opponents, however, were various clerics. There is a long history of clerical intervention when aspects of popular culture, including popular music, have been deemed to be irreligious and/or sacrilegious.[32] Attacks on the Beatles came from numerous churches in the USA after Lennon's 'Christ' remarks. Reverend Thurmond Babbs of Cleveland, Ohio, threatened to excommunicate any of his flock who attended the group's forthcoming concerts (Street 1986: 15) and a number of protests were organized by religious leaders, which included incidents of burning their records.[33] In fact, Lennon's words are still used against the Beatles by fundamentalist Christian anti-rock campaigners: they are mentioned in Eric Holmberg's 1994 study guide on the dangers of rock and roll, 'Hell's Bells', and are also noted in British evangelist John Barnard's 1983 anti-rock treatise 'Pop Goes The Gospel'.[34]

The condemnation helped to make the Beatles' final tour of the USA by far their unhappiest one. Although Lennon did offer a half-hearted apology, the tour was characterized by half-filled stadiums, poor performances, and protests. In Memphis, demonstrations were led by Reverend Jimmy Shand, who organized a counter concert; the Vatican joined in the criticism of Lennon's remarks, although it did accept his apology; sales in Mexico suffered, and there were reports of burnings of Beatles' records there too (Martin and Segrave 1988: 179). However, some clerics defended the group. The Anglican Bishop of Montreal, Kenneth Maguire, pointed out that, in the only popularity contest held in his own time, Jesus came second to

Barabbas; and the Reverend Richard Pritchard of the Westminster Presbyterian church in Madison, Winconsin, commented that the outraged would do better to reflect upon their own standards and values (Sullivan 1987: 313).

Nevertheless, it was clear that for many clerics, Lennon's remarks had confirmed their worst fears about rock and roll – that it was a tool of the devil. One cleric who had already formed this opinion and who was to become possibly the most notorious anti-Beatles campaigner was the Reverend David A. Noebel of the Christian Crusade, an evangelical anti-communist group. In 1965 he toured California, lecturing on the perils of rock and roll, and in an interview with *Newsweek*, claimed that the Beatles were propelling US youngsters into an excited state in which they would do whatever they were told, and that when the revolution was ripe the communists would put the Beatles on television in order to hypnotise US youth (Sullivan 1987: 314). Noebel followed up this by publishing a pamphlet entitled 'Communism, Hypnotism And The Beatles', which was circulated within the John Birch Society. Essentially an attack on rock and roll, rather than the Beatles themselves, it claimed that the music was part of a Soviet plot to undermine US youth's ability to resist communism, and pleaded: 'let's make sure four mop-headed anti-Christ beatniks don't destroy our nation' (Martin and Segrave 1988: 157). Noebel claimed that Russian scientists had used artificial neurosis to break down animals, and that this was what the Beatles, and popular music generally, were now repeating (Sullivan 1987: 314). He argued that: 'The Beatles' ability to make teenagers take off their clothes and riot is laboratory tested and approved. It is scientifically labelled mass hypnosis and artificial neurosis' (Street 1986: 55).

His advice to fans was to put their Beatles' records into the city dump (Sullivan 1987: 315). Rock and roll was portrayed as a tool with which communists could undermine faith in God (Weiner 1985: 12). Following Lennon's remarks about Jesus, Noebel published another pamphlet, 'The Beatles: A Study In Drugs, Sex And Revolution'. This time, he argued that as the Beatles were as gods to teenagers, whatever they sanctioned would be followed by those teenagers; that in the name of art, rock and roll was glorying in drugs, sexual promiscuity and revolution; and that the Beatles were laying the foundations of communist revolution (Sullivan 1987: 317–18). A later work, 'The Marxist Minstrels', is notable for being the only anti-rock text quoted by Mary Whitehouse (1977: 37). Following Lennon's death in 1980, Noebel was to return with 'The Legacy Of John Lennon', which, unlike his previous works, was made available outside the John Birch Society. He believed Lennon's legacy to be the whole of contemporary rock and roll – characterized by the practice of sexual and social revolution, drugs and perversion (Sullivan 1987: 320); this work was favourably quoted in another anti rock text, Rob Mackenzie's 'Bands, Boppers And Believers', which also includes words of thanks to Noebel for his insights.[35]

Mackenzie also highlights another area of concern to Christian anti-rock campaigners – backmasking. This involves the insertion of subliminal messages into tracks, which seep into the listener's consciousness without his or her knowledge.[36] The Beatles have been attacked by many such writers for introducing backmasking into rock. Certainly by the late 1960s the band were experimenting with various methods of putting apparent nonsense – including backwards speech – on to tracks in a series of self-referential jokes and games with their audience. The significance of this for fundamentalist writers is that reciting things backwards is held to be a means of summoning the devil. Christian fundamentalist Jeff Godwin claims that the first track ever to use the technique was 'Rain' in March 1968, and that 'Lennon was the instigator of this whole backmasking mess we find ourselves in today' (1985: 156).

Barnard believes there were subliminal messages on 'A Day In The Life', which he decribes as 'a frightening drug trip song' (1983: 53) and, more plausibly, on 'Revolution 9', from *The Beatles*, an album criticized in many other texts. Aranza claims that the gibberish between 'I'm So Tired' and 'Blackbird' contains the message 'Paul is dead man, miss him, miss him' (1983: 7). And Mackenzie alleges that 'Ob La Di, Ob La Da' played backwards is 'I devil, he devil' (1987: 204).

Although most of these writers are from the Bible Belt, they do have their British adherents. Alex Maloney of the Elim Pentecostal Church runs Face The Music Ministries in Burton-on-Trent. One of its publications claimed: 'FACT: The Beatles were among the first to use this back recording technique and one of their songs played backwards says clearly, "Turn me on dead man, turn me on dead man" over and over again'; the tract went on to denounce the Beatles as 'one of the most anti-Christ groups ever' (Face The Music Ministries, no date). Skynner has argued that 'Helter Skelter' contains the message, 'I like Satan, yea ... and I always like the way you live', and that other songs – 'Revolution 9', 'I Am The Walrus' and 'Magical Mystery Tour' – contain backwards messages; he also notes that on the cover of *Yellow Submarine*, Lennon's character is making the 'Il

Corunto' sign of allegiance to the devil (The Truth About Rock, no date). And the allegations Maloney made about 'Revolution 9' (Face The Music Ministries 1989) are also acknowledged by secular commentators such as McIver (1988: 3) and Walker (1983: 2–3). Interpretation of backmasking then becomes the issue. For the Christian writers it is further proof of the Beatles' satanic inclinations; for the secularists it is merely a series of in-jokes.

Most bizarre of all is the claim that John Lennon's death was predicted just before his murder in the track 'Kiss Kiss Kiss' on *Double Fantasy*. This allegedly contains the lines 'we shot John Lennon' (Godwin 1985: 154). In fact, such writers continued to insist that the group were agents of satanism long after their career finished; and they found more apparent evidence in the group's 1995 'reunion', when it was reported that the 'new' single 'Free As A Bird' contained a few words of Lennon talking backwards (Doggett 1995: 12)

In most of these works, communism is equated with satanism and the Beatles are accused of being agents of both.[37] The texts present communism as a signifier of anything which is anti-Christian, and it is also used routinely as a term of abuse. Thus Godwin refers to 'communist needle junkie John Lennon' (1990:88) as a 'communist dopehead' (Ibid.: 204) and 'a drug abuser, wife beater, a heroin addict, a communist sympathiser, a habitual liar and a drunkard, not to mention being an adulterer and an arrogant, foul-mouthed blasphemer of Jesus Christ' (1988: 193).

Mackenzie notes that the band was praised by the communist press[38] (for 'Back In The USSR') and accuses Lennon of hypocrisy for promoting 'Marxist–Leninist propaganda' (1987: 77) while amassing a personal fortune. Godwin – perhaps the most vehement anti-rocker – opposes all rock and roll, claiming that his argument with the Beatles is not over their lyrics, but the spirit behind the music: Satan (1990: 31). His conviction that every imaginable sin was practised on their tours, that Satan gave them all that they wanted (1988: 69), that drugs were popularized by the Beatles and that the group was a tool of Satan (1988: 74), that 'Hey Jude' is about drugs (1988: 75), and that they made music under the influence of demons, which they unleashed on to others (Ibid.: 200–1) leads to his conclusion that 'Satan used these four sops more than any other group of morons to rewrite history' (1988: 199).

The Beatles' clerical opponents can thus be divided into two factions – cultural campaigners and lyrical campaigners (Sullivan 1987: 321), both of whom might be distinguished by their spectacular lack of success. But the fact that the group is now winning over new generations may well inspire them to even more concerted attacks in the future.

Perhaps the most powerful censors of all are politicians. Many popular musicians have encountered opposition and condemnation from British MPs,[39] but such was the success of the Beatles that political praise for them was widespread, beginning in 1963 from the Conservative prime minister, Alec Douglas Home. After the group began to earn export income, political support was further increased. When the new Labour prime minister, Harold Wilson, awarded MBEs to the Beatles in 1965, the move proved controversial, as many former servicemen returned their MBEs in protest.[40] The private diaries of cabinet minister Richard Crossman later revealed that he thought the decision to give the group their MBEs was justified as the Beatles were 'useful' to the government (Wheen 1982: 23).

The Beatles' respectability and courtship by the political establishment in the West contrasted sharply with their reception in Eastern Europe. In the Soviet Union a burgeoning generation gap was only widened by its youth's enthusiastic response to the Beatles (Troitsky 1987: 14). As illicit copies of their records made their way into the country, many imitation bands were formed, but by the mid-1960s there had been an official clampdown on all forms of popular music (Starr 1985: 295). In 1968, there came evidence that official Soviet attitudes towards the group were softening when, following a series of sarcastic attacks in the official press (Troitsky 1987: 18), the first positive article about them appeared in the magazine *Musical Life*. In the early 1970s the open sale of Beatles' records was allowed, subject to a title change from 'Back In The USSR' to 'Back In Old Russia' (Street 1986: 29). In 1986 their records went on sale officially (Martin and Segrave 1988: 248).

Elsewhere in the Soviet bloc the group also encountered opposition; in the German Democratic Republic in 1966 groups were instructed not to imitate the Beatles (Martin and Segrave 1988: 154). In China the reaction was even less favourable. In 1965 a Peking newspaper described the Beatles as 'monsters' who produced 'an unpleasant noise to satisfy the Western world's need for crazy and rotten music' (Ibid.: 155). Attacks in the East mirrored those in the West in that they were often based on perceptions of the Beatles as representatives of something else rather than criticisms of the group on its own merits.The group described as communist dupes in the West were portrayed as symbols of capitalist decadence in the East.

When they visited Japan in 1966, and performed in Tokyo at a national shrine to the war dead, 'a kamikaze squad of right-wing militant students accused the Beatles of perverting Japanese culture and threatened to kill them' (Martin and Segrave 1988: 155). And in 1964, it was reported that the Indonesian government had placed a ban on Beatle haircuts (*Vox*, February 1991: 61).[41]

In Eastern Europe official censorship was often backed up by attacks in the press – another key player in the censorship process. The Beatles experienced relatively few problems in winning over the British press. After their appearance in the *Royal Variety Performance* in November 1963 the *Daily Mirror* concluded that 'you have to be a real sour square not to love the nutty, noisy, happy, handsome Beatles', and in the same year *The Sunday Times* called Lennon and McCartney 'the greatest composers since Beethoven' (Wheen 1982: 23). The press also played its part in the creation of Beatlemania, loudly heralding its arrival after the London Palladium performance in October 1963. Press claims that between 500 and 1000 fans laid siege to the building were later discounted by the group's official photographer, Dezo Hoffman, who put the real number at around eight (Lawton 1992: 101). While the popular press concentrated on the personal and domestic novelty of the Beatles, such as Donald Zec's *Daily Mirror* article in which, after taking tea with the group, he described them as 'four incomprehensible voices drowned by their own self-inflicted 240–volt amplification' (Ibid.: 108), the quality press was more concerned to discover the secret of their success. *The Sunday Times* announced:

> Sexual emancipation is a fact in the phenomenon, though at the superficial level this may not be important. 'You don't have to be a genius', said a consultant in a London hospital, 'to see parallels between sexual excitement and the mounting crescendo of … a stimulating number like "Twist and Shout" … but I think it is the bubbly, uninhibited gaiety of the group that generates enthusiasm'. (Booker 1970: 217)

In contrast, the Beatles found the US press less positive:

> The music was ridiculed along with the haircuts. 'The Beatles apparently could not carry a tune across the Atlantic,' the *New York Herald Tribune* wrote after their appearance on *The Ed Sullivan Show* in 1964. *The New York Times* found their music 'a fine mass placebo'. (Weiner 1985: 20)

Lennon later complained that they were often forced to meet people – such as the daughters of local dignitaries – in order to prevent vicious stories appearing about them (Ibid.: 18). This was very different from their relationship with the British press. George Melly's review of Lennon's *In His Own Write* for *The Sunday Times* traced Lennon's roots through Carroll, Klee, Thurber, the Goons and Joyce (Booker 1969: 235). The music critic of *The Times*, William Mann, gloried in the group's 'pandiatonic clusters' and 'flat-mediant key switches', and although Lennon later described this as 'bullshit', he also noted that Mann gave the group credibility amongst intellectuals (Wheen 1982: 23).

However, not all intellectuals were convinced, and one of the most savage attacks on the Beatles came from Paul Johnson. Writing in the left-wing *New Statesman*, he referred to the group's fans as 'the least fortunate of their generation, the dull, the idle, the failures: their existence, in such large numbers … is a fearful indictment of our educational system' (1964: 327). His characterization of the fans as fodder for exploitation raised what was to become a common theme of pop critics – manipulation of a hapless young audience by cynical older businessmen.[42] The same journal also published a letter from a teacher in 1965, claiming that the Beatles were turning his pupils into homosexuals (Laurie 1965: 102).

By 1976, it had become evident that something of a pop canon had formed, with the Beatles at the forefront of it. It was ironic that when punk rock appeared, one of the ways in which *it* was attacked was through comparisons with the Beatles; Simon Usher could write in the *Daily Mail*: 'Unlike the Beatles, good enough to take root in the hearts and minds of every generation, punk rock is poor, ungainly, derivative and quite simply no good' (1976: 6) In this way, the Beatles were used to represent an earlier golden age of pop, illustrating and emphasizing that although the press has created problems for many performers,[43] this has generally not been so for the Beatles.

While the press is the last potential censor of popular music, there are other potential, and actual, critics. Certainly, the references to drugs in the Beatles' later work resulted in such criticism. And in 1968, with political uprisings across Europe, the Soviet invasion of Czechoslovakia, and the Civil Rights struggle and war in Vietnam dividing the USA, the principal question raised by the release of *The Beatles* was, for many, the status of the group's contemporary relevance. Cohn was among those who accused the group of pretentiousness (1969: 137). Similarly, MacDonald has cited *Magical Mystery Tour* as not only an artistic failure, but a mark of

> the breakdown of the cross-generational consensus on them, established in 1964 by *A Hard Day's Night*. Notwithstanding McCartney's eagerness to please, this is where parents began to part company with their sons and daughters over the group, rightly suspecting a drug-induced pretension setting in. (1995: 240)

Thus, in addition to their censors, the Beatles also had their critics – a point to remember when today their status in popular music is universally recognized. It was not ever thus.

## NOTES

1. Buckingham (1995) notes Apple's report that 40 per cent of those buying the *Anthology* albums were teenagers.
2. Cloonan (1996).
3. For various bans on post-Beatles work, see bibliographies in Cloonan (1996) and Martin and Segrave (1988).
4. Cloonan (1996: 41).
5. For insights into the internal decision-making process of record companies, see Negus (1992).
6. MacDonald (1995: 41); however, the group was unable to insist that Ringo Starr should play on the track, and early versions of the single feature session drummer Andy White.
7. Compare this with the Rolling Stones, who had to wait until their sixth release, 'The Last Time', before they issued a self-written single; this was some 20 months into their recording career.
8. Because there was no standardized chart at the time, 'Please Please Me' was not Number One in all of the UK charts. See MacDonald (1995: 460).
9. MacDonald (1995: 96, 106, 170).
10. Carr and Tyler (1975: 16) say the recording took 16 hours.
11. All timings taken from MacDonald (1995).
12. MacDonald (1995: 205).
13. This is hardly to deny that it is an important *political* point. My argument is that the Beatles were able to explore pop's potential to a far greater extent than had previously been possible. All the time (and this is the key point) they were earning money for EMI, their artistic freedom was *comparatively* broad.
14. There is a relationship between the commercial status of an act and the amount of artistic freedom it is likely to enjoy, but it is simplistic merely to equate the two. A certain amount of bloody-mindedness is also

necessary. The career of Elvis Presley provides a stark example of how commercial success did *not* engender artistic freedom; the career of the Beatles, on the other hand, shows how it did.

15. Miles (1997c: 15).
16. Capitol was the main label to release Beatles' records in the USA, but the group also appeared on four other labels (Chapple and Garofalo 1977: 249).
17. Stallings (1984: 150).
18. See, for example, the attacks made against pop songs – including 'With A Little Help From My Friends' – by US Vice President Spiro Agnew (1972).
19. Davidson (1995), Donegan (1995) and Sweeting (1995).
20. See, for example, Lennon's accounts of rip-offs (Wenner 1971: 154) and McCartney's own bitter recollections (Miles 1997b).
21. See Cloonan (1996: 122), MacDonald (1995: 199), Melly (1970: 114) and Street (1986: 114). MacDonald (1995: 336) dates the ban from 20 May 1967, 12 days *before* the release of *Sgt Pepper*.
22. Cloonan (1996: 133–4).
23. Martin and Segrave (1988:180) also mistakenly claim that this track was banned by the BBC.
24. Cloonan (1996: 118–20),
25. *Guardian* 8 March and 12 March 1996.
26. See, for example, Martin and Segrave (1988: 189) and MacDonald (1995: 214).
27. Cloonan (1996: 184).
28. This was also true of those who defended the group: see, for example MacDonald (1995: 1–34).
29. Cloonan (1996: 30).
30. Ibid. (217–34).
31. Ibid. (28–9).
32. Ibid. (235–57) and Martin and Segrave (1996: 177–84).
33. Sullivan (1987).
34. Ibid. (323).
35. Mackenzie (1987). For more recent support of Noebel, see Godwin (1990).
36. Cloonan (1996: 248–51), McIver (1988) and Walker (1983).
37. Elvis Presley also accused the group of being communists when he met President Nixon in 1970. He told Nixon that the Beatles had fostered an anti-American spirit (Densclow 1989: 122).
38. In Britain, the *Daily Worker* claimed that: 'The Mersey sound is the voice of 80 000 crumbling houses and 30 000 people on the dole' (Carr and Tyler 1975: 20).
39. Cloonan (1996: 273–83).
40. Martin and Segrave (1988: 118–19).
41. A similar ban was imposed in Britain at Clarks Grammar School, Guildford, which banned Beatle haircuts on the grounds that it made boys look effeminate and moronic (Lawton 1992: 16).
42. Cloonan (1996: 27–8).
43. Ibid. (259–70).

## REFERENCES

Agnew, Spiro (1972) 'Talking Brainwashing Blues', in R. Denisoff and J. Peterson (eds), *The Sounds of Social Change*. Chicago: Rand McNally.

Aranza, Jacob (1983) *Backward Masking Unmasked*. Shreveport, Louisiana: Huntington House.

Barber, Nicholas (1995) 'The Old Kids', *Independent On Sunday Magazine*, 19 November: 22–3.

Barnard, John (1983) *Pop Goes the Gospel*. Welwyn: Evangelical Press.

Booker, Christopher (1969) *The Neophiliacs*. London: Collins.

British Broadcasting Corporation (1981) *The Lennon Tapes*. London: BBC Publications.

Brooks, Richard (1992) 'How "Love Me Do" Nearly Spun Its Way to Flipside of Beatle History', *Observer*, 4 September : 3.

Buckingham, Lisa (1995) 'New Fans Put Beatles on Track to a Record', *Guardian*, 22 October: 2.

Carr, Roy and Tony Tyler (eds) (1975), *The Beatles: an Illustrated Record*. London: New English Library.

Chapple, Steve and Reebee Garofalo (1977) *Rock and Roll is Here to Pay*. Chicago: Nelson Hall.

Clarke, Donald (1995) *The Rise and Fall of Popular Music*. London: Penguin.

Cloonan, Martin (1996) *Banned!* Aldershot: Arena.

Cohn, Nik (1969) *Awopbopaloobop Alopbamboom*. London: Weidenfeld & Nicolson.

Davidson, Andrew (1995) 'Money, That's What I Want', *Independent On Sunday Magazine*, 28 October: 11–12.

Denselow, Robin (1989) *When the Music's Over*. London: Faber.

Doggett, Peter (1995) '1995: John Lennon Sings Again', *Independent On Sunday Magazine*, 28 October: 12.

Donegan, Lawrence (1995) 'Another Bite of the Apple', *Guardian* 21 November: 2.

Face the Music Ministries (1989) *Backmasking*. Burton-on-Trent: Face the Music Ministries.

Face the Music Ministries (no date) *Rock Music: The Truth Behind It*. Burton-on-Trent: Face the Music Ministries.

Gillett, Charlie (1971) *The Sound of the City*. London: Souvenir.

Godwin, Jeff (1985) *The Devil's Disciples*. Chino, Calif.: Chick.

Godwin, Jeff (1988) *Dancing with Demons*. Chino, Calif.: Chick.

Godwin, Jeff (1990) *What's Wrong with Christian Rock?* Chino, Calif.: Chick.

Harker, Dave (1980) *One for the Money*. London: Hutchinson.

Holmberg, Eric (1994) *Hell's Bells: the Dangers of Rock and Roll*. Gainesville: Reel To Reel Ministries.

Johnson, Paul (1964) 'The Menace of Beatlism', *New Statesman*, 18 February: 326–7.

Kureishi, Hanif and Jon Savage (eds) (1995) *The Faber Book of Pop*. London: Faber.

Larson, Bob (1988) *Larson's Book of Rock*. Wherton, Ill.: Tyndale House.

Laurie, Peter (1965) *Teenage Revolution*. London: Anthony Bland.

Lawton, John (1992) *1963*. London: Hodder & Stoughton.

MacDonald , Ian (1995) *Revolution in the Head*. London: Pimlico.
McIver, Tom (1988) 'Backward Masking and other Backward Thoughts', *The Skeptical Enquirer*, **13**(1): 194–231.
Mackenzie, Rob (1987) *Bands, Boppers and Believers*. Harare: Campaign For Cleaner Rock.
Martin, Linda and Kerry Segrave (1988) *Anti-Rock*. Hamden, Conn.: Archon.
Melly, George (1970) *Revolt Into Style*. London: Allen Lane.
Miles, Barry (1997a) 'Yesterday Part 1: McCartney and Lennon', *Observer, Life Magazine*, 14 September 1997: 15–27.
Miles, Barry (1997b) 'Yesterday Part 2: Love, Love, Love', *Observer, Life Magazine*, 21 September 1997: 14–23.
Miles, Barry (1997c) 'Yesterday Part 3: Without the Beatles', *Observer, Life Magazine*, 28 September 1997: 12–21.
Negus, Keith (1992) *Producing Pop*. London: Edward Arnold.
Palmer, Tony (1977) *All You Need is Love*. London: Futura.
Riley, Tim (1987) 'For the Beatles: Notes on their Achievement', *Popular Music*, **6**(3): 257–71.
Skynner, Robert (no date) *The Truth About Rock*. London: Apolistic Ministries.
Stallings, Penny (1984) *Rock'n'Roll Confidential*. London: Vermillion.
Starr, S. Frederick (1985) *Red and Hot*. New York: Limelight.
Street, John (1986) *Rebel Rock*. Oxford: Blackwell.
Sullivan, Mark (1987) 'More Popular than Jesus: the Beatles and the Religious Far Right', *Popular Music*, **6**(3): 313–26.
Sweeting, Adam (1995) 'Let It Be – Again', *Guardian*, 18 October: 2–4.
Troitsky, Artemy (1987) *Back in the USSR*. London: Omnibus.
Usher, Simon (1976) 'The Mercenary Manipulation of Pop', *Daily Mail*, 3 December: 6.
Walker, M. M. (1983) 'Backward Messages in Commercially Available Recordings', *Popular Music and Society*, **10**(1): 2–13.
Weiner, Jon (1985) *Come Together*. London: Faber.
Wenner, Jann (1971) *Lennon Remembers*. London: Penguin.
Wheen, Francis (1982) *The Sixties*. London: Century.
Whitehouse, Mary (1977) *Whatever Happened to Sex?* Hove: Wayland.
Whitehouse, Mary (1982) *A Most Dangerous Woman?* Tring: Lion.
Wroe, Martin (1995), 'Strawberry Fields for Ever and Ever ...', *Observer*, 24 September: 16–17.

# 8 Tell Me What You See: the Influence and Impact of the Beatles' Movies

Bob Neaverson

Television tour documentaries apart, the Beatles starred in or otherwise contributed to a total of five films: *A Hard Day's Night* (1964), *Help!* (1965), *Magical Mystery Tour* (TV movie, 1967), *Yellow Submarine* (1968) and *Let It Be* (1969, released 1970). Given that the group's first album was only released in 1963 and that they had effectively ceased to function as a unified creative force by 1970, that represents a considerable tally. Yet in the wake of their glorious recording career, the Beatles movies (and, for that matter, their promotional films) have been largely overlooked by the critical establishment. While some would maintain that this is not particularly surprising (the Beatles were, after all, primarily a recording outfit), their comparative neglect within film history has not been aided by the group's own reluctance to discuss the films, poor availability in the home video market,[1] and the auteurist bias which still pervades much film history. The only two Beatles films which receive serious discussion are *A Hard Day's Night* and *Help!*, both directed by Richard Lester. I find this situation dismaying – not because I believe that the films reveal a group of great dramatic virtuosity (although Ringo isn't half bad in *A Hard Day's Night*) or that they should somehow be 'reclaimed' as 'classics'. (While I do believe that the films deserve reassessment, I'm not interested in entering into futile debates about what does or does not constitute a film's 'classic' status.) Rather, it is dismaying partly because the Beatles films constituted a vital part of the group's success in Britain and the USA and, perhaps more importantly, because they have exerted an enormous influence over subsequent pop musicals and videos. From a broader perspective, the films were also important to the sustained US investment in British cinema of the 1960s. For the most part, however, they seem almost to have been written out of history, revered by fans yet acknowledged only in passing by the majority of film historians and music journalists, and rarely investigated or discussed in any depth. In this chapter I want to

look at them in some detail, through a consideration of the importance and influence of the Beatles' film-making ventures from both
formal and ideological perspectives.

In what ways were films important to the Beatles' career? From a
purely pragmatic (economic) perspective, making films for interna
tional distribution was the easiest and most cost-effective way to
ensure consistent global exposure and generate maximum box office
and/or television exhibition revenue. Film production provided a
more efficient means of public exposure than touring or making
exclusive television appearances throughout the world, and was ultimately far less time-consuming for a group of the Beatles' global
popularity.The commercial importance of making films became
considerably accentuated in the wake of their unwillingness to tour
after their final concert in San Francisco's Candlestick Park on 29
August 1966. Moreover, by 1966 they had all but given up making
television appearances as a means of plugging single releases,
choosing instead to supply television stations with their own self-
produced promo clips. Although the aesthetic lineage of contemporary pop video can arguably be traced back to the animated shorts of
Oskar Von Fischinger, the Beatles were certainly pioneers of the
independently produced pop promo, and from 1965 onwards a
considerable number of the group's releases were accompanied by
promotional films. The production of feature films and promos therefore became of paramount importance from the mid-1960s, and the
establishment of Apple in 1968 was partly dedicated to this end,
including, amongst its many departments, a film division headed by
production executive Denis O'Dell, who had previously worked with
the group as associate producer of *A Hard Day's Night*.

As well as acting as an intrinsic source of box office revenue, the
films also facilitated the sales of a number of other licensed tie-in
products external to the cinema-going experience. Schatz has examined the rise of this trend, and endorsed the notion that a contemporary hit movie such as *Batman* is 'best understood as a multi-market,
multi-media sales campaign' (1993: 32). While he correctly sees this
ongoing trend as influenced by the enormous synergetic success of the
1970s Hollywood blockbusters (particularly those of Spielberg and
Lucas), the exploitation of tie-in merchandising is neither a new nor
exclusively American phenomenon, and although obviously primitive
by comparison to today's slickly engineered 'high concept' pictures, it
is also possible to view the Beatles movies as multi-marketing tools,
designed, at least in part, to generate substantial profit beyond box

office returns. Indeed, while sales of recordings and sheet music were obviously highest on the agenda (United Artists agreed to finance *A Hard Day's Night* largely in order to obtain soundtrack rights), there were a considerable number of other licensed film-related products marketed – particularly in the case of *Yellow Submarine*, which boasted jigsaws, Halloween costumes, alarm clocks, mobiles, and, of course, Corgi's recently revived die-cast replicas. Although the Beatles movies can hardly lay claim to originating this exploitative approach, they were, like the ever-popular Bond films, certainly important forerunners.

How did the films 'work' upon their audience? From a purely ideological perspective, the movies were obviously – and successfully – used to develop and confirm the Beatles' worldwide popularity. Perhaps more than any other broadcast media, their films were vital in communicating and showcasing the group's ever changing array of images, attitudes, ideas and musical styles. As well as re-affirming their recently aquired international status as recording artists, *A Hard Day's Night* helped to disseminate their then current visual 'look' to a global audience, and to develop their identities as four individuals (rather than a 'four-headed monster') who were by turns amusing, witty, sarcastic, profound and compassionate. In short, it imbued them with the individual personae so vital to the star-audience relationship, which were developed, in a variety of different guises, in their subsequent cinematic outings. While their early identities were to some extent consolidated in the fiction fantasy of *Help!*, their next film, the self-directed (and much criticized) *Magical Mystery Tour* crystallized their newly constructed roles as psychedelic figureheads of the emerging counter-culture. This was again consolidated, albeit in a somewhat more accessible and sentimental manner, by the benevolent and peace-loving cartoon caricatures of *Yellow Submarine*, while *Let It Be* documented a group of taciturn philosophers who, having turned the full musical circle, were now in an advanced state of personal and, to some extent, professional decay. Although the group had achieved a remarkable amount of international success prior to its forays into film, my suspicion is that the phenomenon of Beatlemania could not and would not have been either as substantial or as durable without the identificatory process afforded by cinema.

However, as well as serving an important role within the Beatles' own career, the films have also generated a broader influence. Economically and stylistically, the success of *A Hard Day's Night* and

*Help!* yielded considerable impact inside the British and US film and television industries. The international success of *A Hard Day's Night* contributed greatly to the influx of US capital into British film production throughout the 1960s, and the collective impact in that country of other successful US investments such as the Bond films and *Tom Jones* (1963) 'changed attitudes towards Britain, fostering a belief that London, rather than Paris or Rome or Hollywood, was the place in the world to make a film' (Murphy 1992: 114). In fact, by 1967, around 90 per cent of British productions had some US backing. Consequently, this investment made a major impact upon the ever increasing production and distribution of British pop musicals and, in turn, upon the increasing profitability of the British recording industry in other territories, particularly the USA. 'The influx of American money and interest in Britain coincided with an unprecedented explosion of British popular music, the Beatles spearheading "the British invasion" of the US and Beatlemania signifying the power of the new pop music culture' (Donnelly 1997).

Although the British Invasion was beginning to take place (through the Beatles) before either they or any other British act had produced a successfully exportable film, it is certainly true that the group's first two films, together with such imitative productions as John Boorman's *Catch Us If You Can* (1965), which starred the Dave Clark Five,[2] played a significant, yet frequently overlooked, role in the dissemination of British pop throughout the USA. Despite the increasingly concentrated and integrated nature of the contemporary media, there has always been something of a symbiotic relationship between the film and record industries, so much so that without the popularity of *A Hard Day's Night* and the subsequent imitations which its success encouraged, the British music industry might never have attained the commanding position it did in the USA or, for that matter, have retained it within its homeland. This may be a contentious issue, but it is a general truism that the national 'flattery' of winning over foreign endorsement (especially in the USA) frequently functions as a promotional stimulus for domestic audiences, and *A Hard Day's Night* was certainly central to the consolidation of the Beatles' and, by implication, the British pop industry's international approval abroad.

As well as compounding the success of the British Invasion and heralding a clutch of copycat movies, the first two Beatles films also exerted an important and lasting influence upon British and US television. The most emphatic demonstration of this was *The Monkees* television show which, from its inception in 1966, shamelessly exploited the style of the Lester movies, and featured a four-piece 'bubblegum' pop group whose coldly manufactured 'zaniness' was blatantly modelled on the Beatles' early presentation.

While the Monkees came and (quickly) went, the most lasting legacy of Richard Lester's Beatles movies has been their formal influence upon the visual language and aesthetic values of the pop video. Prior to *A Hard Day's Night*, the majority of British and US pop musicals had relied upon the long-established tradition of song performance derived from the classical Hollywood musical. In the contemporaneous vehicles of Elvis Presley and Cliff Richard, the genre's central musical sequences were inevitably based around the presentation of lip-synched 'performances' of songs by a solo singer which, often combined with minimal onscreen backing sources (in the case of the Presley cycle, his guitar), essentially attempted to articulate the illusion of 'real', diegetic performance. Although such performances were usually, and often necessarily, accompanied by non-diegetic backing (the 'unseen' accompaniment), the underlying importance of this aesthetic was to reproduce the illusory spectacle of performance, as if to reassure the audience of the artist's 'authenticity'. *A Hard Day's Night* changed all that, and was arguably the first film of its genre to fully realize the *illustrative* potential of pop music. While the movie does include a good quota of more conventional 'performances', the 'Can't Buy Me Love' sequence midway through the narrative (which marries the song with footage of the group cavorting in a playing field) broke entirely with conventional approaches and, in the process, freed the musical number from its traditional generic slavery. Lester – perhaps prompted by his own surreal humour – allowed the pop song the opportunity to work in a similar manner to that of conventional incidental music, as an abstract entity capable of emotionally punctuating action which is not tied to performance.

This realization formed an important aesthetic precedent for subsequent pop musicals (including those of the Beatles), and, perhaps most significantly, pop video, which the group itself helped to pioneer from 1965 with the semi-diegetic promos shot by Joe McGrath for 'I Feel Fine', 'Day Tripper', 'We Can Work It Out', 'Ticket To Ride' and 'Help!'. The McGrath promos are important for two reasons. Financed by the Beatles' management agency, NEMS, they were the first independently produced pop promos made specifically for international distribution, thus pre-empting the arrival of the contemporary pop video age. Additionally, their style also anticipated that of contemporary video in their rejection, and partial mockery, of the conventional performance aesthetic favoured by TV shows such as *Top Of The Pops* and *Top Beat*. Although it would be unfair to suggest that they reject performance out of hand (all feature lip-synching), they do seem determined to break from the 'realism' of ordinary 'TV show' performance; they are shrewdly prepared to trade the 'authenticity' of credible performance for visual dynamics, via the non-diegetic positioning of Starr (in 'I Feel Fine' he rides an exercise bicycle, in 'Help!' he wields an umbrella), and the knowing delight the others take in deliberately mistiming their cues. However, the totally illustrative and conceptual use of music pioneered by Lester in *A Hard Day's Night* was developed later by other pop movies and promos and, of course, by the Beatles themselves; *Magical Mystery Tour* contained a number of conceptual musical sequences, and Lester's influence was again apparent in the promos of Michael Lindsay-Hogg and Swedish director Peter Goldmann, whose 'Strawberry Fields Forever' and 'Penny Lane' were wholly conceptual. Without the initial break with performance heralded by *A Hard Day's Night* and *Help!* the history of pop video could well have developed along very different avenues; and it is plausible to suggest that had the illustrative potential of the medium never been realized, the existence of the pop promo might easily have been condemned to an obscure footnote in histories of 1960s television. In this sense the Lester movies established an aesthetic precedent which was to become central to a medium external to that from which they evolved.

Although critically slated in its day, *Magical Mystery Tour* has also been inspirational in its own ways. As well as its importance to the development of pop video, the film's radical rejection of conventional narrative logic helped to establish a precedent for later pop movies such as the Monkees' *Head* (1968), Frank Zappa's self-directed *200 Motels* (1971), the Who's *Tommy* (1975) and Led Zeppelin's *The Song Remains The Same* (1976). But as Medhurst has noted:

> The sacrificing of narrative also meant the sacrificing of audiences as the Beatles found to their cost with the bemused and hostile reaction which greeted *Magical Mystery Tour*. Yet after this radical mid-sixties break, there was no going back to the more accessible naiveties of *Live It Up* (1963) or *The Golden Disc* (1958). Not, that is, if the films were to have any shred of credibility. (1995: 68–9)

Perhaps, then, the film's single greatest achievement is that it played a key role in de-institutionalizing a genre which, to all intents and purposes, had been enslaved by the essentially conventional narrative form and predominantly conformist morality of previous pop musicals.

However, apart from its pivotal role in radicalizing the aesthetics of its genre, one might also argue that here too the formal and generic properties of *Magical Mystery Tour* influenced, or at least pre-dated, other genres of film and television. MacDonald, who like Medhurst is one of the few critics to recognize (albeit in passing) the film's importance, sees it as a prototype of the road movie genre which was inaugurated with the release of Dennis Hopper's *Easy Rider* (1969) at the end of the decade (1994: 204). Its links with British television of the late 1960s and early 1970s can also be seen; for example, elements of the film anticipated the style of comedy series such as *Marty* (1968–9) and *Monty Python's Flying Circus* (1969–74). If instances of *Magical Mystery Tour*'s surreal humour were inspired by programmes such as *At Last The 1948 Show* (written in part by pre-Python fledglings John Cleese and Graham Chapman), it might also be fair to acknowledge the formal influence of the Beatles' film upon the Pythons. This is particularly evident in the second series of *Monty Python's Flying Circus* (1970), in which the constant use of the non-diegetic insert of the applauding crowd seems directly lifted from *Magical Mystery Tour*. Terry Gilliam's inventive surreal animation is very reminiscent of that used in both *Magical Mystery Tour* and *Yellow Submarine*; and the 'Blackmail' sketch makes exactly the same use of the animated 'Censored' sign as does *Magical Mystery Tour*'s strip club sequence. Some years later, when the Python team had branched into full-length features, the Beatles' influence remained apparent – the grotesquely amusing exploding gourmand sketch in *The Meaning Of Life* (1983) recalls Aunt Jessie's spaghetti shovelling dream sequence. That elements of the Beatles' film should have influenced the Pythons is perhaps unsurprising, and in the years following their split, various members of the group have supported or collaborated with the comedy team. Ringo Starr made a brief cameo appearance in a 1972 edition of the show and George Harrison's film production company, Handmade, was responsible for financing a number of Python-related projects. The most notorious of these was their Biblical satire *The Life Of Brian* (1979), which the ex-Beatle rescued from abandonment when the subject matter proved too controversial for EMI, the film's original financiers. Harrison also appeared fleetingly in Eric Idle's spoof documentary *The Rutles* (1978), which also featured acutely observed compositions by Neil Innes who, as a key member of the Bonzo Dog Band, had himself made a guest appearance in *Magical Mystery Tour*.

Similarly, the influences exerted by *Yellow Submarine* are no less important. As well as colouring the eclectic iconography of Gilliam's animation and proving a remarkably successful forerunner to today's product-orientated blockbusters, its chief contribution to British film culture lay in fostering a new subculture that Mark Langer has called 'animatophilia' (Sharman 1994: 15). In tracing the film's influences, Sharman has argued that it was instrumental in popularizing animation within art-house exhibition inasmusch as its success encouraged programmers to buy in independent animated shorts which would otherwise have remained largely unseen outside the festival circuits. In addition, the interest garnered by the film instigated a boom in animation production which resulted in *Yellow Submarine*'s production studio, TVC, becoming 'one of the first large-scale training grounds for young filmmakers, including Diane Jackson, who was later to make *The Snowman*' (Ibid.: 15).

It is thus rather ironic that the Beatles' most 'decorated' film, the Oscar-winning *Let It Be*, should, in some ways, be the most formally derivative. If the animated pop musical feature that was *Yellow Submarine* can be described as one of the most original and adventurous British films of the1960s, then the lineage of the Beatles' final film is much easier to discern, its minimalist verite approach clearly evoking the American direct cinema of Richard Leacock, the Maysles and D. A. Pennebaker, whose masterpiece, the evergreen *Don't Look Back* (1967), has had a huge influence over the pop documentary. What *Let It Be* lacks in originality however, it more than makes up for in voyeuristic magnetism. Although it is alone in having thus far bypassed a British home video release, it is in some respects the most absorbing of the five Beatles films through its fly-on-the-wall approach which provides a fascinating, if harrowing (and flawed), insight into the group's personal and musical relationships as Lennon, McCartney, Harrison and Starr struggle desperately to find a new direction. This interest was certainly not lost on contemporary fans, who flocked to cinemas despite the general hostility of press reviews. Today the film's cultural status rests largely on its claim to 'historical significance' as the only extensive footage of the group in rehearsal/studio mode. Stripped of this trump card, one suspects that the film would not command the same degree of reverence amongst the new generations of hardcore Beatles fans who scour British record fairs in search of pirate copies. However, timing was always one of the Beatles' great strengths, and as one reviewer rightly observed upon its original (and long delayed) cinematic release, *Let It Be* is 'instant history' (*Time*, 8 June 1970), a comment which currently seems questionable, since while it is true that substantial excerpts of the film (together with some outtakes) were utilized in the group's *Anthology* TV series (1995), its lack of commercial availability has to some extent depleted its potential to be reassessed by contemporary critics and audiences as an important cultural artefact.

Yet in spite of their critical and (in the case of *Let It Be*) commercial neglect, the Beatles movies continue to generate both interest and profit. Like the Marx Brothers comedies to which they were initially compared, the films still engage and, for the most part, amuse in a manner which seems to have transcended their period. The current popularity of the first three films in the sell-through home-video market would seem to echo this belief, suggesting that they have found second- and third-generation audiences. For five films which were made with no intention of achieving any sense of permanence, they have dated far more gracefully than many of their contemporaries, and there is no small irony in this. In the spirit of 1960s pop aesthetics, Richard Lester asserted repeatedly throughout that decade that he neither wanted nor expected his films to last. Today, he is justifiably amused by the irony of the situation, and although modestly accepting that he finds it impossible to be objective about his own work, suggests that they may have captured something more 'endearingly representative of their period' (Lester 1996) than a number of other films from the same era. Why do the films retain their popularity with audiences? The reasons, although both complex and numerous, relate predominantly to their continuous influence upon, and existence within, contemporary pop culture.

As the recently released (and heavily Lester-influenced) Spice Girls film attests, the pop musical is not quite extinct. Its popularity has however withered to the point where the release of a film such as *Spiceworld* (1997) is a genuine anomaly. Yet the formal language of the Beatles' films (and their promos) lives on most profoundly in the non-stop global jukebox that is music television. The fact that there have been no textual developments of equal significance since the group's movies has helped them to retain their youthfulness to new audiences, and while video-makers have discovered and employed all manner of new effects and technologies, the fundamentally illustrative, concept-based aesthetic of non-performance established more than 30 years ago by Lester is still very much in place. In addition, the fashions and range of images popularised by the Beatles in their films and promos have become strongly integrated into the post-modern collage of styles which pervades contemporary pop culture. The psychedelic clothing sported by the group in *Magical Mystery Tour* (and their cartoon counterparts in *Yellow Submarine*) has returned to the centre stage of indie pop fashion, and the mid-1960s look of *Help!* (corduroy and suede jackets, sunglasses and leather boots) has also become integral to the look of many contemporary bands. Indeed, to scrutinize the visual style of popular Beatles admirers like Oasis is to witness a near perfect synthesis of fashions culled from different periods of the Beatles' career and reassembled into a bricolage of styles which evokes a disturbingly schizophrenic sense of undifferentiated time. Likewise, the influence of the Beatles' recorded output has never been so prominent, and the Britpop revolution of the mid-1990s (of which Oasis are clearly key players) has at its core a nostalgic pastiche of the Beatles' abstract lyrical allusions and harmonic structures.

But quite independent of the phenomenon of Britpop, the films' soundtracks have retained an eternal youth which has clearly been central to their longevity. While not wishing to enter into speculation about the complexity of reasons for the popularity of the Beatles as recording artists, a number of points are relevant when assessing the soundtrack albums. Like all of the Beatles' recordings, the soundtracks (with the possible exception of Phil Spector's 'revamped' *Let It Be*) benefited enormously from their production values. George Martin's production was so conceptually advanced in its day, and has since been so perfectly and effectively conserved and enhanced by contemporary technology that the sound of the 'CD' Beatles now seems much fresher than that of their peers. Although most of their work was originally recorded on four-track technology, the recordings have been carefully remastered (with the co-operation of their original producer) and have retained a crystal-clear clarity of acoustic which has imbued them with a sense of permanence.

Beyond this clarity of sound lies the Beatles' music, and it is, ultimately, the compositions themselves which, perhaps more than any other factor, have been central to the movies' popularity; and consistent media exposure has ensured that they remain very much part of the 'now'. I would suggest that the central reason for their appeal is rooted in their durability. Unlike a vast number of their contemporaries (and Bob Dylan's early work springs immediately to mind), the songs of Lennon, McCartney and Harrison ran the gamut of lyrical universal abstracts in a manner which transcends contemporaneity. What is more, their approach to songwriting and arrangement encapsulated a far wider musical panorama than had, and indeed has, ever been attempted within pop. As well as developing the germ of their beloved rock and roll into new musical styles and experimenting and pioneering a range of hitherto untried recording techniques, the Beatles were masters of musical pastiche.

Songs written in pre-existing styles cannot, by their very nature, date as harshly as those which are not, and although they were not necessarily designed with this intention, many of the Beatles' soundtrack songs (and particularly those that appeared in the later films) succeed so well for precisely this reason. That the songs were often more memorable than those of the genres from which they derived is extraordinary; the Beatles always had an uncanny knack of not only capturing the essence of their chosen targets, but somehow inexplicably 'improving' them. Soundtrack songs such as 'And I Love Her', 'Yellow Submarine', 'Your Mother Should Know' and 'Let It Be' are (respectively) pastiches of the Latin ballad, the children's nursery rhyme, the music-hall singalong and the hymn. Those who constantly explain the Beatles' current revival as merely nostalgic fail to recognize that whatever else constituted their vast contribution to popular music, an important ingredient of their original cross-generational appeal was *itself* nostalgic.

With the Beatles' official split in 1970 came the end of the world's most successful recording act. Significantly perhaps, it also paralleled the decline of large scale investment into British cinema. The degree to which the Beatles' split influenced this contraction is obviously unquantifiable, but while it has often been rather reductively explained as the result of the internal schisms, decreasing incentives and diminishing returns which characterised such late sixties productions as *Modesty Blaise* (1967), *Performance* (1968, released 1970) and *The Charge Of The Light Brigade* (1968), only the most myopic of commentators would ignore the direct and indirect ways in which the two events were connected. On a purely cinematic level, the end of the Beatles meant that there was one less group of highly bankable British stars for the picking. Yet, even if the Beatles had never set foot in a movie studio, I suspect their demise would still have had some impact on foreign investment into British film.

After all, at the epicentre of the sustained US investment in British cinema were not only the home-grown talents of the film industry, but the country's distinction as a mecca of exportable pop culture, which encapsulated fashion, design, photography, the fine arts and, perhaps most importantly, pop music (most importantly, because pop was the most widely disseminated and 'inescapable' of these media, especially in the USA, where from 1964 onwards, it reverberated around the country as a stern and omnipotent warning to financiers that Britain's new found cultural status was not to be ignored). Throughout the decade, the Beatles were so much the nucleus of the cultural revolution that it is almost impossible to imagine it ever having happened without them. Although the first substantial US investments of the 1960s predated the group's international success by a whisker (for example, United Artists' *Dr No* was released in the same year as the group's first British hit single), it can be argued that the international popularity of the Beatles was the single most important factor in maintaining Britain's perceived cultural credibility throughout the decade; as Richard Lester has insisted: 'It is hard to overestimate the grip of the fab four on the popular imagination of the time' (Lester 1993). Directly or otherwise, the members of the group were key players in virtually every successfully exported and innovative popular artistic medium of their age, not only as film stars and film-makers, but as models for the newly-emerging Carnaby Street fashions, as photographic subjects for David Bailey, Dezo Hoffmann, Richard Avedon and Robert Freeman, as key conspirators in the marriage of fine art and pop, and of course as writers and performers of the most widely exported and distributed music in history. In his reflections on the withdrawal of US funding from British cinema in the early 1970s, Walter Shenson (the producer of *A Hard Day's Night* and *Help!*) explained that:

> this place no longer makes news that is of interest to the world. When society is under stress or going through change, the outlines of what's happening are unfamiliar and exciting, and the artists are under pressure to react to it all. When we are over-familiar with what has been happening, all that is left is a hangover. (Walker 1986: 450–1)

Some would argue that it is a hangover from which Britain has never fully recovered.

The Beatles movies will probably never attain the status of their recordings, and the majority will probably agree that this is no great injustice. My argument has been that much of the Beatles' impact was, by necessity, derived from the marriage of music *and* film. It remains a considerable frustration and a great disappointment that this obvious relationship and its formal, economic, and ideological importance have been so seldom investigated and so frequently overlooked.

## NOTES

1. Although the first four films have all been commercially available at intermittent periods, *Yellow Submarine* is currently unavailable and *Let It Be* has still to gain a home video release in the UK. Furthermore, it has not been broadcast on terrestrial TV for more than 15 years.
2. In some markets outside the UK the film's title was *Having A Wild Weekend*.

## REFERENCES

Donnelly, Kevin (1997) *Pop Music and British Cinema*. Unpublished PhD thesis, University of East Anglia.

Lester, Richard (1993) *Hollywood U.K.* BBC TV.

Lester, Richard (1996) Personal interview with the author: London, 26 March.

MacDonald, Ian (1994) *Revolution in the Head*. London: Fourth Estate.

Medhurst, Andy (1995) 'It Sort of Happened Here: The Strange, Brief Life of the British Pop Film', in Jonathan Romney and Adrian Wootton (eds), *Celluloid Jukebox*. London: BFI.

Murphy, Robert (1992) *Sixties British Cinema*. London: BFI.

Schatz, Thomas (1993) 'The New Hollywood', in Jim Collins, Hilary Radner and Ava Collins (eds), *Film Theory Goes to the Movies*. London: Routledge.

Sharman, Leslie Felperin (1994) 'Animatophilia', *Sight and Sound (Art Into Film Supplement)*, July.

Walker, Alexander (1986) *Hollywood, England*. London: Harrap.

# 9 The Celebrity Legacy of the Beatles

## P. David Marshall

There are peculiar contemporary moments that recall the celebrated past of the Beatles and which reinforce the belief that their influence continues and is vibrantly part of the present. Oasis is probably the most popular band regularly to acknowledge its debts to the Beatles and the Lennon–McCartney songwriting successes. In a similar vein, the New Zealand–Australian band Crowded House was often linked to the Beatles' pop sensibility in its approach to songmaking and its sartorial presence. But more than just adopting and adapting the foundations of a musical style, succeeding generations of musicians and singers have also built upon the public display of self that was a part of the various incarnations of the Beatles – both as a group and as individuals. The popular music industry has in many ways routinized the moments of public display that are part of the Beatles' mythology and has made them representative of youth and contemporary musical culture. This chapter seeks to understand the legacy of the Beatles as celebrity forms for contemporary culture. It is an investigation of the routinization of the pleasures of personality that have become models for the organization of popular music and popular culture.

To start this process it is important to define what I mean by celebrity and, more specifically, how I understand its meaning to intersect with popular music and its discourses. Celebrity is not pure construction, whereby an industry can manufacture a consumable personality; neither is celebrity a total expression of popular will, through which a public determines who is to be elevated into some level of stardom. Celebrity, as I have argued elsewhere (Marshall 1997), is a complex text that contains the tension *between* these two formulations. Moreover, somewhere within the proliferating discourses that define a public personality is the living and breathing individual who makes the projections and constructions that much more complex. Celebrity is not like a film character where there is a limited and original text. It is a presentation of the self for public consumption which accommodates something private and personal. In fact, *revelation* of the private and the personal is the central narrative-like pattern of the ways in which celebrities are viewed by the public. Scandalous disclosures that draw attention to the individual focus media attention and audience attention on what is normally concealed. So, when we hear about another punch-up involving Liam Gallagher, we have one more story that reveals something about the person, and which connects Oasis to a long rock lineage of notorious moments of illegality. Celebrities provide a topic for continuous discussions about the individual and the meaning of individuality in contemporary culture, about the location of the line between public and private, and about the significance of their actions for an audience. Celebrities are sites for the play of identification and identity; the celebrity is producing an identity which forms patterns of identification for audiences and publics.

The popular music celebrity is a particular incarnation of this celebrity system and the Beatles have been instrumental in shaping its construction. Several key elements of celebrity in popular music have been associated with the group's emergence, and it is that relationship which needs to be explored.

In postwar years, popular music has expressed and maintained a clear connection with an emerging youth culture. The marketing to youth, the development of the teenager as a demographic category, and the demarcation of distinctive youth technologies and spaces – from the transistor radio and the jukebox to dancehalls and cars – have all been part of a celebrated differentiation of experience for postwar youth. According to Frith (1983) the teenager is as much a marketing invention as a member of an authentic youth group. Within British culture, as the observations of Hebdige (1988) have suggested, youth became conflated with transformations in class formations through the celebration of the egalitarian spirit in the popular music and culture of the USA during that same postwar era.

The Beatles intervened in this process of the definition of youth-as-marketing segment in a number of interesting ways. Their accents identified them from Liverpool and from the state, rather than the public (that is, private), school system. Accents provide spatial and class co-ordinates within British culture; but the Beatles transcended these co-ordinates to represent something beyond class, something particularly modern that in its transcendence articulated a celebrated status of freedom – a freedom *from something*. In the tradition of postwar British youth, the 'freedom from' seemed to be conveyed through a connection to the black rhythm and blues culture of the United States, which gave its appropriation into British rock and roll a form of double signification: simultaneously, the celebration of something American (specifically in its focus on individual expression) and the celebration of a marginalized part of American culture (which provided the groundwork for the general tonality of rebellion). But this appropriation was without the political and cultural baggage – the very semiotic weight – of a sharply race-divided American society. When transposed into the British cultural mix, with its own residues of class and conflict, the Beatles' style expressed difference, change, and the potential for renewal. Youth, through its public expression in the Beatles, represented a break from the past and a celebration of the future. Although part of the emergence of a teenage marketing category, which might at first seem to be superficial, the Beatles' exuberant power and cultural influence stretched these marketing boundaries into a wider emotive celebration of the renewal of modernity in the 1960s.

I want to concentrate on how the Beatles were a part of the manufacture of the modern public self that has been essential to the maintenance of the myths of modernity. As a cultural phenomenon the Beatles helped to produce persistent patterns with which we interpret public personalities, dialectical tensions that express the inherent instability of public personae, and more specifically the modes of interpretation that we employ to read and make sense of popular music performers. To unravel the connections between the Beatles and our continuing interpretation of celebrities, I have grouped the analysis under specific themes: the formation of affect and connection; the tension between authenticity and fabrication; the expression of individuality.

## THE FORMATION OF AFFECT AND CONNECTION

The emotive outpouring that accompanied the emergence of the Beatles has become the litmus test of cultural significance for most succeeding popular cultural phenomena. The Leonardo Di Caprio moment following *Titanic*'s 1997 release, when adolescent girls and young women returned to see the movie countless times, is in direct lineage with what came to be known as Beatlemania. In a similar manner the pop group Hanson – three brothers aged 11 to 17 – created frenzies of fans at shopping malls throughout North America during 1997 and 1998.

The key connection between these popular cultural moments is that they describe a form of investment that goes beyond the individual into a collective experience. The Beatles, particularly in their international tours of 1964, attracted remarkable crowds, some of which resulted from a combination of promotional strategies and the actions of dedicated fans. It is freely acknowledged that the promoters of Beatles paraphernalia gave a dollar and a t-shirt to each person who came to JFK Airport to greet the arrival of the Beatles in New York in February 1964 (Burrows 1996: 77). Through heavy promotion on radio stations and saturation news coverage, the group's arrival became the equivalent of a major international event. However, between hyperbole and the actual activities of 1964, the Beatles did manage to attract fans whose emotional commitment was undeniable. While at many of their concerts, the level of screaming made it difficult to hear the music, in fact, the music seemed relatively unimportant to the fans; it was ambient to the experience of proximity to their idols.

The Beatles succeeded in producing a peculiarly modern phenomenon that has become routinized and institutionalized in the reproduction of popular music since those early tours. They produced the popular music crowd. The group's concert at New York's Shea Stadium on 15 August 1965, which was attended by more than 55 000 fans, established a standard and scale of emotional connection which succeeding generations of popular music fans have sought to duplicate through the ritual attendance of performances at football and baseball stadia. Despite the physical distance from the performers, the Beatles' legacy was that the moment of the crowd was ultimately more significant. It was a form of solidarity with the performing group. The relationship between recorded music and the live concert consequently fell into a recognizable pattern in the promotion of popular music, in which it was not essential for the music to match the recording quality, since the concert was designed to be a collective experience of support and a moment of declaration that rivalled in devotion the most emotionally charged evangelical tent crusades (indeed, the US evangelist Billy Graham's stadium revivals of the 1950s could be seen as a direct precursor to the popular music concert industry).

Hysteria, the central metaphor in descriptions of what the Beatles created on their first US tour, has been utilized since nineteenth century crowd theorists tried to articulate the transformation of the individual to some form of group behaviour. Around the turn of the century, the accompanying loss of self was held responsible for the creation of a being of lesser intelligence (Le Bon 1960). Often, crowd behaviour was linked to the feminine, in a way similar to the manner in which Huyssen (1986: 44–62) has linked mass consumer culture to the feminine. In the nineteenth-century versions of this argument, there is a clear misogynistic reading of the crowd. Nevertheless, the idea that hysteria was linked to weakness in the female constitution carried on as a cultural connotation from early psychological investigations via crowd theorists like Le Bon and Gabriele Tarde through to the twentieth-century emergence of social psychology. The production of hysteria has enveloped the development of modern advertising as it worked through the process of connecting with the consumer – mass behaviour as fundamentally irrational or, in social psychological terms, appealing to prepotent motivations of the individual.

The concert became an emblem of the moment of irrationality and hysteria essential to the way in which the culture industries operated in the twentieth century. The entertainment industries sought moments where there was a massive effect; in popular music, this patterning came to be described as the hit, where something in the performance produced a huge outpouring of affective connection. The objective of cultural production, as it was organized through the interests of consumer capitalism, was to replicate those moments of massive and collective connection to a particular phenomenon.

Despite the fact that the Beatles were never to perform in concert after 1966, the constitution of their audiences as a cultural memory has remained consistent. While their music may have transformed and adopted aesthetic pretensions and/or emotional maturity, the concerts were the signs of what the Beatles represented in their first years. Predominantly young (pre-pubescent and post-pubescent) girls dominated the image of these concerts and their public appearances on US television, such as *The Ed Sullivan Show*, in 1964. The significance of this representation of fandom is twofold for the organization of popular music personalities.

First, the Beatles produced an audience that helped to define the division between pop and rock in the following 30 years. Pop music, which maintained a closer lineage with Tin Pan Alley and the traditions of the recording industry, was primarily aimed at creating affective sensations that were clearly identified with a female audience. In contrast, rock music grounded itself through an emotional connection to performance that was inherently narcissistic, in that its male performers appealed predominantly to young, male audiences.

Secondly, the Beatles articulated a presentation of personality that played with the construction of public sexuality. Popular music as a cultural discourse of personality became fundamentally a discourse about the construction of gender itself. The female fans' overt and apparently highly emotional connection to their idols underlines the group's play with sexual ambiguity: the Beatles' youthfulness, their girlish moptop haircuts and proper suits made them an amalgam of sexual identity. In some ways, their demeanour made them unthreatening as love interests for young girls and promoted the devotional bedroom shrine that became *de rigueur* for the post-1960s female teenager; but throughout their small efforts to bend the constituent categories of male and female appearance, they were sustained by the media as pleasant boys with a well-developed and well-mannered sense of humour.

What the Beatles produced in those early years through their construction of emotionally charged audiences was a template for an industry. Popular music idols certainly predated the Beatles' emergence; but the concerts and the circulation of images of fan solidarity with, and devotion to, the Beatles became models for the recording industry to replicate. Pop music became the site for producing the teen idol as a phenomenon in the way that movies might have operated more centrally in the 1930s and 1940s. The idols who postdated the Beatles continued the group's play with sexual identity that characterized its international emergence. The Monkees, David Cassidy, Leif Garrett, the Bay City Rollers, New Kids On The Block, Take That, the Backstreet Boys and many others point to the manner in which the affective, even hysterical, moment of the Beatles was routinized into an industrial strategy. (In many ways, this routinization of massive affective moments parallels Weber's [1968] discussion of the routinisation of charisma into political institutions.) The sexual identity of these pop stars has been decidedly between boys and men, and in their play with active sexuality the pop stars who followed the Beatles have tried to repeat the close connection to the pre/post-pubescent girl.

## FABRICATION AND AUTHENTICITY

A central tendency that was further refined by the Beatles was the division between the obviously constructed nature of the celebrity of traditional popular music and some new sensibility of the music performer. The Beatles were instrumental in making the persona of popular music an issue. Unlike folk performers emerging from the USA at roughly the same time, the Beatles were not clearly a public sign of sincerity or authenticity – they operated as signs over the contestation of their own significance. Chambers has underlined the fact that their early music was much more closely aligned with traditional themes of pop tune-smiths (1985: 63). 'Love Me Do', for example, was not a creative advance over the songs produced for Hollywood musical stars of the 1930s and 1940s. But there were differences in the way the Beatles *presented themselves* that established markers for shifts in the meaning of popular music in contemporary culture.

Their media moniker – the Fab Four – provides a clear indication of how the Beatles trod the line between something authentically wonderful and significant (*fabu*lous) and something manufactured and created by an industry (*fab*rication). Their effective blend of this binarism operated through a number of channels. The discourse of the artist as genius-creator was a prevalent definition of something culturally authentic both in contemporary art and, increasingly, in the folk-inflected music cultures of the 1950s and early 1960s. The Beatles were able to ride that form of authenticity predominantly through Lennon and McCartney's songwriting and, in so doing, connected the cultural connotations of the group to the singer-songwriter tradition. Having that control over the production of their music provided a route through which they received a certain credibility in the 1960s and which challenged the traditional Tin Pan Alley distinction between composer/writer and performer. They were also distant from those fabricated singing groups who depended on a manager to orchestrate their music, their venues, and their look; in this way, for example, the Beatles were in clear contrast to girl groups like the Supremes, constructed by Motown. Their ability to play their own instruments positioned them within subsequent definitions of rock performers as opposed to pop performers; their extensive pre-fame work in Hamburg nightclubs accentuated their independence and authenticity as they developed a style and a musicianship which gave them a degree of autonomy from the industry; the fact that they formed their group as schoolboys in Liverpool without the initial help of a manager emphasized that they had roots which predated any Svengali-like transformation.

Despite these impressive claims to the authentic, the Beatles did at the same time represent something contrived and manufactured by an industry that worked to accelerate the power of a new entertainment act. Although their hairstyles came from their Hamburg days and the influence of artist-friends, the suits of the early years (at the insistence of Epstein) were a sign of moulding their personalities into a successful industrial act. Their musical style may have relied on a 'leather and rockers' image; but they traded their leather jackets to present something less threatening. Where Elvis had constructed a more palatable white image for rock and roll, the Beatles moved that image still further, from its African–American creative-though-culturally-threatening source to the boys-next-door. The Beatles, in a very real sense, allowed themselves to be shaped into a product for the proliferation of their fame.

All of these conflicting discourses about the nature of their celebrity converged in their first moments of international fame and, in some ways, their presentations of self did influence definitions of the authentic in contemporary culture. Expansive patterns of fame which represented the antithesis of genuine achievement or real heroism have been presumed to be a source of inauthenticity since the nineteenth century. In the twentieth century, fame through film or popular music reflected a connection to the masses, and was even more clearly associated with something of fleeting importance or a form of commodity fabrication. Fame represented a double break-down in culture: first, the forms of knowledge of the celebrated personality bore little connection to the deeper structural knowledge of the person associated with the traditional community; secondly, the former elites of state and church were no longer in complete control of those who might be celebrated or venerated. What the Beatles signified was a re-reading of the cultural value of fame and celebrity. Instead of possessing a negative connotation, the Beatles became a democratic celebration of the new power of fame. The commodity could no longer be seen as some form of corruption of artistic practice, but it was more *part* of the artistic process. Andy Warhol's blank parodies of fame in his Marilyn and Elvis series was an art-parallel to the Beatles' engagement with their public through the media.

The new authenticity that the Beatles expressed through their own commodification can best be seen in their interviews and in their two Richard Lester movies. The early interviews were an elaborate game with the various press scrums, in which each Beatle performed an evasive manoeuvre as he answered the questions put to him with his own questions or nonsensical answers which played with the rhythmic quality of the original questions. Lennon became infamous for his ability to make nonsense – but funny nonsense. It should be noted that the form of humour followed a long tradition in British comedy, from the music hall to BBC radio's *The Goon Show* in the 1950s.

What was new was its deployment in the presentation of the self for media and public consumption. The evasive but funny interview marked by its sense of non-cooperation with media powers became one of the most dominant patterns in rock and popular music in television and film.

The Lester-directed movies *A Hard Day's Night* and *Help!* served a similar purpose. The basic premise of each film was that the Beatles were playing themselves. Their 'acting' was thus an elaborate variation on their public 'everyday' selves which had grown from their media interview personae. As a narrative, the films represented the capacity of the Beatles to maintain their humour, and thus their authentic selves, in a world which had tipped towards a hysterical relationship to their personalities.

## THE EXPRESSION OF INDIVIDUALITY

These origins of a new authenticity that the Beatles expressed mutated somewhat over the 1960s and affected their status as a group. Indeed, the central narrative of the Beatles as public personalities in that decade was to achieve a form of legitimacy that transcended their group definition and moved the reading of the Beatles into an interpretation of *individual* personality.

The Beatles' migration from a collective identity to a focus on the individual is nothing new. It expresses more than anything else the resurgence of modern conceptions of the individual and their articulation through public personalities. It also reiterates a form of search for authenticity through many of the classically modern motifs – such as scandal.

The development of scandals enveloped the Beatles at various moments of the group's life; there were hints of scandals concerning liaisons with women, and numerous reports of drug use. The greatest scandal was the misinterpretation in 1966 of a John Lennon interview in which he offered the observation that the Beatles were more popular than Jesus Christ. I am less concerned here with the validity of the story, and more interested in the effects of the idea of scandal on the celebrity. Viewed in the usual way, scandal implies deleterious effects; but what has to be understood about the Beatles as celebrity is that scandal, within the discourse of popular music as rock, actually works towards a form of legitimation. This was an emerging part of the idea of rock music as oppositional. Generational divides can become more clearly demarcated through such emotionally charged incidents. The scandal itself can produce a form of publicity that makes the celebrity a richer and deeper text and may allow a form of politicization to emerge from the process. Lyrics may be listened to more closely for intentionality and for their potential political and cultural impact.

Scandal also worked to give the Beatles a sense of autonomy. Again, this conception of autonomy seems to operate counter-intuitively to the meaning of scandal. However, in the case of the Beatles their construction as pleasant, fun-loving personae actually situated them within a clear 'entertainer'–orientated presentation of self – what I have earlier characterized as a clear lineage to the Tin Pan Alley tradition of popular music. In a very real way, the image of the Beatles provided a stereotype that was a form of public strait-jacket for the group. Although Paul McCartney seemed the most comfortable with the tunesmith role, their believed-to-be authentic personae restricted their connection to broader social and cultural movements. Large-scale media scandals actually allowed the group to exercise an independence from the industry it had spawned.

Apple is the most obvious example of this stretch to autonomy. Established in 1968 to foster innovative cultural productions and technological projects – as Paul McCartney labelled it, 'a kind of Western communism' (Burrows 1996: 154) – Apple was crafted to a new cultural politics emerging from the power of the Beatles' contemporary celebrity formation that had emerged from the culture industries themselves. Although generally deemed to be a failure, its status is an important marker of the Beatles' legacy to corporate/artistic autonomy in popular music, if not in other highly commodified cultural forms. Contemporary examples of this exercise of cultural individuality within the corporate structure abound, but probably the most successful in her articulation of a sense of autonomous artistry is Madonna. On more modest scales, the clearly clichéd setting up of the home recording studio is an example of the individual artist reprising some of the power of the corporate music industry world at the level of production.

The invocation of the artist in all its nineteenth-century vainglori-ousness is deeply imbedded in the Beatles' celebrity legacy. The artist has served as modernity's and modernism's heightened expression of individuality. Creativity and innovation have been celebrated in the liberalist conception of the individual and the Beatles were driven to perpetuate the genius-creator myths within a new popular cultural form. In conjunction with their producer George Martin, worked towards a differentiation of their text out of the rhythms of popular music where repetition and appropri... popular and the non-commodified folk traditions were well established; collectively and individually, they worked to construct *differ ence* in their music. *Sgt Pepper's Lonely Hearts Club Band* must be seen as a milestone, not only in popular music production, but also in the shift in audience perceptions of the popular music celebrity. Complicit in this transformation of the meaning of popular music icons was the music press which began to investigate and invest in the inner lives of performers for the inspiration of their artistry in a way which echoed the achievements of their jazz precursors; the fundamental difference was that popular music performers were imbued with the new authenticity of democratic celebrity. Their inner lives became an expression of cultural anxiety, a journalistic shorthand for understanding generational change. Because of their overwhelming popularity, the Beatles were seen – and used – as beacons from which to understand the contemporary. Thus, their experimentation with Eastern mysticism in their Indian pilgrimage heralded a different period of intense scrutiny of the Beatles, when their work and their lives became a journey of self-discovery through which their dispersed and massive Western audience vicariously travelled towards some inner truth about the group and contemporary existence itself. It was a combination of pop psychology, Eastern religion, Freudian psycho analysis and more traditional forms of celebrity gossip. The will to discover the true Beatles was jointly organized by the media, by their fans, and by the Beatles themselves.

The actual fragmentation of the Beatles was a further expression of the role of individuality in popular music celebrity identity. The idea of the pop group continues to be the starting point of the rock/pop music celebrity; but progression is often defined by the movement to solo careers. The Beatles became an unworkable group for all sorts of reasons and it is important to note how the breakup connected to their public roles as celebrities. The Beatles as a phenomenon became, like McLuhan (another 1960s icon), a victim of their own sign crime (Kroker 1984). Ironically, because of their huge success, the Beatles embodied a series of cultural memories that overwhelmed their own present as a group. In a very real sense, the Beatles had to reinvent themselves – as an experimental artist (Lennon), an Eastern-influenced guitarist (Harrison) or an actor (Starr). Re-invention has since become the routine form of renewal for the popular music celebrity. David Bowie's chameleon-like shifts in persona, Madonna's costume and attitude transformation, and U2's trawling of the popart tradition are all examples that have drawn on the transformations of character developed by the Beatles within the lifetime of the group and in the post-Beatle era.

## CONCLUSION

The Beatles in their various presentations of self provide a road map for the organization of the contemporary popular music personality. They successfully integrated previous representations of the popular music performer into a transformed role in the middle of the twentieth century. The constitution of that celebrity form is very much linked to the rejuvenation of modernity in the context of the popular. Although it is difficult to unify the project of modernity, it does have some defining characteristics in terms of social improvement, progress, and positive change towards the future. The Beatles were instrumental in shifting the domain of the modern into the significance of popular culture for the politics of contemporary culture. I have described this shift, expressed through the discourses that developed around their personalities, as a new authenticity that could be best characterized as a democratic celebration of the celebrity. The Beatles demonstrated a new cultural power that was clearly connected to cultural transformations.

This new authenticity of the popular music celebrity has provided a legacy for the meaning and significance of popular music within a broader social context. Popular music has become a major site for debates about sexuality, youth, and the general theme of identity politics. Succeeding generations of popular music celebrity figures (in their invocation of a form of liberalist individualism as artists in conjunction with their popular connection to an audience) have continued to be intense sites or channels for working out contemporary political and cultural meaning. The artistic phenomenon of Beck in the late 1990s, the scandal of Public Enemy in the early 1990s, and the sexual politics of Madonna through the 1980s are all articulations of what the Beatles brought together in their personae. Popular music, through its celebrity icons, became simultaneously the location for the examination of the self, the continuing discourse of entertainment and pleasure, and the recognition of the cultural power of popularity.

# REFERENCES

Burrows, Terry (1996) *The Beatles: the Complete Illustrated Story*. London: Carlton.
Chambers, Iain (1985) *Urban Rhythms*. London: Macmillan.
Frith, Simon (1983) *Sound Effects*. London: Constable.
Hebdige, Dick (1988) *Hiding in the Light: On Images and Things*. London: Comedia/Routledge.
Huyssen, Andreas (1986) *After the Great Divide: Modernism, Mass Culture, Postmodernism*. Bloomington: Indiana University Press.
Kroker, Arthur (1984) *Technology and the Canadian Imagination*. Montreal: New World Perspectives.
Le Bon, Gustave (1960) *The Crowd: a Study of the Popular Mind*. New York: Viking.
Marshall, P. David (1997) *Celebrity and Power: Fame in Contemporary Culture*. Minneapolis: University of Minnesota Press.
Weber, Max (1968) *Economy and Society*, Volume 3. New York: Bedminster.

# 10 Refab Four: Beatles for Sale in the Age of Music Video[1]

## Gary Burns

The millennium approaches, and we have witnessed the second coming – of the Beatles. The group as a whole has been resurrected (after a fashion) and, in particular, John Lennon – he who said the Beatles were more popular than Christ and who sang 'they're gonna crucify me'.

The Beatles have served a quasi-religious function ever since the days of Beatlemania, when they were objects of youthful devotion and sources of comfort to American teenagers after the death of President Kennedy. In their subsequent religious and mythological career, they became a magical brotherhood – Sgt Pepper's Lonely Hearts Club Band, around whom one of rock music's sacred texts (the so-called first concept album) was built. They portrayed wizards in the 1967 *Magical Mystery Tour* telefilm and seemed to act out similar roles in real life, entering the fields of music, movies and literature (via John Lennon's books *In His Own Write* and *A Spaniard in the Works*). Their forays into television were uneven. Their 1967 promotional clips for 'Penny Lane' and 'Strawberry Fields Forever' are considered pioneering works in the field of music video. On the other hand, *Magical Mystery Tour* was generally considered a failure as television, although the music was certainly successful, and the package as a whole contributed greatly to Beatles mythology, especially in the United States, where the television version was not shown until some years after its British broadcast. On US TV, the salient appearances of the Beatles were on *The Ed Sullivan Show* (in 1964 at the start of Beatlemania) and in the worldwide satellite transmission of 'All You Need Is Love' in 1967. This broadcast, coincident with the *Sgt Pepper* album and the Summer of Love, solidified the myth of worldwide love, centered in some way around the Beatles and connected with what we would now call youth culture or the counterculture.

In the United States, there was an urgent need for such a myth with which to combat the unpleasant realities of war in Vietnam and bigotry at home. As the counterculture became more political, it simultaneously and paradoxically became hedonistic. The Beatles eased their way into political topics with 'Taxman' (1966); then 'All You Need Is Love' with its non-specific utopianism; and finally 'Revolution' and other songs from 1968, which sounded unequivocably radical, but were actually ambiguous in their sentiments. And from the standpoint of hedonism, it became known that the Beatles used drugs and had investigated Indian religious teachings. This form of cosmopolitanism – far better than bombing Vietnam – became something of an alternative model to that of the Cold War and regional conflicts. The 1960s slogan 'make love, not war' juxtaposed the imagery of global conflict with that of personal sexual behaviour, thus universalizing 'love', localising 'war', and proposing hedonism as a solution to a political problem. The Beatles were avatars of this worldview, from the vagueness of 'All You Need Is Love' to the more concrete matter of Lennon's affair with Yoko Ono. And through George Harrison's influence, Indian culture remained a major ingredient in the Beatles' image. By 1967, drugs, sitars and mysticism had become ineluctably linked in American popular culture. The Beatles assisted this linkage by juxtaposing Harrison's Indianesque songs about enlightenment with Lennon's oblique drug-trip paeans.

In 1968, the Beatles launched Apple – coincidentally, a Biblical symbol – as their formal venture into business enterprise. Apple was to be primarily a record label, within yet separate from EMI/Capitol. In addition to the Beatles, other musicians – James Taylor, Badfinger, Jackie Lomax, Mary Hopkin – would record for the label. As well as its musical activities, Apple would have a boutique and divisions of film, publishing, and electronics. These ancillary activities ultimately collapsed, but the record label met with several successes. Apple was the Beatles' most audacious foray into an envisioned collective utopia, where, as John Lennon explained, 'people who just want to make a film about anything, don't have to go on their knees in somebody's office' (Cantillon and Cantillon 1996: 73). In effect, the Beatles were seeking to establish themselves as saviours of a sort, using their hard-earned capital to rescue beleaguered film-makers (and other creative artists) from a predatory establishment.

Similarly, they were portrayed as saviours of a fictional Pepperland in the *Yellow Submarine* film in 1968. Scarcely more than a year later, the 'myth of the Beatles' took its strangest turn with rumours that Paul McCartney was dead. These rumours were compounded by a belief that the Beatles had supposedly hidden clues in their records and on their album covers to announce his death and to provide numerous other sensational items of information, including a telephone number people could call to make arrangements to be taken to Pepperland, apparently for life. Where was Pepperland? One theory was that it was in an 'octopus's garden', 'under the sea', inside a 'glass onion' – in other words, a self-sufficient geodesic dome beneath an ocean, built by the Beatles for the chosen, for purposes of surviving nuclear war. In religious terms, this Pepperland was a high-tech Noah's Ark.

When the Beatles broke up in 1970, it was like the Kennedy assassination all over again, or one's parents divorcing. Lennon declared in his song 'God': 'The dream is over'. But it was not. Over the next decade, stories of reunions flourished and promoters offered huge sums of money for such an event. What is more surprising is that the stories persisted even after Lennon's death in 1980. John's son, Julian, who bore an uncanny resemblance to his father, became a pop star in the mid-1980s; hence the reunion rumours could involve Julian joining the three surviving Beatles. John Lennon's death had been tragedy to McCartney's farcical 1960s pseudo-death. Lennon's assassin was a disturbed fan who, like Charles Manson, believed too strongly in the Beatles; Lennon even had his own martyrs – at least two fans who killed themselves because he had died.[2]

The Beatles' story would not be complete without a reunion or without Lennon's resurrection by one means or another. It finally happened in 1995 and was built upon a film and video documentary begun in the 1970s by Neil Aspinall, the head of Apple and probably the Beatles' closest associate. Originally titled *The Long And Winding Road*, the project was postponed for long periods but eventually revived and developed into the *Beatles Anthology* project, broadcast over several evenings on British and American TV in late 1995. An expanded videotape version was released in 1996. The project also includes a book (as yet unpublished) and three double-CD sets released in 1995 and 1996. Most of *Anthology* is archival material, although the TV version also includes recent interview footage. The reunion itself is achieved via the three remaining Beatles' collaboration and expansion into finished versions of some of Lennon's private demo recordings from the 1970s, given to Paul McCartney by Yoko Ono in 1994. They included 'Free As A Bird' and 'Real Love' (which were featured in the *Anthology* CDs and TV series and released as singles), plus 'Grow Old With Me' and (reportedly) another song whose title has not yet been revealed (Gaar 1995: 20).

Music videos were made for 'Free As A Bird' and 'Real Love', and they are, to say the least, interesting specimens by virtue of the unique requirements they had to meet. Almost all music videos promote products – and these videos certainly do – but a Beatles retrospective is a most unusual product. A Beatles reunion is even more singular and notable. Somehow the videos had to promote both the old material and the new and had to do it without the participation of John Lennon.

## FREE AS A BIRD

*Free As A Bird* was directed by Joe Pytka (probably best known as a director of TV commercials). It is the more elaborate of the two videos and was the first to be broadcast. The words of the song are as follows:

*Instrumental introduction*
*Verse 1*
Free as a bird, it's the next best thing to be free as a bird.
*Verse 2*
Home, home and dry, like a homing bird I fly, as a bird on wings.
*Bridge 1*
Whatever happened to the life that we once knew? Can we really live without each other? Where did we lose the touch that seemed to mean so much? It always made me feel so
*Verse 3*
Free as a bird. It's the next best thing to be free as a bird.
*Verse 4*
Home, home and dry, like a homing bird I fly, as a bird on wings.
*Bridge 2 (partial)*
Whatever happened to the life that we once knew? Always made me feel so free.
*Instrumental verse*
*Verse 5*
Free as a bird, it's the next best thing to be free as a bird.
*Coda 1*
Free, free as a bird, free as a bird.
*Cold close (false ending)*
*Coda 2*

The verses are sung by Lennon, with occasional harmony by McCartney and Harrison; the bridges are sung by McCartney. According to the sheet music, the bridge was originally written by Lennon, but with the following words: 'Whatever happened to the life that we once knew? Did we throw it away? Did it just slip away? Whatever happened to the life that we once knew? Can we save anything? Did we lose ev'rything?' The words in the Beatles' version seem rather more optimistic, as befits the occasion, but place greater emphasis upon the individual singer (McCartney) through the words 'always made *me* feel so free'.

In Lennon's original version, the words are probably addressed to a lover, and certainly not to the other Beatles. In the Beatles' version, the lyrics become a dialogue between Lennon and McCartney, with Paul lamenting (and almost apologising for) the passage of the old days, while John celebrates an odd combination of freedom and domesticity.

Lennon's voice sounds tinny and faraway – a function of the poor quality of the original cassette. Producer Jeff Lynne agreed with an interviewer that 'that's the way it should be, with John singing across time ...' (Bonzai 1996: 77). In association with the lyrics, this effect also has a macabre implication. The referent of 'it' is unclear in the printed lyrics but may be 'death' in the CD and video. Lennon would then be saying that being dead is the next best thing to being free as a bird – in other words, not at all bad.

The video elaborates upon the metaphor of the bird by consisting entirely of an ostensibly subjective shot from the point of view of a swooping bird. This effect is reinforced at the beginning with a sound effect of flapping wings. The shot is actually a series of composites created by the FLAME visual effects system (see Krenis 1996). The identity of the bird is probably John Lennon, who sings 'like a homing bird *I* fly'. Possibly he has reincarnated. The video also may be referring implicitly to Lennon's promise, recounted by his son, Julian, that if he found life after death he would send back a message by making a feather float across a room (Lennon 1982: 1–2).

The video promotes the *Anthology* project by including footage from it and by depicting the Beatles' career in roughly chronological order. On the other hand, the production dispenses entirely with many of the customary trappings of music video, particularly lip sync and performance footage. Lip sync identifies the singer, allows the camera to linger on an attractive face, provides an opportunity for direct address (which can mesmerize the viewer), and gives some sense of the singer as narrator or storyteller. Performance footage establishes that the musicians play their instruments well, and sometimes that they are liked and enjoyed by an audience.

*Free As A Bird* instead works by means of razzle dazzle (the simulated long take), nostalgia and contrast (the mostly joyous shots recapitulating the Beatles' career, the mournful voice of McCartney), and a profusion of 'clues' (82 in fact; see Cunningham 1996). The clues consist of such items as a pretty nurse selling poppies from a tray (a reference to the lyrics of 'Penny Lane') and a Blue Meanie appearing from a hole (a reference to the *Yellow Submarine* film). At the end of *Free As A Bird*, John Lennon's voice says, backwards: 'Turned out nice again' (a catchphrase of the British entertainer George Formby, who is the model for the ukulele player at the end of the song).

The clues don't seem to add up to anything but clearly refer to the Paul-is-dead hoax and *its* various clues. Just as the hoax was grounded in semiological excess, so too is the video, which provides the viewer with plenty of opportunity to overlook clues that are there, to see clues that are not there, and to find new information, even after multiple viewings. However, the spoofing of the clue-finding game gives the video an uneasy quality of lightheartedness.[3] Many of the people in the video seem sad, and through much of it we see a grungy, working-class Liverpool, the Beatles' roots. So, the dead John Lennon (with the bird's-eye view) surveys his hometown and his career, into which a game of trivial pursuit repeatedly intrudes.

But not all the clues are meaningless or trivial; there is a poignancy in the Beatles walking along with the workmen at Albert Dock, in the nurse with the poppies, and in the sheepdog (a reference to 'Martha My Dear', which McCartney wrote for his sheepdog Martha). This is the Beatles' lives passing in front of their eyes, and much of the impact of these images derives from the fact that the characters are real, that we have known them for a long time, and that many of them are probably gone.

Thus the video conveys a strong sense of contrast between present and past. The present is the bird and McCartney's nearby voice. The past is what the bird sees and Lennon's distant voice. Mediating the two tenses is much of the Liverpool footage, which was shot recently but artificially aged to resemble the genuinely old footage from the TV series. It appears that all the footage of the Beatles is old. They reappear throughout the video, moving from one location to the next more quickly than is possible, thereby reminding us that they may still be wizards and that the dream is still not over.

## REAL LOVE

*Real Love* is the second video drawn from *Anthology*. It was directed by Kevin Godley and involved filming the recording sessions – the first time the Beatles had played together since 1969. The words of the song are as follows:

*Instrumental introduction 1*
*Verse 1*
All my little plans and schemes, lost like some forgotten dreams.
Seems that all I really was doin' was waitin' for you.
*Verse 2*
Just like little girls and boys, playing with their little toys,
Seems like all we really were doin' was waitin' for love.
*Refrain 1*
No need to be alone, no need to be alone.
It's real love. It's real. Yes, it's real love. It's real.
*Instrumental introduction 2*
*Verse 3*
From this moment on I know exactly where my life will go.
Seems that all I really was doin' was waitin' for love.
*Refrain 2*
No need to be afraid, no need to be afraid.
It's real love. It's real. Yes, it's real love. It's real.
*Instrumental bridge*
*Verse 4*
Thought I'd been in love before, but in my heart I wanted more.
Seems like all I really was doin' was waitin' for you.
*Refrain 3*
No need to be alone, no need to be alone.
It's real love. It's real. Yes, it's real love. It's real.
*Coda*
Yes, it's real love. It's real. It's real love. It's real.
Yes, it's real love. It's real. It's real love. It's real.
Yes, it's real love. It's real. It's real love. It's real.
Yes, it's real love. It's real. It's real love. It's real.
*Fade out*

Lyrically, this song seems to be a restatement of the concerns of 'All You Need Is Love', but in a more domesticated, almost juvenile, vein. The most significant line may be: 'From this moment on I know exactly where my life will go', whereas, of course, Lennon did not know where his life was going. Similarly, although 'Real Love' seems to be a love song, probably addressed to Yoko Ono, it assumes a new meaning when sung years later by the Beatles. As with 'Free As A Bird', the song now appears as a conversation between Beatles. The video contributes to this impression and almost recasts the song as the Beatles' love song to each other.

Unlike *Free As A Bird*, the video for *Real Love* has a fairly conventional structure. Performance and candid shots of the band are intercut with what might be called conceptual footage. The concept is that the Beatles are three (or four) people united as one and that their career has been and still is a dream.

The theme of unity is established early in the video when portrait shots of the three Beatles are 'torn' into each other – a somewhat violent effect that nevertheless is similar to morphing and which echoes a visual motif dating back to the cover shot on the US edition of Hunter Davies's 1968 biography of the Beatles.[4] The idea of dreaming appears in the lyrics and especially throughout the video as musical instruments and other Beatle-related objects float upwards, climaxing near the end with the implication of a rooftop performance not unlike the 'Get Back' event in 1969. There is also a flock of flying hats, reminiscent of Hans Richter's 1928 surrealist film *Ghosts Before Breakfast*. The very first image in the video is of a piano rising (being resurrected) out of a dark pool of water, where it has apparently been buried. This is only the first of many objects that will float upwards, towards heaven.

In this video, however, unlike most others, the performance footage is the most interesting element. This footage seems designed to show that there truly is 'real love' between the Beatles, and that John Lennon is present in spirit; well-chosen lip-sync footage even places Lennon, impossibly, at the recording session. The video reprises some *Anthology* footage and apparently tinkers with the speed of some of the old performance footage so that almost all of it is in time with 'Real Love'. One might conclude that this is the song the Beatles have always been playing.

There is at the same time a sense in which the video plays down the accomplishments of the Beatles. The image of the rising piano corresponds with the words: 'All my little plans and schemes, lost like some forgotten dreams'. Shots of the three Beatles entering McCartney's recording studio coincide with the words: 'Just like little girls and boys, playing with their little toys'. The plans and schemes, and the little toys, are how the Beatles have spent their time as professionals. However, the opposing term, real love, is not associated with any contrasting imagery. It, too, occurs in the recording studio.

Both videos paint an ambivalent picture of how the Beatles feel about each other, about John Lennon, and about their career. In addition, certain issues and people are conspicuously absent. As Peter Doggett complained about the *Anthology* TV series:

> [A]lmost every disagreement was fudged, every rough edge smoothed into blandness. My fantasy is that an alive and kicking Lennon would have sat through the final viewing, and then ripped apart the charade with some well-directed expletives: 'What's that crap? Gimme some truth!' (1996: 23)

The 'rough edges' to which Doggett refers are mainly biographical and career matters – the firing of Pete Best, the Beatles' use of drugs, their legal battles with each other. The videos, created to celebrate a reunion, do well not to dredge up this type of thing, but at the same time they share the TV series' lack of engagement with any relevant social context.[5]

*Free As A Bird*, rather than being an entirely solipsistic exercise, might have focused more on the word *free*, even while retaining the bird metaphor. A bird (especially in a dream) can, after all, swoop over anything – not only the past, and certainly not only the Beatles' past. Even within that self-imposed limit, the creators might have found a way to say something about the more-popular-than-Christ controversy, or the Lennon/Ono bed-in, or Nike's desecration of 'Revolution' (see Weiner 1991a), or the FBI's persecution of Lennon (see Wiener 1991b). This could even be done, albeit perversely, within the trivial pursuit format, whereas in the existing video 'Revolution' is reduced to a distant, fleeting image of someone carrying a large picture of Mao Tse-Tung.

'Real Love' presents a different constraint in that it is a love song, but then the video is all the more problematic because of the relative absence of Yoko Ono (except for a few brief and fairly distant glimpses from stock footage, which merely draw attention to the fact of her non-appearance). Her absence from the TV series was voluntary (Giles 1995: 63), so we might surmise that she also declined to participate in *Real Love*. However, she is present in a few shots and could easily (from a technical standpoint) have been shown in additional archival footage and stills. The failure to include Ono more prominently, for whatever reason, redefines the object of Lennon's love and takes great liberty with the song – probably beyond what Lennon himself would have wanted.

But the real problem is more complicated than that. The well-documented acrimony between Lennon's fellow Beatles and Ono was at least a symptom, and in popular belief a cause, of the group's disintegration. As much of the world saw it, a Japanese woman broke up a pseudo-family of white British men. We now see the men reunited, having forgiven each other at last. The woman is excluded from this unity. Even though we may know that Ono co-operated in the project, the video is an uneasy combination of regressions. The surviving Beatles regress to the male camaraderie they enjoyed as a group, while at the same time they must vicariously join Lennon during his 'house-husband' period. It is as if they are pretending to reunite in the 1970s, without addressing any of the problems that would have entailed, such as Yoko Ono herself, the other Beatles' families, lengthy and acrimonious lawsuits, and the Beatles' divergent career paths. An additional predicament is the general weakness of their 1970s material (including 'Real Love'), especially in the light of their god-like status.

In order to include Lennon, the reunion project had to be built around his songs, but it remains less than clear why those songs had to be poor-quality cassettes from his 'house-husband' days – not that there is anything wrong with being a 'house-husband', but 'Real Love' is hardly representative of Lennon's (best) Beatle songs. Nor does it seem to be an authentic product of the 1990s. It has the effect of transporting the other three Beatles to Lennon's 1970s domestic space and to a time when the Beatles were already ageing. But the video has nothing to say about *issues* of domesticity or ageing – here again the visual absence of Ono (and women in general) is a problem.

## CONCLUSION: THE BEATLES AND THE NOSTALGIC

From a theoretical standpoint, the *Anthology* project represents the ultimate domestication and feminization of the Beatles. Until 1995, the Beatles had been marketed primarily to a youthful audience through a strategy of distinction more than to an adult audience through a strategy of entertainment.[6] They had been stars of film, which is gender-identified as male, more than of television, which is gender-identified as female (Kinder 1987). *Anthology* (the television programme) subsumes hours of film footage of the Beatles, thereby feminizing them, and hours of sound recordings, thereby domesticating them for the family/adult audience.

Kinder identifies music video as a prime arena in the media 'battle' of the sexes and generations. *Free As A Bird* and *Real Love* should therefore have a certain liminality about them – but they too are part of the television programme. Even so, they retain some liminality by being *appended* to the programme and by having 'new' records as their soundtracks.

*Anthology* as a whole is nostalgic. And within nostalgia, '[t]he emotional posture is that of a yearning for return, albeit accompanied often by an ambivalent recognition that such is not possible' (Davis 1979: 21; see also Frith 1996). The Beatles' reunion, in the form of these new recordings and videos, suggests that return *is* possible, a discovery endorsed by Paul McCartney: '[w]hen we'd done it ('Free As A Bird'), I thought, we've done the impossible. Because John's been dead and you can't bring dead people back. But somehow we did – he was in the studio' (Snow 1995: 54). Thus, while the mass character of Beatles nostalgia 'gives testimony to one's prescience, to a heightened sensitivity and oneness with the deepest impulses of an age' (Davis 1979: 43), at the same time the specialness of the Beatles is able to foster a retrospective sense of distinction. The process is explained by Davis:

> Our nostalgia for those aspects of our past selves that were 'odd and different' becomes the basis for deepening our sentimental ties to others and for reassuring us that we are not *that* strange after all. Others, it turns out, were equally 'strange'. (1979: 43)

The trick is to maintain some meaningful strangeness *now*, and this is the burden the new songs and videos are obliged to carry. Alas, the songs and videos succeed only as nostalgia and as marketing devices. They are not transgressive or transcendent; they soften history. As enjoyable and remarkable as they may be in their own way, these are fundamentally conservative texts.

This is perhaps understandable as the 'greying' of the surviving Beatles and their longtime fans proceeds apace. It is nonetheless dismaying in the light of the group's earlier achievements as politically engaged, avant-garde pop stars. Their nostalgic songs in the 1960s – usually McCartney vehicles such as 'When I'm Sixty-Four' and 'Your Mother Should Know' – served to add musical texture to *Sgt Pepper* and *Magical Mystery Tour*, respectively. They also softened and humanized those albums, increasing their mass appeal. This was a benign use of nostalgia.

On the other hand, 'Free As A Bird' and 'Real Love', despite being old works, presented the opportunity for a political or avant-garde coda to the Beatles' oeuvre. Nostalgia was built into the occasion and the music, but the videos did provide a potential forum for comment about conditions in the 1990s and about the relevance of the Beatles' career to the 1990s. This opportunity was mostly squandered in favour of friendly, celebratory clips that regress the Beatles to the mean of MTV-era video pop. The documentary and reunion that were so long in coming deserved videos with more depth and especially more audacity. Instead, like the Beatles' day tripper, these videos take the easy way out – but, in this case, without a good reason.

## NOTES

1. The author thanks Sam Choukri, Tim Connors and Jon Wiener for their assistance. This is a revised version of a paper delivered to the Speech Communication Association, San Diego, 23 November 1996. Portions of this paper previously appeared in the conference paper 'Old and New in the Beatles' Anthology Videos', University Film and Video Association, Orange, California, 8 August 1996.
2. Many of the foregoing matters receive more detailed treatment in Burns (1987); please refer to that article, also, for a thorough citation of sources.
3. In a framing sequence before the video proper, McCartney sets up the spoof by winking at the camera.
4. For an explanation of the tearing effect and other techniques in the video, see Cunningham (1996). Godley pioneered a similar effect in the Godley and Creme video *Cry* (1985). The idea of the Beatles as an uncommonly tight unit has recently been restated by Cohn: 'Watch the newsreels of them de-planing at Kennedy, or of their appearance on *The Ed Sullivan Show*, and they look like the four limbs of a single anatomy. Separate them, and they perish. Only as a group do they have a real life' (Cohn 1996: 13).
5. For a discussion of the television series, see Giles (1995) and Burr (1996).
6. See Attallah (1987). A strategy of distinction involves the creation of an ideology of authenticity and otherness by marketing commodities (for example, sound recordings) to a certain demographic segment (in this case, youth). A strategy of entertainment involves selling a programme (such as *Anthology*) to a distributor (such as ABC), which, in turn, sells its anticipated mass, heterogeneous audience to advertisers; authenticity and otherness are not issues in this strategy except to the extent that they may be undesirable.

## BIBLIOGRAPHY

Attallah, Paul (1987) 'Music Television', in Gareth Sansom (ed.), *Watching All the Music: Rock Video and Beyond*. Montreal: Working Papers In Communications, McGill University: 19–40.

Bonzai, Mr (1996) 'Jeff Lynne: Producing History', *Mix*, May: 76–80.

Burns, Gary (1987) 'The Myth of the Beatles', *South Atlantic Quarterly*, **86**: 169–80.

Burr, Ty (1996) 'Let It Be ... Longer', *Entertainment Weekly*, 13 September: 138–9.

Cantillon, J. P. and Sheila M. Cantillon (eds) (1996) *The Beatles: Anthology of a Band*. New York: Biograph Communications.

Cohn, Nik (1996) 'Introduction', in Robert Friedman and the Editors of *Life* (eds), *The Beatles: From Yesterday to Today*. Boston: Bullfinch P/Little, Brown: 8–17.

Cunningham, Mark (1996) 'The New Beatles Videos', *Record Collector*, February: 136–137.

Davies, Hunter (1969) *The Beatles: the Authorized Biography*. New York: Dell.

Davis, Fred (1979) *Yearning for Yesterday: a Sociology of Nostalgia*. New York: Free Press.

Doggett, Peter (1996) 'Gimme Some Truth: Beatles Anthology 2', *Record Collector*, April: 22–5.

Frith, Simon (1996) 'Introduction: Backward and Forward', in Charlie Gillett and Simon Frith (eds), *The Beat Goes On: the Rock File Reader*. London: Pluto.

Gaar, Gillian G. (1995) 'Roll Up, Roll Up, for the Magical History Tour: a Preview of the Beatles Anthology', *Goldmine*, 10 November: 18–30.

Giles, Jeff (1995) 'Come Together', *Newsweek*, 23 October: 60–7.

Lennon, Julian (1982) 'In His Own Words', *Instant Karma*, April/May (reprinted at <http://www.instantkarma.com/julianissue3express htm>): 1–2.

Kinder, Marsha (1987) 'Phallic Film and the Boob Tube: the Power of Identification in Cinema, Television and Music Video', *One Two Three Four* (Spring): 33–49.

Krenis, Karen (1996) 'Free as a Bird', *Film and Video*, March: 28–32.

Snow, Mat (1995) '"God in Heaven, What was I On?"', *Mojo*, **24** (November):52–9.

Wiener, Jon (1991a) 'Beatles Buy-Out: How Nike Bought the Beatles' "Revolution"', in Jon Wiener (ed.), *Professors, Politics and Pop*. London: Verso.

Wiener, Jon (1991b) 'John Lennon versus the FBI', in Jon Wiener (ed.), *Professors, Politics and Pop*. London: Verso.

# 11 'Sitting in an English Garden': Comparing Representations of 'Britishness' in the Songs of the Beatles and 1990s Britpop Groups

Andy Bennett

A characteristic aspect of many of the songs of the Beatles, especially from 1966 onwards, is the way in which they portray particular notions of British cultural life. Tracks such as 'Eleanor Rigby', 'Penny Lane', the collection of songs on *Sgt Pepper's Lonely Hearts Club Band* and the 'medley' on the second side of *Abbey Road* are linked by the distinctive representations of British cultural life which they contain. Such representations were by no means restricted to later Beatles material, but were a centrally defining aspect of songs by other 1960s British groups, particularly the Kinks and the Small Faces. During the 1990s there has been a resurgence of such musical and lyrical treatments of British life in the songs of Britpop bands such as Blur, Pulp and Ocean Colour Scene. In this chapter I want to consider and compare the images of British life which are presented in the songs of the Beatles and those of contemporary Britpop bands. Without a doubt, the depictions of 'Britishness' portrayed in Beatles' songs – and in the work of the Kinks and the Small Faces – has been a primary source of inspiration for the Britpop phenomenon. It may well be, however, that the meanings and intentions behind the use of such representations in 1990s Britpop are very different from those which underlay their use in the songs of the Beatles and fellow 1960s British groups. The discussion is in three parts. First, I want to set the scene by briefly discussing several studies which have looked at the relationship between music and national identity. Secondly, I shall investigate the role of the Beatles in establishing what came to be regarded as the 'British' sound and will also consider how such musical innovations were complemented by Lennon and McCartney's lyrical explorations of British cultural life. Thirdly, I will consider how the themes and issues explored in the songs of the Beatles have re-emerged in Britpop, and offer a sociological reading of such forms of representation in the context of contemporary Britain.

## MUSIC AND NATIONAL IDENTITY

The history of music as a central instrument in the construction, definition and redefinition of national identities is both long and complex. Perhaps the most typical merging of a musical statement with a statement of national identity is the national anthem (Mach 1994). National anthems provide a common anchoring point for a range of different activities, customs and traditions relating to a nation and its people. In Britain, for example, activities as diverse as the Queen's Christmas Day Speech and the Cup Final are firmly situated as aspects of the nation's culture via a rendition of its national anthem. Folk music too can play a significant role in reinforcing notions of national identity, even in cases where these have been complicated by migration and cultural change. For example, as Frith observes, 'in London's Irish pubs ... "traditional" Irish folk songs are still the most powerful way in which to make people feel Irish and consider what their "Irishness" means' (1987: 141). Music can also fulfil a more sinister role in informing notions of nationality and national identity, as is clearly illustrated in Warren's (1943) study of the role of music in Nazi Germany, wherein he suggested:

> National Socialist songs ... occupy a place of permanence in the national life ... Their primary focus is to arouse the emotions of the singers to a point where they are more sensitive to the impact of the words ... of the speaker. But they also fulfil the derivative function of exercising a lasting influence over the attitude of the individual after they leave the group. (1972: 73)

In this way, argues Warren, music played a vital role in the Nazis' rise to power in Germany during the 1930s. Clearly then, music can work in a variety of ways to inform particular notions of nation and national identity. In fact, Frith has argued that 'only music seems capable of creating this sort of spontaneous ... identity, this kind of personally felt patriotism' (1987: 141).

As the above examples begin to illustrate, music is one of the crucial mediums via which individuals living in particular countries are able to situate themselves both nationally and internationally. Stokes has shown that this is becoming more marked in the context of late modern society, where music plays a central role in informing 'our sense of place' (1994: 3); he refers to Giddens's observation that one of the consequences of modernity has been the '"phantasmogoric" separation of space from place, as places become "thoroughly penetrated and shaped in terms of social influences quite separate from them"' (Ibid.: 3). In Britain, the last 50 years have seen rapid changes in the nation's cultural character. On the one hand there has been a steady increase in the influence of US culture while, on the other hand, various immigrant and post-immigrant populations have introduced aspects of their own cultures into the everyday life of modern Britain. In addition, many of the industries and traditional ways of life which once helped to define the British cultural identity, both nationally and regionally, have all but disappeared. As a result of these combined transformations in the nature of British social life, it is becoming increasingly hard to describe and define British culture. Consequently, individuals in Britain, as in other modern nations which have been subject to the same processes of cultural change, seek ways in which they can culturally 'relocate' themselves. One way in which individuals attempt to do this is through music:

> Among the countless ways in which we 'relocate' ourselves, music undoubtedly has a vital role to play. The musical event, from collective dances to the act of putting a CD into a machine, evokes and organises collective memories and present experiences of place with an intensity, power and simplicity unmatched by any other social activity. The 'places' constructed through music involve notions of difference and social boundary. (Ibid.: 4)

Stokes's comments offer a plausible explanation for the appeal of Britpop in nineties Britain, particularly among the youth of the country. Against a backdrop of industrial decline, concomitant high youth unemployment and an increasing anxiety concerning the fate of the national identity, it could be argued that Britpop, to employ Cohen's (1972) terminology, assists in the 'magical recovery' of the British national identity. I shall go on to consider some of the ways in which this is achieved at a later stage. First, however, it is necessary to trace the historical origins of the Britpop sound and the cultural sensibilities ingrained within the genre. To do this it is necessary to go back to the early 1960s – more specifically, to the beginning of the Beatles' career as recording artists.

## BRITISH POPULAR MUSIC AND 'BRITISHNESS': THE ROLE OF THE BEATLES

Although the Beatles could never be described as the quintessential 'British' pop group, their style being too eclectic for them to be so neatly categorized, they set two important musical precedents which were central to the creation of the British pop sound of the early 1960s. First, the Beatles sang with an accent which was unmistakably 'British'. In 1963, a year when British radio stations were jammed with records by US artists and British US 'sound-alikes' such as Cliff Richard, songs like 'Love Me Do' and 'Please Please Me' stood out because of the 'British' sound of the vocal. However, it was never simply the vocal which defined the Beatles as a 'British' pop group. Equally important was the way in which they redefined the 'sound' of popular music. US popular music was performed either by Afro-American artists or by white artists who drew upon and imitated Afro-American sounds (Gillett 1983). As Chambers sees it, the Beatles combined the bluesy and soulful timbres of US popular music with elements of European classical harmony; the result was a sound which was 'recognisably British in tone ... guitar sounds were frequently "full" ... and employed highly "coloured" chords' (1985: 64).[1] In significant ways then, the Beatles played a major part in creating and developing the musical sounds which were to become standard fare in the British beat music of the early 1960s.

The Beatles were also very much at the forefront during the latter half of the 1960s when British popular music began to move away from the jangly guitar-based three-minute song towards a more avant garde form of pop expressionism. Frith and Horne (1987) point to the importance of the British art school tradition in helping to bring about this change in the direction of popular music, many musicians having studied at art school before gravitating to professional music-making; they suggest that this training was primarily responsible for the shift in thinking among British popular musicians during the late 1960s. Increasingly, musicians began to view the medium of song as a canvas on which they could create particular images and impressions. Both John Lennon and the 'fifth' Beatle, Stuart Sutcliffe, had been students at Liverpool Art College prior to their involvement in the Beatles (Brown and Gaines 1983: 18, 28) and when Sutcliffe left the Beatles in 1960, it was to continue his art studies in Hamburg – a career decision which was tragically short-lived due to Sutcliffe's death from a brain haemorrhage at the age of 21 (Swenson 1981: 48). Lennon, despite his decision to concentrate on music, retained an interest in art, a fact which undoubtedly contributed to the increasingly experimental character of the Beatles' music from 1966 onwards in songs such as 'Tomorrow Never Knows', 'A Day In The Life' and 'Revolution 9'. Such musical experiments by the Beatles, together with their use of orchestral and brass band instruments were to have a profound influence on the sound of other contemporary British pop groups. The shifting focus of the lyrics in their songs at this time also set new standards for British popular music. Indeed, it is this aspect of the Beatles' work which, perhaps more than anything else, set the scene for the themes and issues that began to characterize British pop songs during the late 1960s and which have recently re-emerged in the work of contemporary Britpop artists. From 1966 onwards, songs of the Beatles (and other groups like the Kinks and the Small Faces) became the focus for what Maconie describes as 'a kind of wry vaudevillian chronicling of ... ordinary post-war (British) life' (1994: 71).

   The clearest example of this form of commentary in the work of the Beatles is *Sgt Pepper's Lonely Hearts Club Band*. It is often depicted as the first 'concept' album; and if one listens to the album and studies its lyrics (it was one of the first albums where the lyrics were included on the sleeve) it is possible to discern how almost every song (with the possible exception of George Harrison's 'Within You Without You') is tied by a common thread – their commentary on aspects of British social life. The title track is laden with images of brass bands performing Sunday afternoon concerts in local parks or seaside pavilions. 'Being For The Benefit Of Mr Kite' evokes the atmosphere of the circus, while simultaneously capturing the novelty value of this form of entertainment in the context of British social life – a quality which is enhanced through producer George Martin's use of taped Victorian steam organ music in which the tapes, having been cut, were randomly spliced back together again to simulate the swirling experience of riding on a merry-go-round (Martin 1979: 204). 'A Day In The Life' is a song steeped in British cultural imagery – Lennon's lyrical references to the 'Albert Hall', the 'House Of Lords' and 'Blackburn, Lancashire' are combined with McCartney's cameo appearance as the man who gets up late for work, runs for the bus, and finds his way 'upstairs' to the top deck to have a smoke.

In 'A Day In The Life' everything from the spectacular to the mundane in British social life is graphically documented. At the same time, however, it is difficult to determine precisely how Lennon and McCartney intended this and other songs to be interpreted. While neither could be termed 'social realists', inasmuch as many of their songs merely 'package' impressions of British cultural life for artistic effect, some of their work, particularly tracks like 'A Day In The Life', are clearly meant to be seen, in part at least, as satirical commentaries on aspects of British society. Lennon's descriptions of the slavish counting of the holes in the streets of Blackburn, and his inference in the line 'Nobody was really sure if he was from the House Of Lords' to the double life led by politicians and other members of the establishment, would appear not merely to poke fun at British society but also to criticize it. A similar sensibility is also evident in the work of other British groups of the 1960s. The Kinks' 'Autumn Almanac', with rhyming couplets such as 'I like my football on a Saturday/Roast beef on Sunday – alright/I go to Blackpool for my holidays/Sit in the open sunlight', reads like a shopping list of British cultural traits, and appears to be an affectionate parody of British traditions and cultural habits; whereas other Kinks' songs – 'Dead End Street' and 'Dedicated Follower Of Fashion' (which ridicules the 'Swinging London' Dandy) – have a more satiric tone. The same observation can be made of the Small Faces. While songs such as 'Lazy Sunday' appear to be self-mocking parodies of the band's Cockney[2] roots, these are tempered by the darker, satirical songs such as the anti-war 'Tin Soldier'.

Such conflicting representations of 'Britishness' are further problematized by Britpop. As I have already noted, the Beatles, the Kinks and the Small Faces have been highly influential upon Britpop bands of the 1990s; the British themes and images evoked in the songs of Britpop artists such as Blur, Pulp and Ocean Colour Scene are clearly reminiscent of those employed by Lennon and McCartney, Ray Davies, Marriott and Lane. Seen from the context of the 1990s, however, it could be argued that such treatments of 'Britishness' take on an altogether different resonance which supersedes their function as rhetorical devices in the songs of the 1960s. As noted above, since that decade there have been considerable shifts in the socioeconomic character of Britain, which contain important implications for the nature of the nation's identity. Indeed, 'there is much current debate about the kind of Britain that will emerge in the twenty-first century, and the problems attendant upon putting forward any coherent notion of "Britishness"' (Storry and Childs 1997: 34). One way of interpreting Britpop's re-exploration of the themes and images contained in the songs of the Beatles and their peers could be as a nostalgic turn to an imagined past – to 'that moment before the rot and decline ... set in, when Britain was still "great"' (Chambers 1993: 145).

## BRITPOP: A SOCIOLOGICAL READING

The view that Britpop both 'borrows' directly from the British popular music scene of the 1960s and laments a Britain that we have 'lost' is not uniformly agreed by all commentators. Some have argued that Britpop songs have entirely revised the images of British life portrayed in the popular music of the 1960s. In May 1994, it was claimed that Blur, then at the forefront of the movement, had 'defined a New Englishness ... an attitude based not on a nostalgic Carry On Mr Kipling Britain, but a Britain that you will recognise as the one you live in' (Jones 1994: 42). Certainly, Blur songs, such as 'Boys And Girls' with its satirical commentary on the alleged 'fuck and chuck' mentality of Club 18–30 holiday-makers, might be said to paint a picture of British life which is topical, rather than one which harks back to a lost Britain of the 1960s. Similarly, Pulp's tales of bleak streets and bedsits with rising damp could be said to represent a clear departure from the Beatles' often romanticized accounts of 'Little England'.

It seems to me, however, that such revisions are largely peripheral, and that once Britpop artists' representations of Britishness are subjected to closer scrutiny, they appear to operate on similar territory to those representations constructed by the Beatles *et al*. One fundamental difference between 1990s Britpop and the Beatles is the availability of video (although the video produced to promote the Beatles 'reunion' track 'Free As A Bird' in November 1995 is a telling indication of how effectively much of the Beatles work translates into the video format). Since the early 1980s, the pop video has become an increasingly important marketing tool, with the result that equal effort now goes into the production of the promotional video as into the production of the song itself (Berland 1993). The analysis of popular music video is fast becoming an established area of cultural studies (Kaplan 1987; Frith *et al.* 1993) and I do not have the space to conduct an exhaustive analysis of video here. Nevertheless, I would argue that the use of video in the marketing of 1990s Britpop has allowed for relatively instantaneous connections to be made between it and notions of 'Britishness'. This is not to say that the artists themselves are attempting to dictate directly to audiences particular ways of understanding their material. Invariably, decisions as to how a promotional video is produced and the form which its visual content takes rest not only with the featured band or artist but also with the video director and the production team. Moreover, one must also allow for the fact that audiences themselves will not uniformly read the same meanings into a given video. This point is constructively taken up by Fiske, who argues that pop videos provide 'the raw materials out of which a number of narratives can be produced' (1989: 121). However, as Fiske's observation itself implies, videos can and do suggest basic ways in which to understand a song and interpret its meaning. Such implied interpretations, it can be argued, are evident in Britpop videos. Indeed, an interesting aspect of these videos is the way in which they appear to take lyrical devices used by Lennon and McCartney and convert them into a visual format. Britpop videos are often crammed with images of Britishness which chop and change as rapidly as the lyrical references to British life found in the later songs of the Beatles.

A clear example of this can be found in the promotional video produced for Blur's 'Parklife'. In the lyric we are presented with one particular account of British life – being woken up by the dustmen, having a cup of tea, and feeding the pigeons. At the visual level, however, the song takes on a rather different, yet equally topical character. In the video, we see a typical 'cheeky-chappie' cockney character (Phil Daniels – conveniently borrowed from *Quadrophenia*),[3] driving down the road in his 1970s-style Ford Capri. The scene suddenly changes. It could be an entirely different video, but for the stock of images which uphold the theme of Britishness – the row of terraced houses, the ice cream van, and the individual members of Blur dressed in casual clothes mimicking the typical stance of the British youngster meeting up with friends after school and playing out in the street. In many respects, the video revisits some of the themes and ideas concerning British life explored in the lyrics of Lennon and McCartney. In particular, it appears to touch upon the same sort of utopian reminiscing which informs songs such as 'Penny Lane' where factual characters – the fireman, the banker and the pretty nurse – are written into a story book version of British suburban life (an approach which in some ways pre-empts the 'soap' style of contemporary TV shows such as *EastEnders* and *Brookside*). In keeping with the accounts of British life presented in 'Penny Lane', the video for 'Parklife' uses images which are clearly based upon actual aspects of everyday British life, yet combines them in ways which transcend everyday experience. Like the song which it promotes, it is a surrealistic collage of British life – a cultural pastiche.

Clearly, there is a firm sense in which any attempt to distinguish between fiction and fact in the discussion of culture is misleading; culture is increasingly becoming the sum of its representations. Rather than being a 'given', or something which is simply 'out there', culture, particularly in the context of late modern society, is constructed from sets of images and representations received largely through the mass media in its various forms. The overall consequence of this is that 'all aspects of our lived experience are formulated, made manifest, through the constitutive activity of representational resources' (Chaney 1994: 67). As this observation suggests, however, there is at the same time a firm sense in which such forms of cultural representation resonate with individual experience to produce 'versions' of social reality. Thus, to return to the central focus of this chapter, given Britain's current 'crisis of identity', it may be that the use of visual romanticism and pastiche in Britpop videos serves to provide audiences with a stock of images and ideas about British life from which they are able to form their own views about what constitutes the 'true' British identity. In the case of Blur's video, 'Britishness' is linked both to a strong sense of regional identity, as evidenced in Phil Daniels's typecast appearance as the 'cheeky-chappie' from London, and to the virtues of the simple working-class life – terraced streets where kids make their own fun, and where the highlight of the week is a visit from the ice cream van. During the 1960s, when notions of regional and class identity were still more firmly in place than they are today, they were often viewed ironically, not only by songwriters, but by novelists, playwrights and comedians who also poked fun at the parochial lifestyle of the British citizen (Foster and Furst 1996: 240–63). In the 1990s, however, such images of British life function in a broadly opposite fashion to create a 'golden age' – a process whereby the past 'is lovingly remembered as a time of harmony ... order and security' (Pearson 1983: 7).

In a similar way, the video made to promote Pulp's 'Common People' lends itself to interpretation as a romantic revival of the traditional British working-class identity. The song's story centres around a Greek girl of rich parentage who comes to London to study sculpture and meets a working-class art student from the north of England. The girl is attracted to the student because of his working classness and because she has a self-expressed desire to 'live like common people'. As the song progresses, the working-class student realizes that the visions of proletarian life possessed by the Greek girl are tragically romantic, and that she will never be able to accept the real suffering and hardship endured by 'common people'. Again, however, in its exploration of the lives of so-called 'common people' the Pulp video makes sweeping generalizations about British working-class life which are difficult to substantiate in an age where class identities are becoming increasingly fragmented. The video's references to apparently still 'intact' working-class neighbourhoods clearly conflict with the song's main character who has left his working-class life behind to move to London and study art. At several points in the video we see vocalist Jarvis Cocker walking down a street in what is supposed to be a typical working-class neighbour-hood. The images which pass behind him all reflect scenarios which one might expect to encounter in a working-class street; young boys playing football, courting couples, old women hanging out washing, and so on. It is clear that the video sequence is intended to work as pastiche rather than documentary, in that as many (stereo)typical images as possible are being crammed into the sequence in order to maximize the association with British working-class life. At the same time, however, this section of the video appears to hinge upon the assumption that the exhibited working-class sensibilities continue to characterize British society and to exist in relative isolation from the combined effects of the media and multiculturalization. Cocker, orig-inally from Sheffield, an industrial city in the North of England, is often heard to champion his working-class roots and the people he 'left behind'. In 'Common People' he takes such sentiments to their logical extreme by suggesting that despite their poor life chances, the working classes are quite satisfied, and have no need or desire for contact with middle-class 'trendies' who envy the apparent excite-ment of illicit cigarettes, the pool hall and skipping school. Again, however, once the devices of poetic licence have been removed, it is difficult to identify a coherent social group who correspond with Cocker's notion of the 'common people'.

In many ways the song's account of the urban drama which over-takes the lives of the British working class also appears to hark back to a time when class sensibilities were more widely felt in Britain, and when the petty conflicts of class interest which it documents were much more a part of everyday life. The class-based scenarios featured in the lyrics and video have clear parallels with 'Kitchen Sink' cinema – a move towards social realism in British filmmaking during the late 1950s and early 1960s which resulted in films such as *Room At The Top, Saturday Night And Sunday Morning* and *A Taste Of Honey* (Hill 1986, Stead 1989). Each of these films purported to represent something of the harsh reality of working-class life in the north of England. In a particularly well formulated critique of such cinema, Shields argues that:

> Far from being 'realist' such [films] are entirely selective and *conventionalistic* in that they do not challenge commonsensical, 'folksy', categorisations of the region, thereby framing and presenting a one-sided version of the 'North'. The North is in a sense as disordered as a kitchen sink full of dirty dishes: a place where purified, monological narratives are challenged by the dialogical displacements of codes and recombinations which position actions in improper settings (for example, romantic encounters in a gas-works). (1991: 218)

The point remains, however, that irrespective of the problems inherent in 'Kitchen Sink's' social realist claims, during the early 1960s it was received as social realism by cinema audiences. Arguably this had much to do with the fact that the world it depicted was still a world to which audiences could relate, despite the romantic gloss to which it was often subjected in such films. In contrast, the utilization in 'Common People' of the same romantic devices in the context of the 1990s assumes an altogether more nostalgic air. The fanciful manner of the Greek student's wish to 'live like common people' and her working-class lover's eventual realization that she will never comprehend what it really means to be a 'common person' recalls the central premise of *Billy Liar*, in its assumption that people are effectively trapped within their respective classes, and can only dream about what life would be like if they could manage to break free and become a 'different' person. At the same time, however, Pulp's song acts as a rallying call to those people who consider themselves to be working class (a category which might also include upwardly mobile working-class students and professionals) to recognize their roots and 'sing along with the common people'. As with 'Parklife', 'Common People' might perform an act of 'magical recovery' in that through its idealistic vision of the working class as an identifiable and coherent social group, it helps to rescue and revive an aspect of British cultural life which is gradually disappearing. Viewed from this angle, the dialogue between the two characters in 'Common People' and the overall romanticism of the video become immaterial. Parody and pastiche, rather than distracting from an 'objective' reality, enhance the overall effect, in that the video's appeal is precisely its perceived distance from reality and its harking back to a world where people were much surer of their identity regionally, nationally, and in terms of their class position and place in the scheme of things.

## THE PLACE WHERE YOU LIVE?

There is one additional issue which must be discussed in relation to Britpop and its role in the (re)construction of the British national identity – the issue of race. At several points, I have referred to the increasingly multicultural nature of British society and the way in which this serves to further problematize attempts to define what it means to be British. Significantly, Britpop makes no reference to issues of multiculturalism. Again, there are obvious parallels here between Britpop and the British popular music of the 1960s, which remained essentially 'white', despite its musical and stylistic borrowings from black forms (Hebdige 1976, 1979). Beyond such musical and stylistic acknowledgements, however, British pop music of the 1960s remained essentially indifferent to issues of race. The socioeconomic changes which would make issues of race and race relations a more common aspect of everyday discourse in Britain did not begin to occur until after the 1960s. Awareness among white Britons of the need for racial awareness began to grow during the early 1970s when economic austerity and rising levels of unemployment led to an increasing incidence of racism and racist attacks by white agitators who scapegoated the newly established Afro-Caribbean and Asian minority groups in Britain, blaming them for the country's decline (Back 1996). Such racism and discrimination was in part responsible for the inner-city youth riots of the early 1980s, which again brought home to the white population of Britain the need for improved ethnic relations and racial tolerance.

No such excuse, however, can be made in the case of Britpop which, in emulating the cultural representations of Britishness in the work of the Beatles and other 1960s British groups, glosses over such turbulent aspects of Britain's more recent social history and goes straight back to the 'football on Saturday/roast beef on Sunday' world of the 1960s. This has led to concern that the Britain represented in Britpop is 'being reconstructed around a tradition which is unproblematically white [and] ... from which blacks are systematically excluded' (Morley and Robins 1989: 16; Gilroy: 1986). Cloonan (1995) identifies nationalist tendencies within the Britpop genre and among those who support it; and Batey has suggested that its careless use of the British flag is 'helping to legitimise [Far Right] jingoism' (Sutherland and Batey 1997: 61). Obviously, such arguments carry disturbing implications, not least of all because they suggest a clear connection between the rise of Britpop and the onset of a social sensibility which Samuel sees as a 'born-again cultural nationalism' (1988: 28).

There is, however, another, and perhaps far less negative, way in which the apparent 'whiteness' of Britpop can be interpreted, which has much to do with Stokes's (1994) notion of cultural 'relocation' outlined earlier. If, as he suggests, one of the ways in which individuals culturally relocate themselves is through music, then it would seem that the British popular music scene of the past three decades owes much to the musical and stylistic experimentation of Britain's immigrant populations. Since the early 1960s, new or recently arrived immigrant populations have used music as a way of establishing themselves and their respective cultural identities in Britain. Hebdige (1976, 1979) has illustrated how second-generation and third-generation immigrants to Britain from the West Indies used ska and later reggae as a way of marking out their own cultural territory within the inner-cities of 1960s and 1970s Britain. A study by Kaur and Kalra (1996) suggests that contemporary South Asian dance music is performing similar cultural work for young Asians living in Britain. Employing the term 'Br-Asian', Kaur and Kalra suggest that South Asian dance music, which is essentially all about being Asian in Britain, provides the central focus for the construction of a new cultural identify which is neither British nor Asian. 'Br-Asian' youth come to occupy a new cultural territory which draws on both the traditional parent culture and the cultural sensibilities of contemporary Britain.

Such musical and stylistic innovations, despite their centrality to the cultural relocation of specific ethnic minority groups, have also attracted the interest of sections of white British youth. Hebdige (1976, 1979) and Jones (1988) have both illustrated how white British youth's attraction to West Indian musical forms has resulted in them forging their own forms of hybridized cultural identity which also serve to distance white youth from the more traditional ways of life which characterize their parent culture. Additionally, one cannot overlook the cultural impact of rap music which, despite its origins and continuing cultural importance within Afro-American ghetto culture, has found widespread appeal among youth of all races in different parts of the world (Mitchell 1996; Bennett forthcoming). Indeed, during my own research on hip hop culture in Newcastle upon Tyne in the North East of England, I discovered an almost exclusively white hip hop following, whose common reaction to claims that rap was a black cultural form and therefore inaccessible to whites was to suggest that rap 'isn't a black thing, it's a street thing y'know, where people get so pissed off with their environment that they have to do something about it' (Bennett 1996: 162). The current interest in rap, and related forms of black music and style, among white British youth has prompted some theorists to argue that, from the point of view of the young at least, any discussion concerning the nature of British culture calls for a complete revision of what have convention-ally passed as British cultural traits. This view is neatly summed up by Back, who suggests that: 'Young white people may (now) have more in common with Bobby Brown than John Bull, with the result that it is impossible to speak of a black culture in Britain separately from the culture of Britain as a whole' (1993: 218).

Clearly, if we are to accept such a view, it becomes very hard to account for the appeal of Britpop. On the one hand, writers such as Back (1993) claim that white youth in Britain is moving increasingly away from traditional notions of Britishness, while on the other hand writers like Cloonan (1995) suggest that sections of British youth, through their preference for Britpop, are returning to a 'flag-waving' traditionalist view of the British cultural identity. Both views may contain elements of truth but inevitably suffer from their attempt to impose essentialist interpretations upon notions of identity which cannot be so neatly categorized. Reggae and South Asian dance music forms, which were clearly intended as specific markers of Afro-Caribbean and Asian cultural identities, have by no means excluded white youth. Similarly, Britpop may encourage some of its followers to engage in flag-waving nationalism, but there is little evidence to suggest that this is the only, or the most prevalent, response. Britpop, rather than symbolizing a return to nationalistic values by young people, may be symptomatic of the pluralism which is increasingly becoming a feature of the identity politics of British youth (signifi-cantly, there is still little empirical proof that only 'white' youth in

Britain listen to Britpop). To state this in another way, it could be argued that, like reggae, South Asian Dance music and rap, Britpop is simply another resource via which young people in Britain can choose to culturally situate themselves. This is not to discount the earlier claims that Britpop may function as a form of 'magical recovery' of more traditional notions of Britishness. However, the cultural fragmentation which has led some to seek ways in which to revive such traditional notions of Britishness has, at the same time, given rise to new ways of looking at Britain as a nation and considering what it means to be British. Earlier, I referred to Jones's insight that Britpop is 'about a Britain that you will recognise as the one you live in' (1994: 42). It seems fitting to end this chapter by offering a revised version of his comment: thus, Britpop is not necessarily about a Britain you will recognise as the one you live in; it is rather about a particular 'version' of Britain in which you may choose to live if you so wish.

## CONCLUSION

During the course of this chapter, I have been concerned to compare representations of Britishness and British cultural life in the songs of the Beatles and 1990s Britpop artists. Having considered some theoretical perspectives on the connection between music and notions of national identity, and the historical 'roots' of Britpop in the music of the Beatles and fellow 1960s British groups the Kinks and the Small Faces, I turned my attention to 1990s Britpop. In noting the parallels between Britpop bands and the Beatles in terms of the representations of Britishness contained in their songs, I suggested that in the case of the Beatles such representations could be viewed as a way of ridiculing the institutional fabric of everyday British life, whereas in the case of 1990s Britpop they could be seen as harking back to a lost Britain which seemed to offer a much more coherent sense of national identity. Finally, I considered its seeming indifference to issues of race and multiculturalism – issues which, in many respects, set the Britain of the 1960s and the Britain of the 1990s apart from each other. In doing so, I suggested that rather than simply viewing Britpop as a 'flag-waving' return to nationalism (a point of view which is essentially unfounded) one might more productively see the genre as offering a particular 'version' of Britain and Britishness which co-exists unproblematically alongside a range of other possible versions of national identity facilitated by an increasing musical and stylistic diversity within British youth culture.

## NOTES

1.   The hybridization of Afro-American blues and Western classical harmony in the songs of the Beatles is similarly noted by musicologist Wilfred Mellers in his study *Twilight of the Gods* (1973).
2.   'Cockney' is the term for a native of the East End of London.
3.   In *Quadrophenia*, the film based on the Who's album of the same name, Phil Daniels plays Jimmy, a mod whose total commitment to the mod lifestyle gradually turns sour as he realizes that his fellow mods do not share his enthusiasm for the mod culture.

## REFERENCES

Back, Les (1993) 'Race, Identity and Nation within an Adolescent Community in South London', *New Community*, **19**(2): 217–33.

Back, Les (1996) *New Ethnicities: Racisms and Multiculture in Young Lives*. London: UCL Press.

Bennett, Andy (1996) *Popular Styles, Local Interpretations: Rethinking the Sociology of Youth Culture and Popular Music*. Unpublished PhD thesis, University of Durham.

Bennett, Andy (forthcoming) '"Hip Hop Am Main": the Localisation of Rap Music and Hip Hop Culture', *Media, Culture and Society*.

Berland, Jody (1993) 'Sound, Image and Social Space: Music Video and Media Reconstruction', in Simon Frith, Andrew Goodwin and Lawrence Grossberg (eds), *Sound and Vision: the Music Video Reader*. London: Routledge.

Brown, Peter and Steven Gaines (1983) *The Love You Make: an Insider's Story of the Beatles*. London: Macmillan.

Chambers, Iain (1985) *Urban Rhythms: Pop Music and Popular Culture*. London: Macmillan.

Chambers, Iain (1993) 'Narratives of Nationalism: Being "British"', in Erica Carter, James Donald and Judith Squires (eds), *Space and Place: Theories of Identity and Location*. London: Lawrence & Wishart.

Chaney, David (1994) *The Cultural Turn: Scene Setting Essays on Contemporary Cultural Theory*. London: Routledge.

Cloonan, Martin (1995) 'What Do *They* Know of England? Englishness and Popular Music in the Mid-1990s'. Unpublished paper, *International Association for the Study of Popular Music International Conference*, University of Strathclyde, Glasgow, July.

Cohen, Phil (1972) 'Subcultural Conflict in a Working Class Community', *Working Papers in Cultural Studies 2*. University of Birmingham.

Fiske, John (1989) *Reading the Popular*. London: Routledge.

Foster, Andy and Steve Furst (1996) *Radio Comedy 1938–1968*. London: Virgin.

Frith, Simon (1987) 'Towards an Aesthetic of Popular Music' in Richard Leppert and Susan McLary (eds), *Music and Society: The Politics of Composition, Performance and Reception*. Cambridge University Press.

Frith, Simon and Howard Horne (1987) *Art into Pop*. London: Methuen.

Frith, Simon, Andrew Goodwin and Lawrence Grossberg (eds) (1993) *Sound and Vision: the Music Video Reader*. London: Routledge.

Gillett, Charlie (1983) *The Sound of the City* (2nd edn). London: Souvenir.

Gilroy, Paul (1986) *'There Ain't No Black in the Union Jack': the Cultural Politics of Race and Nation*. London: Hutchinson.

Hebdige, Dick (1976) 'Reggae, Rastas and Rudies', in Stuart Hall and Tony Jefferson (eds), *Resistance Through Rituals: Youth Subcultures in Post-War Britain*. London: Hutchinson.

Hebdige, Dick (1979) *Subculture: the Meaning of Style*. London: Routledge.

Hill, John (1986) *Sex, Class and Realism: British Cinema 1956–1963*. London: British Film Institute.

Jones, Cliff (1994) 'Looking for a New England', *The Face*, **68**: 40–6.

Jones, Simon (1988) *Black Culture, White Youth: the Reggae Tradition from JA to UK*. London: Macmillan.

Kaplan, E. Ann (1987) *Rocking Around the Clock*. New York: Methuen

Kaur, Raminder and Virinder S. Kalra (1996) 'New Paths for South Asian Identity and Creativity', in S. Sharma, J. Hutnyk and A. Sharma (eds), *Dis-Orienting Rhythms: the Politics of the New Asian Dance Music*. London: Zed Books.

Mach, Zdislaw (1994) 'National Anthems: the Case of Chopin as a National Composer', in Martin Stokes (ed.), *Ethnicity, Identity and Music: the Musical Construction of Place*. Oxford: Berg.

Maconie, Stuart (1994) 'Three Minutes', *Mojo*, **7**: 70–4.

Martin, George (1979) *All You Need is Ears*. London: Macmillan.

Mellers, Wilfrid (1973) *Twilight of the Gods: the Beatles in Retrospect*. London: Faber.

Mitchell, Tony (1996) *Popular Music and Local Identity: Rock, Pop and Rap in Europe and Oceania*. London: Leicester University Press.

Morley, David and Kevin Robins (1989) 'Spaces of Identity', *Screen*, **30**(4): 10–34.

Pearson, Geoffrey (1983) *Hooligan: a History of Respectable Fears*. London: Macmillan.

Samuel, Raphael (1988) 'Little Englandism Today', *New Statesman and Society*, **1**(20): 27–30.

Shields, Rob (1991) *Places on the Margin: Alternative Geographies of Modernity*. London: Routledge.

Stead, P. (1989) *Film and the Working Class: the Feature Film in British and American Society*. London: Routledge.

Stokes, Martin (1994) 'Introduction: Ethnicity, Identity and Music', in Martin Stokes (ed.), *Ethnicity, Identity and Music: the Musical Construction of Place*. Oxford: Berg.

Storry, Mike and Peter Childs (eds) (1997) *British Cultural Identities*. London:

Routledge.

Sutherland, Steve and Angus Batey (1997) 'Discredit to the Nation?', *Vox*, **80**:60–1.

Swenson, John (1981) *The John Lennon Story*. New York: Leisure Books.

Warren, Roland L. (1972) 'The Nazi Use of Music as an Instrument of Social Control', in R. Serge Denisoff and Richard A Peterson (eds), *The Sounds of Social Change*. Chicago: Rand McNally.

# Index